The Politics of Knowledge

SUNY Series in the Sociology of Work

Judith R. Blau and Robert L. Kaufman, Editors

The Politics of Knowledge

*Activist Movements in Medicine
and Planning*

Lily M. Hoffman

State University of New York Press

Philip G. Spitzer Literary Agency has generously given permission to quote extensively from *White Coat/Clenched Fist*. Copyright 1976 by Fitzhugh Mullan.

The discussion of housestaff unionization in Chapter 6 was first published under the title "Housestaff Activism: The Emergence of Patient-Care Demands." *Journal of Health Politics, Policy and Law* 7:2 (Summer 1982) 421–39. Copyright © 1982. Lily M. Hoffman.

Photo credits: cover photo of doctors' strike at Cook County Hospital in Chicago, October 29, 1975. Gary Settle/*New York Times* Pictures.

Published by
State University of New York Press, Albany

© 1989 State University of New York

For information, address State University of New York
Press, State University Plaza, Albany, N.Y., 12246

Library of Congress Cataloging-in-Publication Data

Hoffman, Lily M.
    The politics of knowledge: activist movements in medicine and
planning / Lily M. Hoffman.
        p.   cm. — (SUNY series in the sociology of work)
    Bibliography: p.
    Includes index.
    ISBN 0-88706-948-7.   ISBN 0-88706-949-5 (pbk.)
    1. Professions—Sociological aspects.   2. Social change.
3. Social reformers.   I. Title.   II. Series.
HT687.H57   1989
305.5'53—dc19   88-17447
                                                                CIP

10 9 8 7 6 5 4 3 2

For my father
Morris Laufgraben
1906-1963
who came to this country
to be able to become
a professional

Contents

Preface

At a well-attended SDS conference entitled "Radicals in the Professions," held in Ann Arbor, Michigan in 1967, a number of activists got up and spoke about whether professional life was hopelessly middle class and self-serving, or whether it was possible to work within professions and professional institutions for substantive social change.

This book grew out of my own grappling with this issue and involvement in those times. For the generation that came of age politically in the 1960s, the question of "where to" after college involved the desire to retain a political identity and function—to be both political and professional.

In retrospect, the past two decades have been a political and social workshop for professionals. The attempt to combine professional and activist roles has been a goal not only for radicals but for a wide range of dissatisfied professionals. It has involved the introduction of new values, forms of practice and paradigms. Yet the quest has been elusive and contradictory. The internal and external conflicts over the appropriate and legitimate functions of professions and professionals suggest limits to certain kinds of change in American society, and to the possible agents of these changes.

Although we live in more cautious times and characterize young professionals as "yuppies" to underline the dominant interest in making it and spending it, the dissatisfactions raised in the 1960s are likely to recur again both in the lifetimes of individuals and generationally. While the professions, post-1960s, look rather tarnished, the underlying constellation of structural interests has changed and they will again be defended as well as criticized. Although this study confirms the premise that the professions embody money, status and power, it also shows that the professions represent a genuine desire to work and to serve—to profess. But at the same time, professional work is not necessarily compatible with social change.

The collection of interviews and written materials for this book began over ten years ago and there are many people and organizations to thank for help. First, the planners and health activists who spoke with me—some at great length like Drs. Oliver Fein and Des Callan—and who gave me access to their files—among them Walter Thabit, Jackie Leavitt, Dr. Ken Rosenberg. Their commitment and insight enriched this work; the organizations, such as UPA, CIR and particularly Health/PAC, which made their files available; two grants —a Charles E. Culpeper Fellowship at Oberlin College and an NIMH Fellowship at Rutgers—which provided time; and some special debts. Norman Fainstein, for encouraging my interest in another side of urban political movements; Herbert Gans who saw this research through its initial phase and who remains a source of inspiration; Peter Whalley for his insightful comments at several important stages and more generally, for his shared enthusiasm; Robert Alford who brought to the reading of several drafts of this manuscript, his unique blend of rigor and creativity; my sister, Roslyn Bernstein, for her unfaltering editorial and emotional presence. Finally, my family—Joel, Jared, and Margaret—for their patience and impatience, and Tinker who sat at my feet. All contributed but none are responsible for what is finally my interpretation.

Eugene Lang College   L.M.H.
The New School for Social Research
March 1989

Part I

*The Professions
and Social Change*

1

The Professions
and Social Movements

The ability of professions to limit and constrain change in how and whether and to whom they deliver services has become problematic for the public, the academic community, and the professions themselves. Prior to the 1960s, modern societies seemed to be a world in which experts and the rule of expertise were not subject to political attacks.

The 1960s challenged these assumptions. The professions—particularly those which delivered services to minorities and the poor—became a battleground. Professionals, clients, and the institutions which provided services became vocal contenders. Professionals criticized their own professions for self-interest and for class and racial biases. Clients demanded participation in decision making. Institutions tried to hold on to the status quo by arguing that reforms would threaten the quality of service.

The dramatic events of the 1960s—the Montgomery bus boycott and the Selma march, the assassinations of John and Robert Kennedy and Martin Luther King, Jr., and the civil crisis brought on by the war in Vietnam—all challenged established public perceptions of professional behavior as well as institutions and contributed to an alternative consciousness. Prior to the 1960s, for example, people did not believe that professionals would ever strike. To strike was "nonprofessional," at least in the United States. To strike was to be "working class"—to walk picket lines like auto workers, surrounded by police. However, countertrends developed. In 1965, a group calling themselves the Cambridge Committee against the Inner Belt proposed an alternate to a "planned" highway through a low-income area of Cambridge, Massachusetts. They expressed their dissatisfaction with working for those with money and power and their desire to use their skills for those who had no planners—the poor. Also in 1965, a group of doctors organized the Medical Com-

1

mittee for Human Rights. Although their initial objective was to send medical support South to the Civil Rights movement, they soon took up the issues of segregated medical facilities, the lack of adequate health care for blacks in the South, and the American Medical Association's lack of attention to issues of race and poverty.

On a daily basis, newspapers covered this strange new species of professional confrontation. At Lincoln Hospital during July 1970, 30 doctors on the housestaff joined forces with the Young Lords (a Puerto Rican organization), HRUM (a revolutionary organization of minority nonprofessional health workers), and other community groups to stage a 12-hour demonstration. They occupied the nurses residence, administrative offices, and the housestaff quarters to emphasize their demands: no cutbacks in services or jobs, necessary preventative services such at T.B. screening, and "total self-determination of all health services through a Community-Worker Board to operate Lincoln Hospital."

And in 1975, American doctors joined the picket lines for the first time when housestaff doctors at major hospitals in Chicago, New York, and Los Angeles went out on strike. Included in their demands were patient-care issues such as translation services and emergency room equipment. One intern told a news reporter: "We're not doctors-in-training. We are the primary care physicians for poor people in the ghettos."

The general public may have revered doctors but were more skeptical about the work of teachers, social workers, and city planners. Nevertheless, people were surprised that public employees would ever come to contradict the statements and proposals of their employing agencies. Yet in 1969, planners on the staff of New York City's Department of City Planning, testified at public hearings against the rezoning of lower Manhattan. They claimed that their recommendations had been ignored by the department and "hidden" from the public. They argued that the proposals before the Commission "had resulted from high-level political decisions in response to pressure from real estate speculators."

Scenarios such as these reversed the common stereotype. Traditional professionals who defended their own conservative self-interest were being challenged by professionals who also saw themselves as political activists.

TRADITIONAL AND CRITICAL MODELS

The attack on professional institutions was accompanied by scholarly attacks on traditional sociological models of professions. Traditional models, based largely on nineteenth-century ideals, distinguished professions from the lesser occupations by a set of central attributes. These included possession of theoretically based knowledge, altruistic ideals of service, and the right to autonomy in the workplace.[1] Of these, theoretically based knowledge was the chief characteristic as well as the foundation for other claims.

Traditional models have tended to treat attributes such as the knowledge base as structurally given, relatively static, and non-ideological. They were seen as social facts, not as claims; viewed as in the mutual interest of client, professional, and society, not as self-serving. Similarly, professions were seen as homogenous and cohesive communities. These images imparted a sacred quality to professions, a quality captured by the common emphasis in the literature on the importance of trust.[2]

Critics, in contrast, have emphasized political process and outcome rather than intrinsic attributes.[3] They have seen professions as occupations which achieve occupational control by credentialing and licensing.[4] Professions are portrayed as composed of diverse groups or segments with multiple conflicting interests and objectives.[5] From this perspective, knowledge and expertise are not the neutral scientific elements emphasized by traditional theory but political resources in the battle for power and status, constructed and advanced by occupations and segments within occupations to forward collective aims.[6] Critics of medicine, for example, suggested that the reforms of the Progressive period (1900-1917)—notably the changes advocated by the Flexner Report on medical education— institutionalized the "scientific" model of medicine at the expense of competing models and interests.[7]

Macro and historical theorizing accompanied and contributed to this critique. Theories of postindustrial and advanced capitalist society, for example, suggest that changes in organization, technology, production, consumption, and stratification have outdated the concept of professions and revealed its historical and culturally specific origins. Class theorists such as James O'Connor noted the contradictory functions of professions, furthering accumulation and legitimacy.[8] Neo-Marxists, who focused on educated workers and class alignments, predicted *deprofessionalization* and *proletarianization*.[9] Even contemporary technocratic models such as Daniel Bell's post-industrial society, which foresaw professionalism as the transcendent occupational principle, contained some discordant notes. Bell also predicted that the ascent of professionalism as an occupational principle would give rise to populist attacks upon meritocracy and the rule of experts.[10]

The 1960s thus marked a turning point in the traditional career of the professions. Professions have not regained their previous position and continue to be challenged by the issues of that time. Additionally, in the 1980s, a period marked by economic uncertainty and political conservatism, professions are under attack on a number of new fronts—by federal regulatory policies along with corporate rationalization and profit making. This has set off a new round of debate with some arguing that professions in general, as well as "dominant professions" such as medicine, have lost prestige, status, and economic and political independence. There is even a sense that the professions are being deprofessionalized and perhaps proletarianized.[11]

A central issue is the ability of the professions to limit and constrain change. The challenges of the last few decades—from clients, activist professionals, and federal and corporate interests—can help us address this issue since they represent attempts to alter aspects of professional organization and work as well as its outcomes. These challenges provide a series of "natural tests" of the ability of professions to maintain themselves relatively unchanged.

THE RELEVANCE OF
ACTIVIST PROFESSIONAL MOVEMENTS

Activist professional movements are important for several reasons. First, professions have most often been seen as brakes on significant change. During the 1960s, a time marked by the redefinition of services as rights, by demands for participation and control, and by attempts to change and radically transform service delivery and outcomes, insurgents from within the ranks of students, academic and practicing professionals, attempted to orchestrate change and to push their respective professions to the limit.

Second, although protests and political demands came from professionals as well as from the minority and poor communities, we know little about these movements of dissatisfied educated workers or about such internally generated change. The 1960s witnessed the rebirth and blossoming of activism within professions, but most subsequent empirical work has focused upon movements of minorities and the poor. When activist professionals are dealt with, accounts tend to simplify and polarize their activity. On the one hand, they are seen as professional expansionists who collectively benefit from change without regard to the many distinctions among them,[12] or as "agents" of the welfare state despite the considerable evidence of contradiction and conflict in their state funded roles.[13] Other, more sympathetic accounts see them as adjuncts of the Civil Rights and the New Left movements,[14] or as "victims" of capitalism— members of a "new working class."[15]

In all of these accounts, change is attributed to urban unrest, to political interests, to increased or decreased effectiveness—to any and all of the above, but rarely to activists' own efforts. Thus, these accounts diminish the role of professionals as social actors and perpetuate myths about them.

The case studies in this book tell a different story. Although related, the interaction between political mobilization by professionals and community clients was far more complex than the conventional story indicates. They are not reducible to one or the other, nor to the historically specific events of the mid-1960s—the New Left, the Civil Rights movement, or federal social legislation.

A third reason is that internal professional development itself has had an impact on the growth of activism. Increasing federal intervention in professional training, research, and service delivery since World War II has produced contradictions in the functioning of the professions. In the past, the professions were only vulnerable to charges of self-interest and class or racial bias at times of economic recession, when services to accustomed groups were endangered or their needs extended. But the expansion of professional services as part of the welfare state defined low-income and minority groups as categorical clients and made such confrontations inevitable. Unequal treatment became a structural feature of everyday professional life, and generated both internal dissent and external demands.

Thus, low-income and minority clients are important to this tale for their role in redefining and challenging professional positions as well as activists' political assumptions. The fact that activist politics was played out with low-income and minority clients has given it a certain direction and flavor. In a similar manner, the women's movement has been important to the development of an internal politics and feminist concerns have moved activism in specific directions, particularly in medicine, but that history has been well-documented and will not be part of this particular study.[16]

Finally, the study of activist professional movements represents a dynamic view of professions. The knowledge base of the professions has been reified by traditionalists, treated as socially constructed by critics and demoted to historically limited outcomes by macro theorists. A focus on those moments of crisis and change in which activists attempted to push professions to the limits allows us to see the professions in a larger historical context.

In the 1980s, key actors have shifted positions. Some professions are under attack by the private sector as well as by the government and owing to their profitability as well as their costs. Critical views stemming from the 1960s have been picked up and used by different actors for differing and even opposing ends—from victim-blaming to the reduction of services. We are now in an even more complex situation, but its roots can partially be understood as an outcome of the professions' reaction to both internal and external pressures.

PROFESSIONAL WORK AND
ACTIVISTS' POLITICAL STRATEGIES

Much of the work on professions has been either classificatory or has studied professionalization as a process to the relative neglect of the examination of professional work itself. For the traditional model and its critics, the structuring of professional work around claims to knowledge and expertise, control of the client relation, and autonomy in the workplace, has been a focus of polemical debate.

As traditionally defined, professional work is the work of "experts"—those who apply a given body of abstract knowledge to specific problems, situations, or cases. Translated into a more or less standardized set of social practices, which is commonly referred to as *professionalism*, the traditional model asserts that the dependence of the client, the knowledge of the expert, and the importance of the task, make it necessary to maintain an impersonal orientation to the task at hand, a hierarchically structured relation between client and professional, and professional control of most if not all aspects of professional work.[17] For critics, on the other hand, professionalism is not a "best solution" to an inherent set of dilemmas, but a form of practice that maximizes professional control to maximize professional self-interest.

Critics and traditionalists have differed in their conceptualization of knowledge and expertise, including whether they are the same thing. For my purposes, I regard them as equivalent. By and large, knowledge leads to expertise and the exercise of expertise leads to further knowledge. Both critics and traditionalists have linked knowledge to autonomy and to labor market control. For both, it is a stabilizing element. This has meant that significant threats to knowledge are presumed to be external.[18] Along the same lines, few have explored the limits or "dysfunctions" of knowledge based work and most have equated scientifically based knowledge with professional security.[19]

One consequence has been that neither traditionalists nor critics foresaw the development of critical knowledge nor the possibility of political radicalization from within professions themselves. Freidson's discussion of the politics of professions in *Professional Powers* is limited to institutionalized politics just as his discussion of knowledge is limited to formal or institutionalized knowledge. But professional politics also occurs in the marketplace where professionals and clients interact and where authority must be confirmed.

This raises the question at the substantive heart of this book— the compatibility of political activism and professional work. What actually happened as activists set out to improve services to minorities and the poor? What constraints did they meet and how did they react to these constraints? Did their beliefs and behavior change and with what results? To address these questions, my analytic methods were twofold: First, I identified three general political strategies of activists and examined them in terms of the central dilemmas or issues of professional work—claims to knowledge, ideals of service, and autonomy. Second, I compared the activist experience in two dramatically different professions—medicine and planning.

In Chapter 2, I introduce the players, medicine and planning and activist organizations of doctors and planners. These professions were chosen because they fall at opposite poles in terms of their knowledge base and occupational control as well as historical development. Chapter 3 examines the historical and developmental context of activism in medicine and planning in the 1960s. This involves tracing federal-professional relations in the post-World War II period with particular attention to how medicine and planning have handled the issue of equity.

Activist professional organizations were guided by a variety of assumptions about the nature of the problems they sought to correct and the solutions they should apply. Whether these assumptions were implicit or took the form of explicit statements, in each case they gave rise to a program and thus became a political strategy. To identify these strategies, I asked two questions of activist organizations for the period under consideration (1960-1978): Why did activists believe their professions had failed to serve minorities and the poor and how did they seek to redress these inequalities? I found that, over the course of almost two decades, activists used three major political strategies: they delivered services, empowered people and attempted to transform society. Chapters 4 through 7 analyze these political strategies and present the case histories in narrative form so that the reader can follow their political development. These case studies were constructed by means of interviews, participant observation, and the use of organizational files.

Chapter 4 begins with delivery strategies, among the first adopted by activists who blamed institutional malfunctioning—professional monopoly and bureaucratic rigidity—for the inequitable distribution of services. The activist roles were advocacy—to incorporate the poor into the market of services by giving technical aid, and professional reform—to put pressure on the professional establishment (represented by national associations and schools of professional education) to fulfill their service claims.

Chapter 5 examines empowerment, a second strategy which emphasized process not outcomes. Professions were seen as bureaucratic actors in organizations which served dominant interests. Professionalism, defined as a system of dominance and dependence, was the culprit, and deprofessionalization, the solution. The problem for minorities and the poor was not lack of experts and services per se, but awe of professionals and service bureaucracies. The activist roles were to mobilize client communities to help themselves and to democratize service delivery by transferring expertise.

Chapters 6 and 7 deal with a third strategy. Social transformation was an explicit socialist analysis in which the problem was identified as the changing economic and political requirements to maintain a capitalist society. The activist solution was to create a political movement for systemwide change, either by workplace organizing (Chapter 6), or by the creation of an intellectual vanguard to demystify and politically educate workers and clients (Chapter 7).

Chapters 8 and 9 draw from the case studies to develop an argument about the ways in which these strategies responded to a variety of forces and events, internal and external. Activists' shifting political strategies were related to issues central to their work—client relations and autonomy, but particularly claims to knowledge.

Although the overt aim of activists was to weaken or radically transform professionalism, radical changes in practice proved to be self-limiting because of their tendency to undermine claims to knowledge, the basis of the legitimate authority of experts. Despite attempts to radically change both ideology and practice, activists could not break out of the constraints of professional work without dissolving their distinctive positions. Thus, attempts to innovate in these areas threatened activists' ability to work, not only their status and prestige.

This is a double argument: the fact that activists "failed" shows the strength of professionalism as a form of organization of skilled services and suggests that critics have gone too far in claiming professionalism to be an "emperor's new clothes" phenomenon. On the other hand, the impact these movements did have undermines the image of a sacred or "inherent" quality to the professions.

2

Medicine, Planning, and Activist Organizations

This book rests on case histories of activist organizations in medicine and city planning over an 18-year period beginning in 1960. I chose two professions which fall at opposite poles on a number of criteria used to define a profession. Medicine closely resembles the traditional model with its standardized body of scientifically based knowledge, required training period, collegial control, service ideals, and until recently, fee-for-service delivery. Planning, which lacks all those features, is typically called a "semiprofession,"[1] a "minor" profession,[2] or a "professionalizing" occupation.[3] Medicine and planning also represent different historical and developmental types.

OCCUPATIONAL DEVELOPMENT OF PLANNING

Planning has its roots in both the social reform and city beautiful movements at the turn of the century. But the institutionalization of planning has been linked to the narrow and more technical perspective which stresses land use and physical planning rather than the broader concern with problem solving or the formulation of societal goals.[4] Progressives in the 1920s saw planning and the independent planning commission as substitutes for corrupt political decision making. Planners were expected to replace machine politics with neutral expertise, and professionalism was promoted along the lines of the models provided by more established professions such as medicine.

The ascendance of technical professionalism was symbolized by the creation of a professional association—The American City Planning Institute—and its separation from the broader movement organization, the National Conference on City Planning, in 1917. Members of the newly minted American City Planning Institute were expected to have "at least two years of experience in some form of city

11

planning activity." The organization's objective was to provide a scientific forum for the presentation of "carefully prepared papers on timely subjects."[5]

Until recently, technical professionalism with its focus on physical or land use planning was the dominant perspective within planning, and the social reform tradition, associated with the quest for public housing, remained a minor but alternative perspective. Social reform briefly gained prominence during the Depression when national priorities meshed with attention to the poor, with housing, and with social problem solving in general.[6] Although the technical model brought planning a measure of institutionalization, growth, and public acceptance, claims to full professional status have always been somewhat problematic for planners.

The debate about what special knowledge and competence planners have, or what planning is, has been temporarily decided one way or another at various historical moments but has never been resolved.[7] One strategy was to stake out a narrowly delineated area of knowledge and specific techniques. While this sort of rationalization enabled the development of professional training programs, specialization was also less flexible and quickly outdated. Planners have also viewed themselves as generalists who contribute a "comprehensive approach" to urban development. As generalists, they have sought coordinating and leadership roles. As generalists they have also stressed the interrelatedness of social and physical factors and methods for predicting and controlling growth.[8]

The midcentury explosion of the city as both cause and site of social problems fueled this debate. On the one hand, urban crises and the resulting national attention increased the perceived functional importance of planning. In lieu of a professional monopoly over licensure[9] or a social mandate, planning was legally institutionalized by federal programs which required city plans as a prerequisite for urban renewal money and which defined the scope and content of planning. On the other hand, rapid change, increased governmental intervention, and the increasing competition of other occupations for dominance within the urban field reinforced the counterclaim for some sort of general and overreaching theoretical or methodological base.

What is the nature of planning's service claim? In contrast to professions such as medicine and law, which offer tangible personal services to individual clients, planning has traditionally offered indirect or impersonal service to a collectively defined client—the public-at-large or to specific areas and neighborhoods. The plan itself has been intangible—a document whose implementation depends upon political processes. Furthermore, until recently, large-scale national planning has been associated with socialism in the United States and has been ideologically blackballed.

Confined to the limited arena of municipal planning, to "counteract the effects of industrialization and urbanization upon the environment," planners have been "aligned with the middle-class, business, home-owning, largely suburban forces, because this was the only segment of American society that had need for planning, if only in a severely restricted role."[10] Planners, for the most part, have ignored the distributive effect of their services and claimed that planning served a unified public interest. Questions of "in whose interest," or the impact of planning on minorities and the poor, remained in the background until the 1960s. There was a corresponding lack of attention to urban research. In contrast to medicine and law, where the explicit market mode of organization encouraged the institutionalization of reformist or social justice claims (legal and medical services for the poor), planning neither recognized separate interests nor institutionalized such services. The reality of public employment and the corporate service ideal meant that the legitimacy of planning often rested with public policy or its implementation—and thus out of the reach of planners' hands.

What of autonomy? Control over the content and performance of work as well as training and entry into the profession have all posed obvious problems for planning. It is said that planning has no real autonomy; that as a bureaucratically located semiprofession, planning has only advisory power to government or corporate interests. Moreover, that the placement of the planning function in decision-making systems is determined largely by forces outside the planning field.[11] Additional support for a civil service designation comes from the observation that the career aspirations of planners tend to lie within administrative ladders as opposed to individual employment.

This means that even if planning were to advance along a model of professionalization as some have claimed—from "adolescent" or aspirant to full professional status—the benefits of such a status are doubtful.[12] Institutional autonomy and legal monopoly are paradoxical as goals for planning. Without entering into the political process, plans may be proposed and printed but need never be implemented. Given the fate of many Master Plans, this issue came into sharper focus during the post-World War II period when planners came to question first the efficacy, not the morality, of a neutral or apolitical stance.

OCCUPATIONAL DEVELOPMENT OF MEDICINE

In contrast to planning, American medicine has been characterized by a scientific knowledge base and market control. It has been the profession *par excellence*, providing sociologists with a model for the professions as well as personifying professionalism to the general public. Revisionist social historians and critics of the "march of science" approach to the history of medicine, have documented historical and political aspects of medicine's success, pointing out how competing models of medical care were displaced and "scientific" medicine gained its dominant position.[13]

In nineteenth-century America, medicine was not credited with much knowledge or expertise. Medicine was fragmented into rival schools, each with competing models contending for public favor.[14] In the tumultuous Jacksonian period, medicine's generally low public esteem and intense factionalism coincided with widespread antiprofessionalism, an expression of class antagonism. Occupations were not seen as areas of expertise but as avenues of mobility which could and should be open to anyone. This meant that requirements such as credentialing in medicine and in law were viewed as exclusionary mechanisms and were popularly attacked.[15]

It was not until the scientific breakthroughs of the late nineteenth century—the bacteriological studies of von Behring, Pasteur, and Koch—that it began to make a difference whether one saw a doctor.[16] Basing their claims on the new laboratory science and on such techniques as the control of infectious disease, a segment of the profession successfully asserted control over training and credentialing. The 1910 Flexner Report on medical education was a key document in this movement.[17] Flexner had surveyed medical schools to find one satisfactory school in the nation, John Hopkins. His report, which called for restructuring medical training and practice around a standardized curriculum with an emphasis on laboratory based scientific medicine, resulted in the subsequent closing of two-thirds of the medical schools in the country. For the most part, these were non-university affiliated "proprietary" schools. The Flexner Report marked the institutionalization of the scientific model of medicine.[18]

While the explicit rationale for the Flexner reforms was to advance and upgrade medical care, the reforms had a notable impact upon the supply and demand aspects of medicine. They eliminated a proliferation of medical schools and competing ideologies and limited the number of physicians. This raised the general cost of care and reduced access for many poor clients.[19] In addition to its self-serving functions for the profession, some critics have suggested that a reformed medicine served early capitalists as well. Philanthropic support for a rationalized and coordinated system of medical care by entrepreneurial figures such as Rockefeller was seen to offset the inequalities and social unrest of the emerging industrial order.[20] Whatever the motivations and whoever benefited, critics agree that it was not by scientific advance alone, or by the survival of the fittest, that scientific medicine gained dominance within medicine. Rather, a combination of philanthropic and guild action, under the banner of an improved medicine, helped to eliminate competing sects and to allow the regular or allopathic physicians to gain control over both medical training and licensure.

An alternate model of "social" medicine emerged in Europe in the mid-nineteenth century with the work of Rudolph Virchow.[21] In contrast to the narrower "scientific" model with its focus on individuals, organs, disease, and single bacteriological causes, the social model of medicine outlined by Virchow took group and class as units of analysis, emphasized multifactoral causation with social as well as bacteriological factors, and looked at prevention and health as well as disease. Virchow's assumptions led to different modes of intervention—to political action such as social insurance, to establishing local health centers, and to family treatment.

This alternate social perspective on medicine was well-developed in Germany and Scandinavia, but was slow to develop in the United States for reasons relating to the dominance of laboratory science techniques and the prevailing nineteenth century ideology of individualism.[22] In the United States the social medicine perspective has been historically associated with industrialism, urbanism, and immigration and with the problems and reforms related to these massive social, economic, and political changes.[23] To the extent that a social medicine approach has developed, it has been narrowly defined as *public health* and reduced from a competing paradigm or overview of medicine to one of many medical specialities—a low prestige specialty.[24]

Historians of medicine have pointed out that stratification of medical care has always existed—with folk practitioners for the majority of the people and the more skilled craftsmen for the upper classes.[25] The impact of the Flexner reforms was to eliminate a variety of intermediary practices and practitioners and to institutionalize an informal two-track system. This meant that the majority would pay for services received and the poor would be treated as charity patients by doctors volunteering their time at municipal or private hospitals. Medicine's code of ethics prescribed charity care and this prescription complemented the need for "practice" patients at the growing teaching hospitals.

Social medicine, on the other hand, has been centrally concerned with poverty and the poor, both conceptually (in terms of etiology) and organizationally (in terms of the delivery and financing of services). Virchow, who saw medicine enmeshed in social activity, put forth a program for public health that included political, economic, and social demands as well as the more limited provisions of care itself.[26] In the United States, attempts to provide more adequate and more broadly defined health services for the poor have taken organizational shape in the Neighborhood Health Center movement of the 1920s and 1930s, the health insurance movement beginning in the 1920s, and in group medical practice.[27] For the most part, these efforts have remained the concern of a socially minded stream of physicians located in public health and somewhat at a remove from mainstream American medicine. These concerns have also remained in the background, claiming public attention only at times of social, economic, or political crisis.[28]

How successful has the scientific, fee-for-service model been that has characterized American medicine until recently? Several issues have emerged over time that relate to the knowledge base, mode of organization, and delivery and service claims.

Scientific medicine has been a hospital based, capital-intensive mode of medical development and treatment. This has meant that despite antipathy to government intervention on the part of the majority of physicians and their representative organization, the American Medical Association (AMA), medical research, training, and service delivery, became increasingly dependent on federal funding. Increased federal funding, in turn, brought with it regulation and control—not only of the clinicians represented by the AMA, but also of the academic medical establishment and of medical research.[29]

In a similarly contradictory manner the scientific medical model, which has focused on organisms that cause disease and on the individual as unit of diagnosis and treatment, has proved both costly and ineffective over time. Critics within the profession as well as governmental and consumer groups have begun to question past statistics and future gains. Has the reigning medical model gone as far as it can go? Do heart disease and cancer require broader definitions of health and illness? Do we need a paradigm which includes social and environmental factors? Some have suggested that socially engineered preventative health measures should replace the current focus on individually oriented diagnosis and care as a major societal effort.[30]

Solo fee-for-service practice has also been a factor in the relative loss of power by physicians to corporate medical interests. During the Depression, for example, when neither hospitals nor doctors were paid by their middle-class patients, the introduction of the principle of third-party payment limited to reimbursing hospitals and hospital practice (as opposed to reimbursing home or office care as well) helped to make the hospital financially independent. A similar point about the shortsightedness of defensive strategies as compared to strategic reform can be made as escalating costs (and profits) in recent decades pushed the federal government and corporate interests to encourage forms of national health insurance, prepaid group plans, and increased competition in the delivery of medical care.[31]

Finally, the organization of a vital service such as medical care as a two class, segregated system of delivery made American medicine vulnerable to demands for reform and change at times of social, political, and economic crisis. Such demands were reinforced by increased federal intervention into various components of the medical system.

These historical overviews suggest that medicine and planning represent opposing structural types. Medicine's knowledge base, for example, is relatively homogeneous and standardized. Its core is "scientific" and, for the most part, produced by the medical profession. Access to prescribed training programs is also professionally controlled. All in all, this creates a large gap between what the expert and the layperson know.[32] Planning, on the other hand, lacks a unified or a standardized knowledge base. A common complaint of the planning literature—who are we and what is planning—reflects this general state of dissension. Training programs differ in the content of what they teach and in how they train planners. Unlike medicine, planning has developed in response to external stimuli such as economic development or expanding governmental functions, and like engineering, from a functionally diverse as opposed to a homogeneous core of knowledge.

Medicine's prized knowledge base has been used to gain occupational control over practice as well as training and entry.[33] Doctors "dominate" the health-related professions with whom they typically interact.[34] They have also been able to retain control over their work in such bureaucratic settings as hospitals. Planners, in contrast, have typically remained unlicensed and professional entry has been by a variety of routes in addition to university training programs.[35] Among the related disciplines with which the planner comes into contact, there is no generally agreed-upon consensus as to the authority of the planner who is often low man on the totem pole.[36]

Typical modes of organization and service delivery also differ. Although historical investigation has qualified the concept of the "free" professions, doctors, until fairly recently, have been predominantly self-employed, solo practitioners while planners have been salaried members of public sector bureaucracies.[37]

If we look at claims to service in terms of the client-professional relation, there are equally dramatic differences. City planners have not traditionally offered direct personal service to the objects of their services.[38] In planning, an intermediate client or consumer who can also be an employer, is often interposed between the planner and the public. This has raised questions of conflicting loyalties.[39] As a public employee, the planner most typically operates as staff without supervisory line authority. As a public employee, the planner also faces a client or consumer whose identity is intangible and problematic—an area population and their representatives. In the 1960s, the location and definition of this client became controversial, giving rise to the question "in whose interest."

The typical interaction of doctor and patient is direct and private; this has organizational significance. Privacy traditionally makes for low visibility and greater autonomy.[40] Although the increasing prevalence of group and hospital practice for doctors has qualified this distinction, planning, which is situated in the heart of the political arena and publicly visible, remains more open to both regulation and attack. Planners' clients are easier to mobilize because they already have a collective identity and planning has traditionally had a greater degree of client as well as governmental regulation.

Another comparative dimension is the relative importance of the service to the population at large. Most would agree that health is the more salient concern since it is a universal, deals with life and death, and gives rise to a seemingly limitless demand for service. Medicine and planning also have different societal connotations. Medicine has been associated with the conquest of disease and increased longevity, with science, modernization, and progress. It has been ideologically as well as organizationally congruent with the market in a capitalist society. Planning has less positive connotations. Associated with both capitalism (protectionist zoning regulations) and socialism (centralized planning and state expansion), it has been ideologically challenged by the left and the right on both these accounts.

Finally, medicine and planning also represent different historical and developmental types which are commonly referred to as "old" and "new" professions. Medicine is the classic nineteenth-century "free" or market profession which began as part of the self-employed middle class and has only recently become salaried. Planning is a prototype of the newer organizational or state sponsored professions whose emergence and advancing fortunes have followed the growth of large-scale organizations and governmental functions in advanced industrial society. As a consequence, it has been located predominantly in the public sector.[41]

The rationale for the choice of medicine and planning is that a comparison of patterns of activism and their outcomes in two such differing professions should help us understand the capacity of professions to constrain and shape change. Traditional models, for example, assert the importance of attributes, particularly, the knowledge base, but does a strong knowledge base or control over work make for a greater ability to resist change? If so, how much of a difference does it make and is the difference in the direction expected by traditional theory?

Alternately, critics have argued that attributes do not define professions and that it is the successfully defended claim that matters. This line of reasoning suggests that activists can dispense with traditional claims. Also, if claims crumble or can no longer be successfully defended, there will be change for all professions, even those "closest" to the model.

At another level of analysis, macro theorists have argued that differences between professions which are related to their historical origins (organizational or free) and to so-called inherent characteristics (knowledge base) are being outweighed by economic, technological, and political forces, making for a convergence of occupations composed of educated labor. A comparative framework which utilizes widely divergent cases also permits us to consider the impact of large scale changes on the work situations and politics of doctors and planners.

The limits of professionalization have generally been thought of as either internal to the profession—the inherent limits of a particular set of attributes such as its knowledge base, or external to its control—the result of long-term trends such as increasing bureaucratization or a more educated and demanding public. These case studies describe an alternate scenario in which liberal and reformist groups within professions are shown to have been active agents over the past several decades, both initiating and facilitating change.

They set limits to professionalization (they *deprofessionalized*) as well as to deprofessionalization (they *reprofessionalized*).

CHOOSING ACTIVIST ORGANIZATIONS

My data consist of 19 case histories of activist organizations over an 18-year period beginning in 1960, 8 in city planning and 11 in medicine. Although the groups, mostly in Boston and New York City, are not representative in a statistical sense, I familiarized myself with the character and scope of activism in other areas as well during that period through extensive reading and interviews. That plus my own experience of the 1960s and 1970s leads me to conclude that they represent typical activist strategies and dynamics.

In planning, the selection of activist organizations was influenced by the particular case history of Urban Planning Aid (UPA), an early and well-known advocacy planning group in Boston. Organized in response to threats to homes and community posed by plans for highway construction and urban renewal in a poor neighborhood, UPA spanned the period under examination and went through several significant changes which correspond to the political strategies described in Part II. This led to the decision to let UPA serve as a model for planning activism over the period and to treat it as a major case study in planning.

UPA's usefulness is also related to its longevity. Its organizational history cut across the differing policies of successive federal administrations, the rise and fall of political and social movements, the aging of individual members, and the entry of new cohorts. Organizational longevity also meant that UPA was resourceful and survived various crises.

In addition to UPA, I made a series of briefer case studies of a number of activist groups selected on the basis of their analytic or empirical interest. Groups such as the Newark Community Union Project (NCUP) and Planners for Equal Opportunity (PEO) present us with differing responses to the pressures of the Civil Rights and the New Left movements, movements increasingly critical of technical aid by professionals, particularly white professionals, and of reform in general.

The Urban Field Service (UFS) at Harvard University is included because it represents an example of an attempt to locate advocacy within a university setting. Although the university came under attack in the 1960s, it has also been viewed as a seedbed for innovation and criticism and as a sheltering institution for activists in a number of fields. The experience of UFS provides some insight into the tensions between the growing academic component of planning and those desiring community change. I also use UFS to discuss the relative advantages of strategies of social transformation compared to benefits strategies for planners in academia.

The shift from communities and community clients to institutional sites and professional constituencies reflected activists' experience with community based efforts; changes in the opportunity structure for activism as federal monies ran out; and changes in the Civil Rights and New Left movements—the emergence of Black Power and of a branch of the New Left, the Movement for Democratic Society (MDS).

Attention to organizing planners (and other professionals) as a constituency in the late 1960s owed much to the New Left, which intersects planning activism with two different strategies. NCUP represents the first or antiprofessional phase in which the main thrust was community organizing projects in the ghettos with planners hired to work directly for the movement.

The second phase, MDS, focused on the position, needs, and change potential of the "alumnae" of the student movement. Organized by a maturing generation of student radicals who sought political continuity, its main concerns were to define "radical roles" for those who had left school and joined the middle-class labor force and to articulate models of radical life in the professions as an alternative to the established professional community.[42] As a direction within the New Left, MDS was liberated by the failure of the ghetto strategy.

The Urban Underground represents one of the earliest and most successful of the MDS groups. The Urban Underground organized primarily within the New York City Department of City Planning and attacked the myths of planning. This involved public testimony by city employees on the use and misuse of their technical reports.

Another example of work based activism was an ongoing attempt to politicize the technical guild of a municipal civil service union composed primarily of city planners and engineers. The experience of the Urban Underground and the Technical Guild address the viability of a strategy whose constituency are planners in bureaucratic settings. Both also tell us about the impact of the fiscal crisis on public workers in the 1970s. In addition to these politically initiated efforts. I introduce several studies of bureaucratic insurgency or reform to give further insight into the possibilities and limitations of institutionally based modes for activist planners.[43]

The Planners Network and Homefront allow us to explore activists' impetus to create more overt political and theoretical frameworks as a basis for action, as well as the problems and contradictions stemming from these attempts.

In medicine, unlike planning, I did not find a prototypic case to use as a model of activist political development. So I have selected organizations which represent typical strategies as well as those of particular analytic or empirical interest. Two organizations with a national presence, the Student Health Organizations (SHO) and the Medical Committee for Human Rights (MCHR), marked the start of a decade of renewed health activism.[44] Originating in the 1960s in the context of Civil Rights and the student movements, these organizations addressed social contradictions within medicine that had been exacerbated by federal policies of the post-World War II period.

SHO and MCHR were both empirically and analytically important. They were both large-scale efforts that involved doctors, medical students and other health workers; they both had local chapters as well as a national office. Each had a direct impact on the medical establishment as well as on the cohorts of medical students and doctors who were active members. Both began as liberal movements of professional reform and over the course of time changed their assumptions and strategy. Given its constituency, SHO directed its attention to medical schools while MCHR addressed the AMA and the broader professional establishment.

Attempts to create alternative decentralized service delivery ranged from federally funded Neighborhood Health Centers (NHC) to store-front "free" clinics staffed by volunteers. For the most part, the NHC were initiated and controlled by medical centers. I selected the North East Neighborhood Association (NENA) Health Center in New York City, one of the few genuinely community initiated and controlled efforts and one that kept its independence from university medical centers. In choosing NENA as a case study, I was interested both in understanding its initial success as measured by its independence, and in using NENA as a deviant case to illustrate the limits of even a community initiated and controlled health center as a strategy for medical activists. I also compared NENA with the Martin Luther King, Jr. Health Center in New York—a medical school initiated and controlled health center.

Institutionally based organizing was a logical as well as a chronological next step for a generation of SHO activists. I selected the Lincoln Collective—one of the most publicized medical collectives—and the Committee of Interns and Residents (CIR), the first and largest housestaff union, as examples of work based efforts. Both are in New York City.

Although collectives and housestaff unions emerged elsewhere,

New York City was central to this phase of activity for several primarily historical reasons. First, New York City had a well-developed system of public hospitals alongside a growing private and voluntary sector. The existence of this dual hospital system and the political dynamics uniting the two sectors, gave rise to policy analysis of the trends of the public and private sectors. This made New York City hospitals a focus of attention and a proposed model for the country.[45] Second, the existence of numerous city hospitals affiliated with prestigious medical schools meant a concentration of housestaff slots in New York City in the public sector. This was conducive to organizing and consciousness raising. Finally, New York City, with its dwindling tax base and its relatively generous welfare services, was the first of our cities to experience the fiscal crisis of the 1970s. This encouraged activism in the public sector among workers over jobs and conditions, and within the community for groups whose services were being cut.

To gain additional perspective, I compared New York City's CIR with two other politically active housestaff associations—the Los Angeles County Joint Council of Interns and Residents and the Cook County Housestaff Association in Chicago. At the national level, I also examined the Physicians National Housestaff Association (PNHA).

In choosing research organizations, I selected two whose analysis has been most influential in shaping the health movement—the Health Policy Advisory Center (Health/PAC) and the East Coast Health Discussion Group (ECHDG). For a good part of the period under study, Health/PAC was the organization responsible for providing political analysis and leadership. Health/PAC popularized the "medical empires" analysis of the health care system and in 1989 was still publishing the *Bulletin*, the "longest continuously publishing insurgent health publication in the United States." The ECHDG broke with Health/PAC's concrete, mid-level analysis of actors and interests to emphasize theory building, ideology and culture as "political battlegrounds," and to make explicit use of Marxist analysis.

The variety of the cases described above raises the issue of comparability. Can we compare a loosely knit communications network mailed to several hundred radical planners to a housestaff union? Some of the activist organizations existed more on paper while other met full-time staff payrolls and had mandated objectives and activities. Some were small in size—even one-person efforts— while others were large organizations. Some were open in membership and relatively informal while others involved dues, collective lifestyles, and political commitments. Some were short-lived while others lasted many years.

Because my objective was to sample representative types as well as to examine analytically and empirically important examples of activism, variety was inevitable. Variety was also an integral part of the study—the phenomenon to be explained—since at different times I saw that activists sought different organizational solutions to their needs. This meant I became interested in organizational structure particularly when it became an issue for activists. For example, when an "intensive" live-in collective was seen as crucial to the viability of a community project or when a local organization felt that without creating a national organization it would not be able to move toward its social transformation objectives, even if the national organization remained a "paper" organization.

Another methodological point is the use of comparative analysis and deviant case analysis to strengthen and maximize single cases. For example, I compared the CIR with two other major "radical" housestaff associations in Chicago and Los Angeles. This enabled me to evaluate the impact of historical, legal, and political differences. Then, by examining the national association, PNHA, and interviewing a range of less radical and nonradical housestaff leaders, I was able to put the radical experience into the broader context of housestaff unions with less political leaders, in different types of hospitals, and in a variety of geographic areas, nonurban as well as urban.

The use of deviant case analysis is illustrated by the selection of the NENA Health Center. By examining one of the few genuinely community initiated and controlled health centers, I was able to illustrate the limits of even a community initiated and controlled health center as a strategy for medical activists. I also compared the experience of activists at NENA with a more traditional model, a medical center affiliated health center, Dr. Martin Luther King, Jr.

The cases, for the most part, were drawn from the New York City/Boston area. While remaining regionally bound to the northeast might limit generalization to activist organizations in other parts of the country, it enabled interviewing and collecting written data, and also helped the longitudinal analysis. Given the complexity of issues, political environments, and actors, a regional focus made it possible to hold some of these factors constant over time, allowing me to follow a historical and developmental progression of issues, strategies, and organizational forms within a given geographical area. Moreover, this study does not claim to sample statistically or to come up with scientific generalizations. This study is explicitly historical, comparative, and developmental and its aim is to generate theoretical observations from the data.[46]

In addition to selected local case histories, I included major attempts at national organizations of activist doctors and planners during this period. While problems and dynamics at the national level can differ, the inclusion of these organizations is particularly important in directing attention to the interplay between activists and national level actors such as the professional establishment (the American Medical Association [AMA] or the American Institute of Planners [AIP]) and the federal government. National efforts also provided a broader view of activism to help counteract any regional bias.

The actual case analysis follows the dynamics of activist ideas and actions over time. I have organized the case materials by asking the following questions: (1) What did activists want to change and how did they go about doing it? (2) What was the activist experience over time? By this I mean, what dilemmas or contradictions emerged in the course of action and what modifications followed? (3) What was the success or failure of various types of efforts? My focus is on both the dynamics of particular cases and the overall trajectory of activities and ideas over time.

ACCESS TO PEOPLE AND PAPER

To construct case studies of activist organizations, I interviewed participants and leaders, inspected documents and files, and became a participant observer.

Because the unit of analysis is organizations, locating and gaining access to records and files, including minutes, correspondence, newsletters, magazines, published reports, and in some cases membership lists, was crucial. This proved difficult to do for a variety of reasons. Given the diversity of these organizations in terms of size, duration, organizational structure, and visibility, I found that some were virtually undocumented but for a few leaflets and were "alive" only in the memories of their participants. Others, such as the Student Health Organizations, published numerous volumes of annual reports from projects at multiple sites across the country. These reports, which include personal essays by participants and comments by sponsoring community organizations, proved to be rich resources. In one well-known organization, a history of political controversy as well as the appropriate caution of people on the Left made it difficult to get interviews or files. As with many action projects, scorn for keeping written accounts meant that recordkeeping was not done in an organized way. Thus, the researcher had to be lucky enough to find a former leader or participant who had "kept papers." Finally, the passing of time along with the mobility of middle-class professionals—activists included—meant that participants and papers were geographically dispersed.

The nature and often personal location of the data meant that I had to travel by a reference route—from one person's friend to another's. Whether for interviews or records, I found that entry into the radical community took credentials. Mine were antiwar and antisegregation activities in Ann Arbor, Michigan and Shreveport, Louisiana in the 1960s and the network of people I knew from that period. Without this shared grounding in what turned out to be a formative period for many of the activists I spoke with, it would have been much more difficult to gain empathic access to many informants, and perhaps impossible with a few. In fact, several interviews with activists who subsequently gave me other names and telephone numbers, felt more like interrogations than interviews. They focused on my past—who I knew and what I had done—and only after having established my background credentials did we begin to talk.

My involvement in two health organizations and one planning organization became another source of access to people and paper. I began to collect material on planning and interview planners in the spring of 1976. During 1976-1977, I served on the voluntary steering committee of the New York Area Planners Network, interviewed planners involved in other activist efforts, and attended a number of planning conferences to become more familiar with the issues and attitudes of planners in general and activist planners in particular.

Although my work on activist medical organizations overlapped with planning, I began to wind down commitments in planning at the end of 1977 and became more involved with medical organizations in 1977 and 1978. In the fall of 1977, I began to examine Health/PAC's files. During the same year, I also helped with fund-raising efforts which culminated in a 10th anniversary celebration in spring 1978. In spring 1978, I began to attend the East Coast Health Discussion Group. At the time, the group had just opened its doors to new members. My work on CIR—the New York City housestaff union—had actually begun in 1975 during its "historic strike," when I had interviewed union leaders and collected material for an earlier paper. In 1977, I reestablished contact with CIR, interviewing executive staff and officers. In spring 1978, I attended the national meetings of the Physicians National Housestaff Association where I was able to sit in on executive meetings and interview housestaff leaders from organizations across the country. When I was in San Francisco in 1978, I interviewed housestaff officials at the San Francisco General Hospital, along with several other local health activists to compare health activism on the West Coast with activism on the East Coast. At that time I also interviewed Chester Hartman, who had organized the Planners Network, about Network activities in the Bay Area. The lack of travelling funds kept me from interviewing perhaps a dozen more leaders and organizational participants with whom I would have liked to speak, and in some cases, I was able to conduct interviews over the telephone.

In the course of my fieldwork, I gained access to many personal files. The unexpected kept happening. Someone gave me three boxes of material on one seminal organization no longer in existence; another person gave me folders full of publications by the Radicals in the Professions project of the New Left. People whom I interviewed, identified and found key letters, memos, or documents that I was able to duplicate. One organization allowed me to make use of their extensive files. Rather than the dreaded dearth of materials, there came a time when I felt I would never get through what I had. Not only were the records very engrossing; intermixed with agendas and formal letters, I came across personal notes, letters, poems, and, at times, photographs that brought the period alive. Reading through these scattered and incomplete files was like working on a jigsaw puzzle. When the picture had gaps, I had to find people who could help me fill it in.

Interviews

I conducted 25 interviews with planners and 36 interviews with medical activists. The interviews were with leaders of activist organizations and with key organizational participants. When accounts differed, I made certain to interview several leaders or participants to get a fuller story. In almost all cases, I was able to get several accounts of each organization studied. Interviews lasted approximately two hours and in several cases, I needed more than one interview from an informant. One doctor spoke with me for four lengthy sessions.

My procedure was to take notes during and after the interview rather than to use a tape recorder. The advantages of full replay and of being able to look up more often were outweighed by the reluctance of some informants to be recorded (I had tried the tape recorder at the beginning), the lack of funds for transcription, and by my own past experience with both methods. I felt comfortable taking notes in my own shorthand and filling them in afterward.

The interviews, which were oriented toward getting organizational case histories, were semistructured. For a general guide, I had a series of questions or topics to be discussed. For specific organizations, I prepared several key issues or events that I wanted to focus upon.

Informants were asked first for a brief personal history. Here, I explored their linkages with social and political movements, schools and organizations, and other activists. Then, they were asked to describe each organization—how it began, its leaders and members, organizational structure, ideology, strategies, and goals. We explored the organization's external and internal politics—inter-actions between clients and activists and among activists as well as between activists and sponsors, social and political movements, professional associations and schools. I asked for specific examples of controversial issues. To clarify whose response I was getting, I would ask the respondent what he or she felt, and then the official organizational position. I looked for and probed all comments related to changes in goals, means, or points of view. I also asked informants for their personal assessment as well as the organization's assessment of its failures and success. The analysis of why they and their organization thought a given strategy had succeeded or failed become important as I began to see that the subsequent strategies of individuals, organizations, and the activist movement as a whole, had to be viewed, in part, in the context of activist self-assessment. I asked informants about their own involvement with the organizations. When and why it had started? When and why it had ended? Whether they had continued to do alternate work?

The interviews were the most challenging and rewarding part of the study. To begin with, some of my informants had devoted themselves to activism since the 1940s and 1950s. Many were still involved in alternate work, although in some cases, its nature or form had changed because of changing life cycle needs or lack of appropriate jobs. In other cases, activists under similar pressures had turned their particular expertise and even their radicalism into profitable careers. I found that radical commitments were sustained over time by the existence of a loose network or community among fellow activists who shared past and current experiences. Like musicians and artists whose careers are characteristically "hard times," radicals in the professions seemed to get by "with a little help from their friends."

Among those interviewed were activists who also described themselves as "burnt out for radical work" or "taking a rest." This seemed to be more of a problem for doctors than for planners, and among doctors, for those wholly involved in clinical work. For one doctor, alternate work, chosen years before at the cost of a career which promised much greater financial success and status, was at the time of the interview, a cause of embitterment. He felt that the community efforts he had given his life to had become both bureaucratized and poor quality medicine. "Maybe," he said, "I would have done better if I had had a conventional career, earned a lot of money, and given it to other activists."

For planners in general, alternate careers were less costly. Planners did not have clearly identifiable career lines, nor experience a large gap in either money or status in moving between alternative and main line careers. There was much less stigma attached to alternative work, and it was easier to go into and out of establishment positions. One planner, who was forced to leave an eight-year commitment to a radical organization for financial reasons, was delighted with the mainstream job, found it a source of new ideas and perspectives, and felt that perhaps more radicals should get out into the "heart of the capitalist system."

3

The Postwar Context
of Activism

The 1960s were marked by innovative federal service delivery programs and new social and political movements as well as by the rise
of activism directed at professions. Before turning to the case studies,
these developments must be placed in the context of changing state
involvement with professions and professional work and the wider
political significance of this activity. While the professions have been
vulnerable to intermittent charges of self-interest and class or racial
bias in the past, I argue that their growth as part of the welfare state
has made such confrontation a structural feature of everyday professional life.

Social historians have often pointed out that the growth of the
professions has been intimately related to that of the state. Still, the
post-World War II period reflects a watershed both in terms of
federal involvement and professional expansion. After World War II,
federal policy with respect to the professions and professional services can be divided into three roughly defined periods: the "pro-
growth" period from the war to the early 1960s, the service strategies
of the 1960s, and retrenchment and cost-containment beginning in
the 1970s.[1]

In the immediate post-war period, legislation funded urban
renewal, hospital construction, and biomedical research at the
National Institutes of Health (NIH) and the National Science Foundation (NSF). This legislation encouraged research based growth and
expansion in medicine and planning. By contrast, the War on Poverty
legislation of the 1960s created new channels of service delivery for
minorities and the poor with such programs as Office of Economic
Opportunity (OEO) funded advocacy planning programs, Neighborhood Health Centers, and Medicaid. These programs often specified
community participation and planning initiative. Minorities and the
poor were to become clients rather than objects of services. In

further contrast, cost-containment policies of the 1970s initiated a variety of mechanisms to rationalize, regulate, and cut back on the costly services and programs of the 1960s. Examples include the Community Development Act, Comprehensive Health Manpower Training Act, Professional Standards Review Organization (PSRO) program, and the Health Maintenance Act as well as local and informal "planned shrinkage" policies.

Professional activism occurred in the context of these federally sponsored programs and was often dependent upon or grew out of federally funded community based action. Moreover, changes in clients, roles, the organization of work, and the scope of activity, must be seen in relation to these federal programs and policies.

The 1960s also marked the reemergence of social movements. These movements influenced professional activism in a number of ways. The Civil Rights and the student or New Left movement established a general ideological context critical of dominant institutions and favoring substantive social change. In comparison to the right-wing ascendancy which characterized the McCarthy era of the 1950s, and which was responsible for "killing off" a number of activist groups in medicine, architecture, and planning, the political movements of the 1960s supported the emergence and spread of left-wing groups.[2] In addition to a favorable ideological environment, these movements contributed specific strategies to groups struggling for change. They also served as a training ground for a generation of students, many of whom entered professional schools within the same decade.

The Civil Rights movement had a similar direct impact upon reform-minded professionals. Civil Rights provided the original legitimacy for many organized efforts in the early 1960s. The movement's turn toward Black Power was equally important. As ghettos repudiated white professionals, activist organizations oriented toward civil rights split along the lines drawn by these issues. Central questions for activist professionals over the course of the decade became: Who is our constituency? What is our role? Are we a service group for other organizations or are we actors in our own right? Can we legitimately act on behalf of others or should we limit ourselves to correcting our own institutional practices?

The opportunities and threats these events posed for planning and medicine, and the activist response, raise a number of issues. First, how did each profession handle the issue of equity—the provision of services to minorities and the poor. What claims does the profession make, what modes of service delivery exist, and what is the relation of dominant and alternate models of professional knowledge to the question of who benefits? Gouldner and others have suggested that scientific and technical rationality is a weak base for social legitimacy and that experts must generate a larger morality.[3] To explore this issue, medicine and planning will be examined as service delivery systems and as political formulas, going back to the formative Progressive period.

Second, what is the relation between increased government intervention and professional development—including activism? What was the impact of successive federal policies upon the delivery of services, on knowledge base, and on the relations between producers and clients? For example, did federally funded expansion diminish or accentuate class and racial biases in service delivery and outcomes? To what extent did new federal programs provide a collective experience for many planners and doctors? What was the impact of shifting federal programs upon activism? To address these questions, I examine the relation between federal programs and professional development starting with the post-World War II period, as the war seemed to mark a turning point both for federal intervention and for professional expansion.

CONDITIONS GIVING RISE TO
ACTIVISM IN PLANNING

For most observers, World War II marks the "great divide"—the beginning of a "golden age" and the "coming of age" of planning in America.[4] Most writers credit policies of federal intervention for the period of occupational growth: federally sponsored education and research in general, and urban renewal and highway transportation legislation in particular. Among the factors that favored both state intervention and planning were successful wartime experience with planning, postwar needs for economic growth and development (particularly for housing, education and jobs), and the decline of central cities relative to their faster growing suburbs.[5]

Beginning with the Housing Act of 1949, successive legislation tied federal funds for cities and transportation systems to planning activities.[6] According to the rhetoric of the Housing Act, the rationale for an enlarged federal role in urban rebuilding was a composite promise of greater rationality, efficiency and equity (social justice) to be achieved by planned growth.[7] The legislative mechanisms that expanded planning included requiring plans from areas seeking funds; allocating funds for planning staff; earmarking funds for education, training, and research connected with planning; and creating new planning agencies at city, state, and regional levels.[8]

This federally funded expansion later provided the context in which mounting public criticism and self-criticism of planning occurred.

Postwar policies were associated, first, with human and technical capitalization. The increased number and variety of employment opportunities led to a desperate need for planners. This meant that planning agencies hired persons holding B.A. degrees and trained them on the job.[9] There was a corresponding increase in the number and size of academic programs turning out planners.[10] During this same period, the U. S. Civil Service Commission recognized city planning as a profession and gave exams for department and field positions for planners in the federal government.[11] Finally, the growing importance of planning led to the creation of the federal Department of Housing and Urban Development (HUD) in 1964.

The growth of the academic planning establishment was associated with the increased importance of research as "an adjunct to city planning." In the postwar period, research institutes focusing on urban problems emerged. At these institutes, planners developed new knowledge to give planning more power and relevance. One form this took was the introduction of social science perspectives into planning.[12] Complementing these changes, was a shift in the background of planners—from predominantly architecture and engineering to the social sciences.[13]

In addition to the growth of both supply and demand and the rise of an academic establishment oriented to research, the social organization of planning changed. As planners became involved in carrying out legislatively mandated programs, the structural locus of planning shifted closer to decision making and to the centers of power: "Plans have become the companions of policy and the planner has moved inside government into a position similar to that of a general staff in an army."[14] Along with politicization went new roles and functions. As one enthusiast said, "Planners are increasingly abandoning their aloof role of unloved civic vestal virgins. . . . Plans are ceasing to be the civic New Year's resolution and embalmed work of art . . . and [are] becoming the action programs of a problem-solving community."[15]

Looking back with the advantage of hindsight, some were far less positive about this change. Beyle and Lathrop, for example, found politics and planning an "uneasy marriage," conducive to political patronage and to even more conservative functions.[16] State intervention made the planner more of a vehicle than the arbiter of the "ideals" of the city beautiful or efficient. Although planning gained in efficacy in that plans were now funded to be carried out, there were complementary losses in autonomy as the government became the taskmaster. Federal programs, for example, redefined planning roles and methods by requiring community participation as a requisite for funding.[17] Class relations were also affected. For example, federal mandates designated categorical clients—minorities and the poor in slum areas. Housing legislation further defined the relationship of planners to the poor: planners were to redevelop the slums and blighted areas and to relocate the poor.[18] By underwriting activities oriented to specific clients, such mandates fractured the planner's ideology of a "unitary public interest." One consequence was that the profession could more easily be implicated in the outcomes of the programs, both their success and failure.

Finally, as gatekeepers to federal funds, increased power and prestige accrued to planning activities and planners. Expressed more cynically, politicians found that planning constituted "gold."[19] This period saw the rise of entrepreneurial figures or "power brokers" such as Logue in New Haven and Moses in New York, who packaged land, developers, and federal funds for the benefit of city interests.[20] Along with the entrepreneurial role went another new image—that of planner as bureaucrat, the person with expertise in filling out forms, writing proposals, and pushing the requisite paperwork through the bureaucracy.

The postwar transformation of planning can be summarized as an expanding professional body with an academically based, social science oriented segment, interested in innovation and seeking authority commensurate with their increasing numbers. While internal change was complemented by a federally sponsored expansion of opportunities, the increased demand, efficacy, and status of planning carried a certain price.

Accompanying these changes in the objective conditions of professional work, were changes in the dominant ideas and consciousness of planners. Federally sponsored activities such as urban renewal and transportation legislation did not begin controversy for planning. Questions such as "in whose interests" or the relation of planning to minorities and the poor had been raised before.[21] However, large-scale public funding of planning activities, widespread employment of planners in these efforts, and the subsequent gap between the rhetoric of the legislation ("a decent living environment for every American family") and the reality of who got what, made a latent issue into a matter of general public concern.

Urban renewal and transportation programs benefited central business interests and private developers at the cost of minorities and the poor and did so in a highly visible fashion and at a time when ghetto populations were beginning to be mobilized by Civil

Rights. This raised a series of issues. Criticism was directed not only at the specifics of the legislation, its advocates, and at local implementation, but also at dominant models of planning. For example, social scientists looking at urban renewal suggested that the theory and methods of traditional physical planning were inadequate. Physical planning was too narrow a conception of the scope of planning and might be a consequence rather than a cause.[22]

Second, the outcomes, variously described as "Negro removal" or "aid to the rich at public expense," raised questions about the class and racial biases of core assumptions such as the concept of *slum*. Slum was criticized as an evaluative not an empirical term and planners were asked what they knew about the needs of low-income people. There were similar questions about the alignment of planning with politicians and with business and real estate interests.[23] Critics suggested that the doctrine of a monolithic public interest on behalf of which planners act, and which they are presumed to know, was at best a generalization of middle-class experience, and at worst, a screen for the play of private interests.

Urban renewal served as a source of conflict for planners as well as for a more general public. While Jane Jacobs, associate editor of *Architectural Forum*, popularized the criticism of redevelopment for its destruction of neighborhoods, she objected mainly to tall buildings and "projects." The first wave of critics included planners and other professionals, many of whom had been involved in various aspects of the renewal programs.[24] Drawing upon his experience in Boston's West End, Herbert Gans wrote the first criticism of redevelopment to appear in the *Journal of the American Institute of Planners* (*JAIP*).[25] He attacked the cultural biases of middle-class professionals and asked "who benefits?" Members of the same West End project (Chester Hartman, Marc Fried, and Peggy Gleicher) put forth similar perspectives in *JAIP* as did John Seeley, Peter Marris, and Walter Thabit.[26]

The criticism and self-criticism supported and helped direct a progressive analysis put forward by the expanding, social science based academic wing of the profession. For part of this group, urban renewal issues provided the mandate for desired change—for a broader social planning and for research and social action.[27]

Analysis of *JAIP*'s contents during this period shows successive attempts to remake the professional formula in response to urban problems; also the emergence of a call-to-arms regarding minorities and the poor. Early critics called for a pluralistic, mid-range, goal-oriented planning which, while strong on user orientation, did not specify the particular needs of minorities or the poor. Later critics identified poverty and race as key variables and examined the impact of planning on minorities and the poor.

Gans and Seeley's work on urban renewal was with predominantly white, working-class neighborhoods. Marris, who had worked on urban displacement in Africa, raised questions about the racial and class consequences of urban renewal in the United States. Both Marris and Gans questioned the traditional solutions put forward by planners. They suggested that the poor might want jobs and income more than housing or education and raised the issue of the planner's responsibility to the low-income populations most often hurt by redevelopment.[28]

By the mid-1960s, Frieden, Rein, and Davidoff directly addressed poverty. Asking what planners could do, Frieden answered, "identify the impact . . . on the poor and on minority groups."[29] Davidoff, who developed the concept of advocacy planning, continued: "At a time when concern for the condition of the poor finds institutionalization in community action programs, it would be appropriate for planners concerned with such groups to find means to plan with them."[30] By 1968, the issues of race and poverty had "arrived" on the pages of the *JAIP* and were treated from a variety of perspectives. This paralleled rising racial tension and black militance, the growing "comprehensiveness" of federal legislation, and the development of activist movements within the profession.

The seeds of more radical criticism were also planted. Gans's work, for example, provides an increasingly more structural understanding of what is wrong with urban renewal and with planning.[31] Beginning with the "caretakers" who define and solve problems by reference to their middle-class values and who would rather offer the traditional planning package of housing and transportation than jobs, Gans goes on to attack poverty and racial discrimination as a consequence of national priorities and policy making.

This progression suggests that urban renewal challenged a generation of planners to increasingly critical perspectives. As expansion occurred, political activism as well as criticism, developed among planners.

CONDITIONS GIVING RISE TO ACTIVISM IN MEDICINE

World War II marked a divide for medicine as well as for planning. Although the roots of change go back further, during the postwar period there was significant growth at all levels of the health system. Here, too, observers have cited the importance of the wartime experience in enabling postwar policies of federal intervention.[32]

The war, "like the Great Depression, dramatized medical needs."[33] When physical exams showed that one out of three draftees was medically unfit, attention focused on the poor health and level of medical care of the public.[34] Unlike the Depression, however, it was possible to demonstrate new ways of attacking these needs during the war. The experience of 15 million armed services personnel with a comprehensive and well-organized system of medical care—many of them for the first time in their lives—probably raised everyone's postwar expectations regarding medical care.[35] These findings and the successful experience with planned or "socialized" medicine, lowered the credibility of the AMA, which had consistently linked the fee-for-service mode of organization with American medicine's superior performance.

Wartime organization of medical services accelerated the trend to specialization among doctors and introduced a generation of doctors to salaried medicine, group practice, and to the importance of social-psychological variables such as stress.[36] At the same time, the war demonstrated to policymakers, physicians, and the general public that planning and organization could make resources more effective and improve care.[37] The war also encouraged the growth of voluntary and commercial insurance plans for hospital care. At a time of wage squeezes, the National Labor Relations Board (NLRB) allowed collective bargaining for fringe benefits such as employer-paid health plans. As a result, hospital insurance, initiated in the 1930s by Blue Cross for the middle class, was extended through union contracts to part of the working class.[38]

The postwar period also marked the beginning of major federal intervention into the health system. Outside of carefully delineated areas of public health, the government's prewar stance to medicine was laissez-faire, partly out of disinterest, partly due to the AMA's political strength.[39] After the war, President Truman voiced the changing view when he proposed a five-point national health plan to include support for medical schools and students, research funding, hospital construction and health insurance.[40] The Magnuson Commission, appointed somewhat later by Truman to determine the health needs of the nation, came up with a similar agenda and stated as its premise that "access to the means for attainment and preservation of health is a basic human right."[41]

Although certain sectors of the health establishment were in favor of federal aid, the opposition of the AMA and Congress successfully limited government funding to the two most "neutral" areas: research and hospital construction.[42] In both these areas, federal intervention also served postwar development needs. Voluntary hospital construction had been almost nonexistent during the 1930s and 1940s and research, prior to 1940, had been both small scale and privately funded.[43] Wartime efforts had demonstrated the successful collaboration of the government with private universities in the discovery of penicillin, sulfa, and gamma globulin.[44]

Beginning with the Hospital Survey and Construction Act of 1946 (Hill-Burton) and the various pieces of legislation which funded the biomedical research apparatus of the NIH and NSF, federal programs and policies moved into successively more controversial areas, the financing and delivery of new services and direct support for medical education and health manpower development.[45]

These federal policies and programs were, in turn, associated with a series of transforming structural changes. First, there was a shift from solo, office based medicine to hospital based medicine, with its focus on the medical center complex.[46] The accelerating scientific and technical orientation of medicine meant a growing dependence upon complex equipment and procedures requiring large-scale settings. As research and medical center facilities gained in importance and prestige within the profession, physicians sought both the facilities as well as the status of these institutional affiliations. Between 1950 and 1969, the percent of salaried physicians more than doubled.[47] In addition to federally funded hospital and research facilities, proliferating health insurance plans made these institutions financially viable and independent during this period.[48]

Social and political reorganization accompanied hospital centered medicine. In the hospital setting, medical practice became more visible than in the privacy of the office, coming under increased scrutiny by a variety of occupational figures. As organizations became a more frequent setting for the doctor-patient interaction, the public view of medicine also began to change and a common complaint was the impersonality of modern medicine compared to the family doctor of former times.

Along with change in the mode and locus of work, there was increasing fragmentation within the medical community coupled with a shift in the balance of power away from the clinically oriented practitioners who were the traditional leadership of the AMA, to the newly prominent research oriented, academic wing of the profession.[49] The interests of this expanding academic wing diverged from those of the practicing physicians. While research physicians aligned themselves with policymakers in the Department of Health, Education and Welfare (HEW) and with other groups seeking federal intervention as a basis for expansion and growth, the AMA remained adamantly opposed to federal intervention.[50] Other actors in the health arena fell out along this divide as their interests more clearly diverged from those of the AMA. The hospitals, for example, favored federal aid for hospital construction, Medicare and Medicaid, and increased manpower.[51] The commercial and the nonprofit sectors of health along with academic and research physicians were in favor of government financed growth and expansion (with private control).

In addition to the changing balance of power between academic and practicing physicians, there were other sources of strain within the medical community. Interns and resident physicians became a "weak point" in the system during this period of hospital based growth and expansion.[52] Due to the AMA's resistance to increasing the number of physicians, hospitals were understaffed and interns and residents overworked. This meant that they received less training and provided more service.[53] Medicare and Medicaid legislation exacerbated this situation.

Medical students became another weak point. Medical schools had become federally funded scientific and research complexes by the 1950s and 1960s. This meant that the impact of technical medicine was felt most immediately in medical school. Students did not get to see patients until relatively late in their training. For many of them, the emphasis on research was at odds with the more humanistic expectations (and backgrounds) with which they entered the profession.[54]

The shifting balance of power within the profession affected the ordering of medical priorities and the distribution of services to the public. Hospital based, specialized medicine led to a growing disequilibrium of supply and demand, both in relation to the medical needs of the public and to the geographic distribution of medical services. Scientific research refined expensive treatment procedures for relatively rare problems and encouraged the production of ever more narrowly trained specialists while whole area populations lacked coverage for everyday medical needs. The clustering of physicians in medical centers while a "crisis of medical care" was proclaimed in surrounding urban slums underlined the imbalanced distribution of medical resources in what was now a publicly financed system.[55]

Institutional relations were also affected. Over time, changes in organization, production, and financing led to an erosion of autonomy as legislative mandates were introduced along with state regulatory mechanisms. These changes, which appeared as a series of "unanticipated consequences" to some, were viewed by others more dialectically. For example, unregulated underwriting of hospital construction in the 1940s, 1950s, and 1960s, was blamed for cost escalation and overbedding in the 1970s, and inspired federal legislation to control hospital construction decisions.[56] Medical research, at a time of fiscal constraint, led to the questioning of research as well as the evaluation of research priorities.[57] The cost of delivery programs such as Medicaid led to a pullback from "access to medical care as a right" and to the institution of regulatory devices such as PSRO legislation.[58] The introduction of direct federal aid to medical schools and the general subsidization of medical education was accompanied by a number of federal mandates regarding the regional distribution of physicians, the production of general versus specialty physicians, and the length and nature of the training program.[59] In sum, introducing public money into a privately controlled system led to the questioning of priorities and to the demand for public regulation and control.

Medicine became more overtly politicized. Although the medical system had been a two-class system from (at least) the time of Flexner reforms, new federal legislation and programs exacerbated racial and class based inequities and made them more visible. At the same time, federal intervention provided the means for redressing some of these inequities. For example, the Hill-Burton Act contained a separate-but-equal clause which allowed federal funding for segregated hospitals in the rural South. This same clause later became the focal point for attempts to change the segregated structure of medical practice in the South.[60]

Federal intervention both directly and indirectly affected class relations. Policies which favored heavy research funding, medical specialization and the consolidation of power by medical centers, increased the problems of providing service for minorities and the poor, particularly in urban settings. The priority of the medical center complex was research as opposed to medical care in general or service to surrounding communities. As these medical centers began to expand their facilities with federal funds, expansion cut into surrounding neighborhoods and incited anger directed at the policies and priorities of the institutions.[61]

The public hospitals which served minorities and the poor were also under pressure. In the postwar period, the public hospital system faced a successive series of crises—difficulties in financing, in staffing, and in clientele—which led to a series of solutions at different levels of the system. In New York City, for example, affiliation contracts assigned the public hospitals to medical centers, but these contracts led to increased costs and medical center priorities.[62] At the national level, changes in the immigration laws in 1965 to allow foreign trained physicians to fill the less prestigious slots in the public system led to charges of a dual labor market as well as a two-track delivery system.[63] Even voucher systems such as Medicaid, which were specifically designed to end the two-track system and to allow the poor to buy into private care, increased the problems of providing care for minorities and the poor. Voluntary and nonprofit institutions screened off desirable patients (those with Medicaid coverage) hastening the trend out of the public hospitals.[64] During New York's fiscal crisis in the mid-1970s, "empty beds" contributed to hospital closings leaving certain sectors of the population without any hospital or medical care.

In short, the general underwriting of the growth of the medical system both directly and indirectly affected the institutions that traditionally provided care for minorities and the poor. For a variety of reasons, attempts to change this system often aided those very sectors they set out to reform. This led to conflict centered on these institutions and to critical attention directed at the class structure of medicine and at the impact of state intervention.

Accompanying structural change and the politicization of the medical sector, was a rise in "consciousness" about medicine within the profession as well as among the general public. Critics first attacked the AMA for successfully blocking national health insurance. They also attacked the dominant "scientific" ideology because of the gap between medicine's professed public interest and its apparent self-interest. As in planning, the critique of organized medicine provided the ammunition for sought-after change that included a broader "social" medicine, redistribution of services, and socially responsible roles for physicians. This agenda became the basis for federal intervention in the 1960s by a coalition of progressive medical figures and Washington policymakers.

As in planning, the seeds of more radical criticism were planted as well. As the reform based expansion of medical services starts, activism appears within the left wing of the medical profession. Activists questioned the liberal coalition, the emerging medical center "empires," and the functions of medicine and medical personnel. They also questioned medical paradigms and methodology.[65]

This examination of the historical and developmental context of activism in medicine and planning has shown that distributive benefits were a weak spot. Planning claimed to serve a unified public interest. Medicine was organized along a two-track system with market services for those who could pay and charitable care in public institutions for the poor. Both professions had a social reform as well as a scientific model. While the scientific perspectives represented by physical planning and "scientific" medicine helped occupational institutionalization, they presented problems as models and reality.

This examination has also shown that issues of equity were exacerbated by increased federal intervention in the post-World War II period. Although federal intervention was associated with occupational growth, federal programs also introduced minorities and the poor as categorical clients, setting the stage for social conflict and for activist efforts. This is the context in which social reform emerged within planning and medicine.

Part II

Strategies of
Change

4

Delivering Services

Advocacy in planning consists in developing and presenting
plans that advance the interests of a particular group or class
rather than that of 'the public interest' or 'the general good'
however defined. We have argued that all planning is advocate
planning, whether it recognizes itself as such or not; and we feel
that the growing movement of advocacy planning on behalf of
the poor is a step forward in broadening the process of planning
to include formerly unrepresented groups. To the extent that
planning is carried on, it should be carried on in behalf of the
poor as well as the rich.
Paul Davidoff and Linda Davidoff
Social Policy (July/August 1970)

The responsibility of the health professional goes beyond the
provision of health services to political action: to obtain and
insure the right to adequate health care for all members of
society; to provide programs which extend adequate health care;
to recognize and oppose those aspects of society which prevent
provision of adequate health care; to eliminate those conditions
which destroy life and health.
1967 *California Student
Health Project*

The first generation of activists criticized medicine and planning for
the inequitable distribution of services to minorities and the poor.
They felt that inequality was the direct result of institutional malfunctioning—professional monopoly and bureaucratic rigidity, and
defined their new role—to incorporate minorities and poor into the
market of services by giving technical aid and putting pressure on
the professions to reform.

47

Activists were drawn from the ranks of professionals and students involved in the Civil Rights and student movements and from a preexisting base of liberals in schools of medicine and planning who had long wanted to create a "social medicine" and a "social" planning. Planning activism also attracted planners involved in the much debated urban renewal projects.

In vivid contrast to the prevailing "value neutral" orientation to clients, overly technical models of professional knowledge, and ivory tower training, activists sought to broaden their knowledge base to include social, economic and psychological aspects of planning and health care. In contrast to the prevailing professional rhetoric that planning serves a unified public interest, or that medicine provides equivalent charitable care for those who cannot pay, activists argued that the interests of minorities and the poor were not being served; that professionals and students of the professions must leave the schools, offices, and laboratories for the communities where they could identify needs and target services to neglected and underserved groups. Optimistic about the possibilities of reform, activists sought to relink professional claims with the reality of who got what.

But as advocates began to work with low-income communities, they became increasingly politicized. Community clients challenged their assumptions and their services, and the advocates themselves became critical of their initial analysis and strategy. The case materials that follow illustrate the dynamic quality of delivery strategies directed at minorities and the poor. I look first at planning by examining three advocacy groups which developed in radically different contexts.

Urban Planning Aid (UPA), a well-known advocacy planning group in Boston, was organized to counter threats to people's homes posed by plans for highway construction and urban renewal in a poor residential area. Because UPA covers the period under examination and went through several shifts in strategy (which will be chronicled in this and subsequent chapters), UPA will serve as a model. Like UPA, many advocacy groups moved toward community organizing. Similarly, the focus on constructing political and theoretical frameworks for local issues, which characterizes many contemporary groups, can be seen to develop at UPA in response to its experience with advocacy and organizing as well as to specific historical events.

URBAN PLANNING AID:
A TRANSITIONAL CASE

UPA began as the ad hoc response of a group of professionals to the threat of an inner-belt highway through a lower-class neighborhood in Cambridge, Massachusetts. Formed in 1965, the Cambridge Committee Against the Inner Belt proposed an alternative route that would reduce the number of homes taken by the highway. A member of the original group, which included planners and related professionals, some of them academics, described the initial motivation as altruistic and reformist. "All were committed to using their professional educations and positions to help promote movement in America toward greater equality and freedom."[1] They shared "a common dissatisfaction with the narrowness of [our] work," with working "for the rich-and-powerful and organization classes," and with the class bias of professional services in general.[2]

In 1968, the group went from being a single-issue organization staffed by volunteers to become an independent nonprofit advocacy planning organization which offered free planning services to middle and low-income groups in the greater Boston area. Beginning with a small grant in 1967, which covered one full-time professional staff member, a secretary, and an office, UPA received federal funding two years later as an advocacy demonstration project.

Although the creation of a planning organization for minorities and the poor seemed to offer a solution to some of the problems raised by planners at the time, UPA's developmental history raises questions about the viability of advocacy. Many planners who started out as advocates, as the term was first used, became politicized as did the organization as a whole. UPA went through several significant shifts. These shifts, reflecting changes in goals and means, affected the role of professionals in the organization.

Technical Assistance and the Alternate Plan

At the start, UPA consisted of the voluntary services of professionals who offered their technical skills and prestige on behalf of deprived groups. The products of these efforts were plans—alternatives to the plans of the official highway and urban renewal agencies. UPA's objective was to produce a design as "technically feasible" as that of its adversary, the planning department.[3]

Client involvement was initially *pro forma* and symbolic. In the Brookline-Elm highway controversy, the planners were concerned with participation only to the extent that it was necessary to legitimate their activities. Citizen groups were informed of dealings between planners and city officials and were called upon for support purposes. The local people and organizations entrusted themselves to the volunteer professionals. The initial relation of the planners to the community was "benevolent paternalism."[4] Planners spoke for and acted for but did not consult with or educate community groups. Although opposed to the highway, the community voiced little protest at the start of the antihighway committee.

This situation rapidly changed as low-income communities emerged as a more organized and critical voice—critical of advocates as well as government planners. At the same time, advocates themselves began to see the limits of a "technically feasible counterplan." For the community, the emergent issues were differences in goals, cultural styles, and strategies. Whereas the planners sought an alternative route for the Cambridge section of the Inner Belt, one that would take fewer homes, the citizens' position was "no road" at all. One advocate described the early period this way: "At regular meetings and at rallies, the only proposal that was consistently cheered was any statement to the effect, "we don't want any highways at all through Cambridge."[5] But the planners thought this "unrealistic." It was only as the citizen protest groups—both those formed by advocates for support and those which arose in response to similar problems and efforts elsewhere—gained momentum and coalesced into a citywide effort that the community voice began to have weight with UPA. At this point, UPA gave priority to the "no road option" and to community participation in general.

Broader and more general criticism from below was directed at cultural or class biases in strategy. Client groups in various UPA advocacy efforts found professional plans, discussions, and explanations overly technical and "hard to understand." CAUSE, a South End client, fighting against forced relocation outside the community, criticized UPA's quantitative and statistical presentations as a "nonfeeling" way of dealing with the issue of relocation.[6]

Working with community groups such as CAUSE also raised questions about alternative plans as a strategy toward urban renewal. The increased demands from more vocal low-income and minority groups led UPA to redirect its efforts toward getting the community, not the advocates, into direct contact with the urban renewal agency. This removed UPA from the political as well as the technical aspects of planning, made UPA a behind-the-scenes adviser, and put emphasis upon the community's role in making government bureaucracies do their job.[7]

The advocates also began to question their role and strategy.

Some of the most trenchant criticism of advocacy planning came from first-generation UPA planners, among them, Hartman, Peattie, Fellman, and Goodman. Peattie wrote that "to attempt to plan in terms of the interest of specific local communities by no means does away with the political conflicts and ambiguities which, in the first place, gave rise to the notion of advocacy planning."[8]

Many of the same problems of conventional planning—who are the clients, what are the issues, whose definition of the problems, plagued the advocate planners. Speaking of a successful UPA project, Peattie pointed out the ambiguity involved in claiming to "represent" the community. "Nonparticipants were not randomly selected; they tended to be the poorest of all, the most marginal, those with least stake, while the community organization was dominated by, although not exclusively composed of, persons who owned their own little homes in the area."[9]

Summing up the impact of early UPA experience on planners, Fellman said:

> They soon realized, however, that reason alone was not enough to change the Belt design. Gradually understanding that government decision-makers respond to pressures from institutions behind-the-scenes, [they] sought to build a power base to counteract the forces favorable to the Brookline-Elm location.[10]

They moved, he said, "from a purely technical definition of the problem to a political one." But to have experts playing what Fellman called "institutional politics" might be an ineffective strategy as well as one which created additional dangers for minorities and the poor. Clearly, power accrued to the advocates who acted as "political brokers or middlemen," translating between the minorities, the poor, and the "organization class."[11] In a debate on advocacy planning in *Social Policy* in 1970, Piven called the movement from politics to planning a diversion from "types of political action by which the poor are most likely to be effective."[12] Although a road was rerouted, the poor community could remain as voiceless and alienated as before.[13] Critics such as Piven would add, even more so.

A larger question loomed in the minds of these planners. Was the goal to be measured in "outcomes" or should emphasis be put upon the "process" of getting a community involved with the political and technical aspects of their problems? Should UPA educate residents about political struggle rather than organize them as supporters?[14] These questions challenged advocacy as a strategy. If dependence on experts was part of the problem, then advocate planner were implicated as well as governmental bureaucrats and a transfer of skills might be required—cultural change as well as a "politics of protest."[15]

Advocates also found that fighting highways suggested "larger frameworks" and "issues of even greater scale."[16] The problem was not alternative roads, but the federal policies and the powerful interests supporting these policies. Peattie noted: "Indeed, looking at the whole thrust of public policy in the area of transportation, it was possible to argue that there was a basic class bias in the pattern of allocating federal funds for very large problems of highway building."[17] If this was true, "all that advocate planning did was to allow the poor to administer their own state of dependency."[18] In this context, the planner as local advocate functioned as a pacifier to a system in need of more basic change.

THE URBAN FIELD SERVICE:
ADVOCACY IN THE UNIVERSITY

Delivery strategies ran into difficulties within the academic establishment as well as the community. The Urban Field Service (UFS) at Harvard was one of the first attempts to bring advocacy planning within the regular curriculum of a school of planning.[19] Begun by Chester Hartman in 1967, UFS was an outgrowth of a variety of pressures: Hartman's commitment to changing planning outcomes by changing professional education, student demands for a relevant curriculum, and the increased emphasis on urban problems in other university departments which "threatens to attract students . . . and at the same time makes obsolete many of the courses that were once thought to be the special province of professionals trained in "city planning."[20] The net result was a program whose objectives were to aid and work with community groups, to educate or reeducate students, and to challenge professional elitism.

UFS began with the proposition that:

> the community is best able to express it own demands and that it is the task of the trained professional to help translate these needs and desires into reality, relying to the greatest possible extent on the involvement and participation of local people themselves.[21]

This meant that in contrast to prevailing professional norms, "we let them call the shots." Secondly, UFS was an attempt to take the student out of the ivory tower studio which "all too often provided students with a narrow and unsatisfactory simulation of professional work and real-life conditions." In contrast, the "community-based studios" were "an attempt to structure the learning situation around different types of problems and to provide contact with a type of client and professional working relationship and style that can probably be furnished only in vivo." Lastly, there was a deliberate attempt to "nurture a critical spirit" among the students. "UFS explicitly and implicitly challenges the elitism of the planning and design professions, their values and typical clients, the 'track record' of the immediate past." This was to be accomplished by means of a seminar in which student work was examined and related to more general issues of "social change and political analysis."

Typical projects included providing the "impact" research, alternative planning, and design to support a community's fight against an urban renewal project; providing technical support for a group fighting university expansion and rising rents; developing recreation plans for community groups; aiding tenants' groups to organize and staff a statewide federation of tenants' associations in public housing; and developing plans and designs for teenage or community centers. In all cases, community groups requested the aid of UFS.

According to its founder and first director, Chester Hartman, UFS was "by no means an unqualified success."[22] Although much was accomplished over two years, UFS ran up against some of the same problems advocacy encountered elsewhere, as well as discovering what might be "inherent limitations" for this mode in the university setting. Among the planning faculty, there was opposition to giving departmental credit for field service. More was at stake than a dislike for the politics of community work. Hartman felt, "One of the most threatening aspects of community-based planning and design work is the 'deprofessionalization' or decentralization of professional skills and power that is its conscious and inevitable accompaniment."[23] Its objectives were perceived as threats to knowledge, skills, and status, which were insecure in the first place. Thus, the courses remained extracurricular, listings were omitted from the catalog, and finally the director was dismissed. There were other conflicts: the interests of the planning faculty, as consultants, were at odds with their interests as community advocates.

The educational value of the service program also engendered debate. One issue was the differing nature of the design professions involved in UFS. Because architecture and landscape design students required a higher level of technical skills than planners, they had less to offer the community during their early years of training. This made their placement on the projects more difficult and prompted their faculty to keep them in traditional studios.[24]

The community was no more pleased with the projects than was the university. There were problems in commitment and continuity. Projects did not neatly fit into university time schedules, and students were not always on call for the community groups. Participating faculty and students were themselves frustrated. The disorganization of community groups made projects fragile and meant that an inordinate amount of time was spent organizing. Finally, self-critical faculty and students questioned whether "short-term discrete victories and achievements had any lasting effect" or merely "fostered the illusion of change."[25] In sum, the university did not free advocacy from many of the problems that arose in other settings; moreover, it contributed the general academic bias against efforts based on values as opposed to knowledge.

The subsequent history of the UFS and its assimilation into an ongoing regional service program seems representative of the fate of advocacy within most university training programs. Although community fieldwork has become an accepted part of the curriculum of many planning schools, it usually takes the form of more structured internships that work through already-established organizations and institutions rather than directly for community groups.[26] From the activist perspective, these internships present a watered-down version of advocacy minus the adversarial role. Community clients have become an alternative set of clients, the rules of the game are given, and planners facilitate or negotiate the plan. In this context, the institutionalization of community fieldwork is less a reflection of activist values than of the growing importance of these alternative clients, given the increased number of planners and the existence and/or possibility of federal funding on their behalf.

Coming from a different end of the political spectrum than UPA or UFS, the Newark Community Union Project (NCUP), a New Left ghetto project, tested the role of the professional as social change agent in much the same "intensive" format turned to somewhat later by UPA. Because many of the criticisms of advocacy planning concerned its lack of a politics, we gain additional perspective on advocacy as an activist strategy to the extent that similar problems were encountered at NCUP, where advocacy planning was sponsored by radical movement groups.

THE NEWARK COMMUNITY UNION PROJECT:
PLANNERS WORKING FOR A
POLITICAL MOVEMENT

In the summer of 1965, Students for Democratic Society (SDS) sponsored a project to supply technical/professional help to several groups involved in organizing the poor through the National Committee on Full Employment.[27] The Newark Community Union Project (NCUP) was one of these groups. It consisted of a loose confederation of community block associations, program committees, and a staff of students and community organizers.

The student movement had a strong bias against professionals at the time and there were several reasons for concern about introducing them into the project.[28] Minorities and the poor were viewed as the agents of change. As members of the middle class, professionals knew nothing about these groups. It was felt that "the professional will undoubtedly be taught more than he teaches . . . [he] really comes in with very little, let's face it . . . with fairly arid methodological skills and a vacant sense of reality and virtually no understanding of the Negro community."[29] Professionals were also believed to introduce a division of labor between mental and manual work that inevitably became hierarchical. Translated into activist strategy, this meant that research should not get priority but had to "grow out of organizing activities" and had to be done by the organization as a whole.[30] This also meant that goals should relate to process, not outcome. The objective was "to let the people create their own plans for housing, schools, parks. . . . We want politicians to base themselves on the needs of the victimized, not on the needs of banking, business and the respectable classes."[31]

Given these views, what was the motivation for introducing professionals such as planners? Antipoverty proposals had to be developed from "the grass roots up" but to date, the project had been unable to organize the poor. It was felt that technical aid was needed to enable the community to take advantage of the federal funds.[32] The rationale given for the introduction of professionals was to "test" their relation to social action movements; to see whether professionals chosen for their political responsiveness could work with "the people" at NCUP, in a way they could not when attached to government funded efforts.[33]

A newly trained planner, Jacqueline Leavitt, was introduced into the community as a "resident" planner. Her account of the attempt to develop a proposal for a community center shows the problems that live-in planners in a movement project encountered at this time.[34] The loose structure of both the movement and the community meant that there was no organized client with whom to work. In lieu of existing organizational vehicles, Leavitt was continually confronted by the need to create the client—to organize. This meant that the planner had to reconcile two "incompatible styles and outlooks—organizing and professional work." Related to this was the issue of acceptance or legitimacy. Acceptance within the movement and within the community was not based upon expertise or getting a job done, but had to be won by commitment. This meant "being there" and doing what "had to be done" from babysitting to advocacy. The job thus called for a different lifestyle. Leavitt also described a conflict between the political goals of the staff and the community's own interests. Caught between the pressure to act on "real community problems" as opposed to doing what the staff thought was "good for the community," the staff at times manipulated the community's expressed interests. In her words: "Rebelling themselves against middleclass goals, they are reluctant to let the people decide to become middle class." She also noted that NCUP's primary concern with participatory democracy and process often conflicted with getting a job done.

Over and beyond these role conflicts and conflicts of interest, Leavitt criticized her intermediary function in the project as "makework" and misplaced activism. Writing proposals for poverty agencies was a "bureaucratic hassle" that the professional ultimately ended up doing for the community. NCUP should have made the governmental staff do this work.

The issues raised by the planner at NCUP were similar to those experienced at UPA. There was the lack of community organization to contend with as well as questions of conflicting interests and staff manipulation. There was also the larger issue of whether the whole effort was misguided. Rather than mediate between the government and the poor as federal legislation itself encouraged, should not pressure be put upon government agencies to do their job?

Health advocacy and reform played out a similar trajectory. The Student Health Organizations, (SHO), which successfully created large-scale federally funded health advocacy projects in urban and rural poverty communities across the country, marked the start of a decade of medical activism. Between 1964 and 1968, SHO moved from a position of alliance with medical schools and the federal government, working for change within the system of health care, to a position to the left of the progressive coalition, critical of sponsoring universities, the federal government and their own advocacy and reform efforts. SHO's development illustrates activists' rejection of health advocacy and creative federalism when it is seen to contradict a needed "medical politics."

STUDENT HEALTH ORGANIZATIONS: REFORM,
POLITICIZATION AND WITHDRAWAL

SHO began simultaneously in Los Angeles and Boston in the fall of 1964.[35] Part of the general student awakening that characterized the early 1960s, health student activism was particularly influenced by the Free Speech movement at Berkeley and the Civil Rights movement in the South.[36] The health students' first efforts were to hold forums and lecture series at which nationally prominent speakers addressed topics such as abortion and birth control—topics relevant to medicine and to students but "conspicuously absent" from the medical school curricula.[37] Forums were followed by action projects which involved health science students with medically underprivileged populations. The emergence of similar organizations and activities at medical schools across the country during 1964 and 1965 led to the convening of the First National Assembly of SHO in the fall of 1965. These yearly national assemblies continued through 1969.

Beginning in 1966, a SHO summer project sponsored by a coalition of medical schools received $200,000 in OEO funds and placed 90 health science students from all over the country in primarily rural poverty spots in California.[38] The funding was continued so that the project would remain open year round. By the summer of 1967, there were three projects (New York, Chicago, and California), increased funding ($700,000), and 260 students. In 1968, summer projects peaked with 600 students in nine cities and more than $1 million in federal funds.[39] There were two projects in the summer of 1969 and none thereafter.

After the demise of the summer projects, there was an attempt to strengthen the organization at the national level by establishing a national office in Chicago oriented to research and communication. This office ceased to function in 1970. At its height (1968), SHO had local organizations in more than 40 states with 3,000 to 4,000 members, of whom almost 60 percent were medical students.[40] Many of these organizations published magazines and newsletters. Many were actively involved with curricular reforms and maintained student service projects during the rest of the year in addition to the more publicized summer projects.

Why did SHO, which started so forcefully and gained so much momentum and establishment support, stop rather abruptly at its height? Part of the answer to this question relates to the social and historical context—the Civil Rights, student, and antiwar movements. But we must also look at SHO's own experience providing medical services to minorities and the poor, attempting to reform medical school curricula, and working on delivery projects with federal and medical school sponsors. This experience helped politicize SHO and contributed to the decision to drop the summer projects and go out of the advocacy business.

The Student Reform Model:
Bridging the Gap between Science and Service

> *Medicine has had a remarkable scientific success in the past quarter century, but it seems to have been far less successful as a social instrument. One of the most urgent problems confronting the nation is the distribution of health services to all of the people—services which we know how to provide. I am delighted to see the creation of these student health organizations which will involve all of the health professions and which will direct their energies towards solutions of the social problems of medicine.*
> Robert H. Ebert, M.D.
> Dean, Harvard Medical School
> *SHO Bulletin* (Spring 1966)

From the start, the dual objectives of SHO were self-education and health advocacy: to develop "a politically responsive and progressive student community" and to extend medical services to minorities and the poor.[41] These goals stemmed from two critical observations about the state of American medicine: the failure of service reflected in "the staggering gap between what we know and what we do for many citizens" and the lack of service delivery to specific segments of the population.[42]

Health science students were among the first volunteers to work in the South with the Civil Rights movement. They brought back North with them a new sensitivity to culturally and racially diverse clients, an awareness of their differential treatment within medical institutions, and a basic exhilaration at being out of the classroom and working with people. Most typically, the medical students' first two years took place in the laboratory. Although motivated to alleviate human suffering,

> For the health student, the growing emphasis on scientific technology has further separated his learning process from daily life and human needs, building in him an intolerable conflict. . . . as he senses the incompleteness of his formal training which emphasizes the disease process, isolated from social realities.[43]

The villains in the student critique were both the new and the old medical establishment, the medical schools and the AMA. Students viewed the AMA as resistant to change and committed to the concept of health as a privilege, not a right.[44] The medical schools were criticized for having failed to provide a model for a committed and responsible medicine. They were to blame for the excesses of scientific medicine and for the relative neglect of social and environmental aspects of health.[45]

While the student critique implicated the whole medical system, teaching institutions were the pressure point and health science students, the change agents, not only for medicine, but for the wider student movement. Health science students were in a "unique position." They were linked, according to this analysis, by "vocational choice" to "a lifelong responsibility in the service of alleviating human suffering." At the same time, they were faced daily with the medical school, "the educational institution par excellence which most offensively deviates from its theoretical obligation to the public."[46]

The reform agenda called for a broader definition of health, a socially responsible medicine, an interdisciplinary approach to learning and care and the practice of community medicine. Activists began by attacking the prevailing narrow definition which they linked to medicine's disengagement from humanistic aspects of medical practice as well as from the larger environmental and social aspects of health. The post-Flexnerian curriculum, with its emphasis on establishing laboratory science as the basis for medical practice and its exclusive attention to biological and organic etiology, was faulted for promoting a sharp division between scientific and clinical training.[47] At SHO's First National Assembly (Chicago 1965), student activists adopted the definition of health used by the World Health Organization—"a state of total physical, mental and social well-being, and not merely the absence of disease and infirmity."[48]

Health students also called for a socially responsible medicine. They claimed that their curriculum was deficient because of the "absence of important and timely topics of the day such as abortion, population explosion, discrimination in health care, and chemical and biological warfare." The curriculum created an ivory tower effect by neglecting the relation between poverty and health, the organization of health services, and the economics of medical care.[49] The net result was that the medical student educated inside the research hospital had little understanding of the social, political, or economic context of her work and this lack of early exposure set the stage for later neglect.

> Physicians will not be trained to meet society's needs until medical educators become part of the community, believe themselves accountable to the community, and train physicians with the same attitude.[50]

Student activists argued that the responsibility of the health professional went beyond providing health care to

> political action: to obtain and insure the fight for adequate health care for all members of society . . . to recognize and oppose those aspects of society which prevent provision of adequate health care; [and] to eliminate those conditions which destroy life and health.[51]

There was also a strong feeling among SHO activists that the failure of teamwork among the health professions was rooted in students' early socialization into the rigidly hierarchical organizational structure of medicine. They suggested an interdisciplinary approach which would "combine the various health science students during their formative educational years."[52] To promote this, the founders of the First National Assembly chose the more inclusive term *health student* for the organizational title. SHO projects were also interdisciplinary from the start.[53]

At the heart of the student critique and of SHO strategy was the medical scientists's isolation from the world outside the medical school.[54] The community was to be the "new school" for the health science student. This focus met both prongs of the student critique—the failure of the medical delivery system and student alienation. The failure to serve the community was a cumulative process. It began with the failure to teach community medicine—to deal with social and psychological factors of medical care and illness or to require appropriate language skills from personnel or institutions. It was reinforced by the way in which fee-for-service medicine isolated minority groups and the poor from mainstream medical care and brought them into contact with doctors as teaching material in training situations.[55] The net result was that doctors inside the medical research complex did not know the health needs of surrounding populations or the barriers they experienced in finding and receiving care. "The affluence of the profession and its training schools has created a shocking remoteness from the people."[56] By promoting responsiveness and change, health activists sought to relink "medical reality to ideals."[57] In this sense, SHO's initial focus was student alienation and their organizations were "built around meeting the needs of the students which they themselves defined."[58]

The first project.   The Student Medical Conference (SMC), a multischool organization in the Los Angeles area, created a model for both the organization and the student health project. Multidisciplinary teams were placed in various work situations with a maximum of autonomy and leadership. Limited by their lack of degrees, licensure and clinical knowledge, they inevitably stressed screening, patient advocacy, and the collection and distribution of relevant health care information. Participants also had to submit written reports evaluating their experience. The projects attempted to create "myriad possible roles which health science students could play in and out of schools."[59]

Several of the initial projects are worth describing. SMC conducted an audiovisual screening of more than 1000 Head Start youngsters. They arranged for referrals and follow-ups and presented their data to the State Health Department. SMC also distributed information about a proposed therapeutic abortion bill to all medical students in the state. The leaflet, which consisted of a legislative review of the bill along with analysis of the pros and cons, informed students of a key political health issue. SMC members also initiated and staffed a family planning and birth control facility in a Mexican-American neighborhood on the basis of a prior survey which documented the need for such a clinic.

Between 1964 and 1965, similar projects to gather information and institute needed services started independently in Boston, Chicago, and Mississippi.[60] While this movement led to the creation of a national organization, SHO, from the start, chose to remain a loose national confederation with a local emphasis. SHO's mandate was to recruit students for community action health projects in the South, to "mount a large national summer project in California along the lines of the Student Medical Conference," and to function as a "communications network" for health student activists all over the country.[61]

The progressive coalition.   The student health projects received immediate and enthusiastic support from medical school deans and faculty across the country.[62] This group of liberal doctors and medical educators represented a progressive faction within medicine who desired change and who had previously debated the AMA over the need for community medicine and for some form of health insurance.[63] This group forged links with New Frontier administrators and politicians in Washington who also wanted change and who welcomed a socially progressive alliance.[64] The coalition envisioned for SHO, the same role that SHO saw for itself: a catalyst for urgently needed change in the medical system.[65]

The first large-scale summer project (California, 1966) received "direct encouragement" from OEO and a $200,000 research and demonstration grant to mount a "project concerned with health care for the poor in California."[66] In 1967, the student health projects were funded through OEO, the Neighborhood Youth Corps and Job Corps; in 1968 and 1969, through the Regional Medical Program.

Federal sponsorship added the OEO mandate of community action for social change to the student objectives of self-education and community service.[67] Federal funding also introduced Neighborhood Youth Corps workers in 1967, and in 1968 and 1969, added the Regional Medical Program's objective of gathering information on community groups. These funding agency mandates and objectives contributed to politicizing and radicalizing the student health projects from above and within.

Student Health Projects: Health Advocacy to Medical Politics

Between 1966 and 1968, significant changes took place in the student health projects (SHP): in types of placement sites and preceptors; in the relation between projects and communities; between SHP and the sponsoring progressive establishment (both medical schools and the federal government); and in participant satisfaction. Initially, the goals of education, service, and community action were seen as complementary. Over the course of time, however, the goals were reevaluated as ambiguous and contradictory and, by the close of the summer of 1968, the projects were torn by criticism from below, above and within. Beginning with the first large-scale national summer project, I examine successive SHPs in terms of their evaluation by students, preceptors and relevant community groups, and the direction of change.[68]

The 1966 California pioneer project placed students from all over the country in predominately rural areas of the state, working for county health departments, county hospitals, and private doctors whose practice was the rural poor. Project preceptors were primarily medical staff and 14 community workers were used to "introduce the students to the communities."[69] The goals, as stated to recruits, were to educate health science students about the poor, to aid the communities by providing health services, and the official OEO mandate—to stimulate community action for social change.

The orientation program held at Asilomar was declared a "milestone for American medicine."[70] There was a consensus among those gathered on the need to change the status of health care from a commodity to a basic human right. All were optimistic about the support of "creative government," critical of the AMA's "hard line" toward change, and supportive of students as vehicles of professional change.[71]

At the close of the summer, communities, participants, and sponsors all considered the projects successful. The final reports by medical preceptors and students showed that they had adopted community action as an objective. The problem was not just the distribution of services but the "attitude" of all involved—health workers, the poor, and relevant service organizations. Professional change was also deemed necessary and participants called upon the "medical centers of America to assume their rightful place as leaders in the development of new approaches to community health."[72]

The recruitment literature and orientation conference for the 1967 California project underlined the same themes. However, several changes were made relating to funding and legislative mandates which proved important in "shaping SHO thinking on community health and slum problems" throughout the summer.[73] Urban sites were added in Chicago and New York; more students were placed in "independent," nonclinical settings, and ghetto teenagers were included along with health science students.

The use of local teenagers, initially a device to give SHO entry to communities, was expanded in 1967 partly as a result of funding through the Neighborhood Youth Corps (NYC). These teenagers became the most difficult, controversial, and, according to some, "successful" part of the summer project.[74] One medical student wrote:

> The confrontation of SHO prejudices and inabilities to relate to teenagers (freely and honestly) demonstrated the real communication problems of working in the ghetto. The NYC's were more than an entry into the community—they *were* the community to the SHO's who had to work with them. The NYC's were a focus for learning about transcultural relationships.[75]

Although many students felt that "the NYC program pushed SHP into a new relationship with the community" and helped

uncover attitudes of incipient racism, elitism and class consciousness, from another perspective the introduction of the NYC represented externally induced conflict. SHO suddenly had a new responsibility—to provide "meaningful interpersonal experiences for the
NYC." This diverted attention from the projects to the interactions
between the two groups of students.[76] From the start, there was no
clear sense of what the NYC should do and the relationship was
defined in advance by unequal salaries and timecard responsibilities.

Participants responded with a "politics of guilt" syndrome.[77] A
big debate about whether to include the NYC in a final conference
personified the quandary for white middle-class activists at the time.
Not to include the NYC raised cries of prejudice and a lack of
acceptance. To include them would make it difficult and perhaps
impossible to conduct the conference as SHO had planned. In
comparison to the summer of 1966, SHO had lost its clear sense of a
professional role vis-a-vis the "community" or the sense of who the
community really was.

The increased use of placements with self-help community
groups and the more generally assertive tone of these groups raised
the issue of who benefited by the projects. Critical participants felt
that staff deemphasized community needs and arranged services for
their own convenience or for the benefit of "future resumes." Others,
looking beyond the good work, felt that SHO must face the danger
to the community of "post summer letdown"; that short-term projects should not be attempted "without rigorous attention to follow
through."[78] Community leaders inquired into the motivation of
SHO. What was SHO trying to ascertain? Were they merely paid
snoopers in poor communities? Why did almost every interdisciplinary team conduct a sex education class? Was this an attempt to
"keep the birth rate down in the ghettos and barrios?"[79]

In comparison to 1966, the 1967 projects with more urban sites,
community organization placements and ghetto participants, were
characterized by uneasy relations between health science students
and poor and minority communities. SHO's attention turned toward
trying to fill community rather than student or establishment
needs.[80] However, the projects were still described as important and
"eye-opening experiences for students" and although issues arose,
participants were not yet saying that health does not matter.[81]

Between the summers of 1967 and 1968, there were clear signs of
dissatisfaction and soul-searching within SHO. The Third National
Assembly held in Detroit in February addressed the question,
"Where are you going SHO?" The keynote speaker in 1968 was the
outspoken activist Benjamin Spock, in contrast to the gentlemanly

clinician, Paul Dudley White, who spoke at the initial 1966 confer-ence.[82] The meetings were marked by intense debate on a number of issues including whether to take a stand on the Vietnam War, the virtues of organizational centralization, and the role of lay partici-pants in planning the summer projects. A black caucus presented demands for summer 1968 that called for one-third representation at all policy and planning sessions and for contact, prior to the summer, with community groups. Robb Burlage of Health/PAC presented a paper criticizing health advocacy without political content and call-ing for an analytic research role for health activists.

In the spring of 1968, the Stanford University SHO cancelled their planned summer project with an accompanying statement that declared that large-scale federally funded programs "determined by a coalition of students, university and the federal government" were antithetical to the movement for self-determination and community control which they were "coming to believe is necessary," and which communities will begin to demand. They announced their decision to open a "dialogue" with the community prior to any plans.[83] In New York City, student SHO leaders at the Einstein College of Medicine quit over the issue of medical school versus student and community control of the summer project.[84]

During the summer of 1968, the projects both peaked and exploded. The final project reports for sites scattered across the country revealed much criticism of SHP goals, strategies, and actual functions by participants, preceptors, and community groups. A "distinct evolution" had occurred, according to one SHO organiza-tion, "in the attitudes of each succeeding group of student project participants."[85] After four years of demonstration programs, self-education, and "sensitization," the conclusion that "I did nothing but I learned a lot" was no longer a viable rationale for the heavily funded program, neither among the students nor the more organized and aggressive communities.[86]

Students had learnt that documenting and publicizing the link-age between poverty and ill health or the nature of care available to the poor did not produce significant change. Their surveys and documentation of the extent of lead poisoning in ghetto children, for example, did not create sustained long-term attention to the problem by either local hospitals or public health facilities, but at most, short-term flurries of interest.[87]

Even if the students wanted to learn in the ghettos, they began to feel increasingly unwelcome in this role. Community organiza-tions were resentful of being studied by outsiders with government money. Why give summer stipends of $900 to white, middle-class students as opposed to channelling the money directly to community groups or to minority students?[88]

The cumulative weight of experience with health advocacy moved SHO's analysis beyond the original assumptions of the student reform model. The problems of health care and the poor health of minorities and the poor were redefined not as "anomalies in an excellent system, but rather, as predictable by-products of a system of values directed to the entrepreneur and to pure research."[89] This meant that a different strategy was indicated. SHP concluded that it would take political confrontation to force a change in priorities and that "neighborhood groups needed to struggle."[90]

DILEMMAS OF ADJUNCT STATUS
AND PROFESSIONAL REFORM

Along with delivering services, activists created national organizations to serve as a support structure for individual efforts and as pressure groups within the profession. These organizations called attention to the impact of professional activities on minorities and the poor and encouraged broader social and political responsibility. Like advocacy, these organizations did not represent "radical breaks" with the professional mainstream but maintained professional roles and services and sought to make use of professional influence and prestige. Like advocacy, they too became politicized.

Both Planners for Equal Opportunity (PEO) and the Medical Committee for Human Rights (MCHR), began in response to appeals for support and presence from the Civil Rights movement. Oriented toward serving the Civil Rights movement from the start, both organizations illustrate the problems of reform efforts whose politics is to serve other political and social movements and whose goals and constituency are dependent on these movements. Although Civil Rights provided the initial legitimacy and focus for these efforts, the turn to Black Power and the subsequent repudiation by black communities of white activists in their midst threw these organizations into disarray.

Organizational responses differed. Denying the concept of a separate professionalism, and choosing neither to broaden nor redefine their role, objectives, or constituency, PEO, which sought to retain a technical role and to focus on the redistribution of services, was left to counter organize around the national planning organization—the American Institute of Planners (AIP). MCHR, on the other hand, survived the changes in the Civil Rights movement by broadening its focus and constituency and adopting an antiwar program.

Buffeted by the antiwar movement as well as the Civil Rights movement, MCHR ultimately rejected a support role. Refocusing on health, MCHR attempted to become a mass organization by offering an alternative health platform to build a movement for change based on restructuring health care.

PLANNERS FOR EQUAL OPPORTUNITY:
CIVIL RIGHTS AND PROFESSIONAL REFORM

PEO was one of the spate of professional groups to organize on behalf of minorities and the poor. Founded by Walter Thabit in 1964, as a counter organization to the AIP, PEO modeled itself after similar national organizations of medical and legal professionals.[91] In its statement of purpose, PEO declared itself a forum and support structure for already individually engaged planners, to examine "programs and actions of public and private agencies and institutions" in order to identify the impact of planning on minorities and the poor and remedy these wrongs.[92]

Beginning with the assumption that planning could assist in the struggle to equalize opportunities just as it had been to blame for exacerbating inequalities, PEO supported the advocacy model with its criticism of traditional concepts of a unitary public interest, narrow technical scope, and professional neutrality. Because many planning decisions were made by the state, planners needed to broaden their role and become politically informed as well as socially responsible. This meant attending to public policy since the villains were federal legislation and administration as well as professional practice.[93] PEO also argued for "the planners' right to speak out on public matters." Since the majority of planners were publicly employed, this issue arose at the time of PEO's formation when planners with government contracts expressed concern about joining PEO, and some planners were specifically enjoined by their supervisors from PEO membership.[94]

Oriented toward reforming the national professional associations—AIP and American Society of Planning Officials (ASPO)—to meet the objectives of the Civil Rights movement, PEO ran into difficulties due to changes in Civil Rights, the professional establishment, and federal policy and programs.[95]

The Civil Rights movement presented problems for PEO from the start. As a guest speaker from MCHR pointed out, "their internal politics makes any sort of consistent relation difficult."[96] PEO's first efforts were aimed at technical assistance and took the form of Freedom Planners South and a projected 10 cities project. These projects had trouble with funding and legitimacy. It was difficult for a new national organization to "step into" local communities. Where individual planners and local chapters already had ongoing advocacy, these projects ran the gamut of success, failure, and stalemate detailed in the growing and critical analysis of advocacy. But even PEO's successful efforts began to be severely strained as the Civil Rights movement turned toward Black Power.

At PEO's second annual conference (March 1968), black advocate planners "challenged the role of white professionals in a black movement and challenged PEO to become a tool of the black liberation movement."[97] This theme was repeated in discussions of advocacy, Model Cities, housing, and metropolitan development. Advocacy by whites in black communities represented "another instance" of professional dominance and made use of planning as a pacification tactic. The alternative would be to give these communities real resources and control, not just planning services. PEO members were unsettled by the confrontation. One workshop broke up over the question of

> what PEO's own role is and should be . . . whether it has a legitimate role in the black liberation movement . . . whether its best role is as a forum for discussion . . . or should be limited to educating and shaking up the white controlled institutions for the purpose of facilitating black liberation.[98]

At a joint meeting of citizens and planners sponsored by the Pittsburg Model Cities Community and PEO (October 1968), a similar confrontation occurred, making it clear that "planners of *any kind* would need to prove themselves before they could be accepted by such a beleaguered community."[99]

PEO responded to these confrontations in a conciliatory manner. While denying the concept of a separatist professionalism for the ghetto, PEO increased black participation on its Policy Committee, increased its attention to the recruitment and employment of minorities in planning schools and agencies and stated that "the advocate planner should bow to the community wishes although its demands may be incongruous with his professional views or leave the project."[100]

By the fourth conference in 1970, it looked as if the problem had been solved. The theme was "New Cities for Black and White," and the conference leadership was described as

> a who's who of advocate and local community planners in both black and white communities and in every phase of local and national

planning interest. More than one-third are black or other minorities. . . . Whereas other conferences have their black/white confrontations, this conference will bring blacks and whites together on a mutually agreeable and . . . jointly planned program.[101]

But repudiation by the black community and black professionals critically undermined PEO, leading to a loss of focus and initiating a period of drift.[102] PEO did not shift to new goals or strategies but instead reaffirmed black and minority participation as the "key to relevancy" and "with the planning world falling apart," looked to black planners "as a model."[103]

A second major issue for PEO was its relation with AIP. From the start, PEO's efforts were directed at persuading the major professional planning association to attend to the relation between planning, social inequality, and racism. As a counter organization, PEO assumed moral as well as political leadership. The first direct confrontation occurred at AIP's Fiftieth Anniversary Convention in Washington, 1967. In contrast to AIP's theme, "Planning in the Next Fifty Years," PEO called its conference, "Planning—Black and White Today." In contrast to AIP's tour of Reston and New Town, PEO organized a tour of Washington slums or "Now Towns" to demonstrate the impact of urban renewal. PEO's counter workshops attacked Model Cities, discussed racial equality, housing and the poor, planning and politics, even the relation between Vietnam and domestic policy. Media coverage found AIP proceedings "stuffy and irrelevant" as compared to the burning issues pressed by the radicals. More than 400 attended the counter conference and 100 new members joined the organization. According to the president, "it put PEO on the map."[104]

But "AIP learned quickly."[105] By the next conference, AIP had included the issues of race, poverty, and equal opportunity on its conference agenda. While there were still enough "zero" items left to make holding another counter conference worthwhile, zeal and momentum were lost as the larger organization began to respond to the "now" challenges. Before long, PEO members addressed similar topics as speakers from AIP and ASPO platforms. When the AIP took a stand for peace and new priorities in 1970, PEO responded by saying, "what we advocated five years ago is now part of the establishment line." AIP adopted a Code of Professional Responsibility, which included a statement about the claims of "those who have least."[106] In an attempt to build upon these moves and establish itself within AIP, PEO endorsed a slate for the AIP election, but the slate lost.

AIP's pattern of cautious response and incremental change can be interpreted as PEO's success. In this sense, both organizations were engaged in what Edelman has referred to as "symbolic politics."[107] But many activists felt that the superficial assimilation of timely issues deflated PEO's ideology and mission. This led to a call for more vigorous analysis: for "an alternative ideology" not a cooptable set of reforms, for an "alternative" not a reformed institution.

Shifting federal policies also created problems for PEO and its members. The Nixon administration's pullback of funding from existing programs, meant the collapse of many of the strategies that sustained advocate planners. As OEO and HUD supported advocacy "dried up," the problem became how to advocate. "How does the radical planner function in today's cauldron of urban no show?"[108] The newsletter *Equalop* turned its attention to a "jobs for advocates" column as the 1970s came into focus. By the fifth conference in 1971, PEO's theme was "watchdogging" as an alternative to advocacy and the proposed strategy was to form a professional lobby in Washington to lobby for funding and favorable legislation.

Although Civil Rights provided instant starting power, many of the problems described above were related to the fact that PEO defined itself and acted as an adjunct to that volatile movement. Shifting federal priorities and AIP's assimilationist style also suggested the need for an independent political analysis.[109] By the early 1970s, many advocates felt that they had "fought the wrong battle."[110]

THE MEDICAL COMMITTEE FOR HUMAN RIGHTS: ADJUNCT TO INDEPENDENT STATUS

MCHR began as a "direct appeal for medical support and presence" by the Civil Rights movement to established doctors during the 1964 Mississippi Freedom Summer.[111] Among the founders were a generation of doctors with old left affiliations who favored giving physical support to Civil Rights workers; medical care progressives who were interested in health conditions in the segregated South; and a younger group of insurgent health care workers who desired to focus less on the South and more on the nation as a whole.[112] The former prevailed. An initial fact-finding mission to the South suggested two directions for medical efforts: medical presence to provide emergency first aid for Civil Rights workers in the South along with back-up support and fund-raising in the North, and a direct attack upon the discriminatory and segregated patterns of health service in the South.[113]

After a summer of sending shifts of medical personnel South, MCHR formally became a national organization in September 1964. The consensus of the founders was for a federation of affiliated local chapters with "maximum local autonomy consistent with a functioning national body." Fearing exclusivity, but concerned that "we keep a medical committee image," membership was defined somewhat ambiguously as "health personnel who are deeply concerned with the health needs of the socially deprived." The general sense of the group was that the health professions "include at least M.D.s, nurses and dentists."[114]

MCHR's statement of purpose included broader objectives. Along with physical presence, MCHR would undertake research, education and pilot projects to promote the "elimination of racial segregation and discrimination in all medical activities and health services," and establish itself as a counter organization to the medical establishment.[115] The minutes also stressed that the new MCHR be linked with both activist civil rights organizations as well as liberal medical organizations and explicitly provided that members act as liaisons to these groups.

Although the two strategies proposed by the fact-finding team— medical presence for the Civil Rights movement and the broader attack on segregated patterns of health service delivery—did not necessarily conflict, they reflected a split among the original members as to how MCHR should proceed. MCHR attempted to move in both directions. A model health clinic was started in Mississippi in 1964, staffed by MCHR personnel. Members also carried out surveys of health needs and conditions in Southern communities (and later in the North).[116]

On the whole, the attack on segregated and second-class health care took back stage to "medical presence" which was defined as the more radical position at the time, by virtue of its association with such groups as the Student Non-Violent Coordinating Committee (SNCC).[117] The doctors involved in the pilot health clinic turned to the federal government for support, and although MCHR was later criticized for turning its back on the broader program, this is a difficult criticism to assess. It is unclear whether a majority or a faction of the membership chose to go with the militants or whether those involved in the pilot project "sold" the strategy to a receptive federal government sensing the limitations of MCHR for large-scale institutional change.[118] Even if MCHR had sponsored the broader health program, it is unlikely that it would have been able to "hold on" to a large federally funded program any more successfully than SHO.[119] At any rate, the attack upon segregated and second-rate health care was picked up by the federal government as part of the War on Poverty strategy, and became the Neighborhood Health Center program.[120]

Related to whether MCHR should define itself as service and support to an increasingly militant Civil Rights movement was the role health professionals should play. At first, MCHR abstained from direct political involvement believing that such involvement would compromise the support it offered the nascent Civil Rights movement.[121] Professional influence and prestige were the basis of the original understanding of "medical presence." But, with the influx of a number of young medical and nursing students and housestaff into the organization, the issue of political involvement arose. A proposal at the First National Assembly in 1965 declared that MCHR denounce the war in Vietnam. Narrowly defeated in both 1965 and 1966 under the old guard leadership, the resolution was passed in 1967.

The Meredith March in 1966 marked the end of MCHR's first phase of neutral presence. The emergence of Black Power alienated a number of its liberal supporters and hurt the organization's financial base. Black Power also undermined the initial rationale of service and support to the Civil Rights movement as black militants told white liberals to look to their own institutions in the North. By 1967, there was "an almost entirely new cast of characters" at MCHR.[122] Many of the first generation of doctors, including public health and activist black doctors had left MCHR to work in organizational contexts more relevant to the tasks they envisioned. They were replaced by an influx of "student movement types," younger doctors, nurses, and nursing and medical students. Many of these were SHO graduates, committed to political action in general, and specifically to antiwar activities. The leftward drift of MCHR at this time was marked by new leadership and by the shift of the national office from the original New York base to Chicago.[123]

Political Advocacy and Counter Institutions

From 1967 to 1971, a politicized MCHR reached out to and supported a variety of movements on the left in a blend of political activism and counterculture characteristic of the times. Searching for a viable politics, MCHR moved on several fronts: it attacked the positions and policies of the professional medical establishment, supported alternate modes of service delivery, and became political advocate for ostensibly nonmedical issues such as the Vietnam War.

As Civil Rights shifted from voter registration in the South to "economic conflict in the North," MCHR attempted to follow the mandate to look to its own house.[124] This meant health care delivery and the health care politics of the AMA.

The programmatic focus of MCHR's Fourth Annual Convention, entitled "Health and Society" (1968), was the economic and social aspects of health care. Adopting the slogan, "health is a human right," MCHR launched an attack upon the AMA for having proclaimed that health was a privilege.[125] Although MCHR had picketed AMA meetings since 1965, the confrontation became more focal. In 1967 there were 500 pickets in Chicago; in 1968, MCHR gained access to the speaker's platform to condemn racial discrimination in medical societies and the lack of health facilities for the poor.[126] In 1969, in combination with other health and human rights organizations, MCHR confronted the AMA in New York with the burning of an AMA card, and in 1970, at Chicago, MCHR organized a People's Health Care Convention. Twelve community clinics in areas of Chicago otherwise without medical service, held a counter convention analyzing the barriers to good community health and presenting their solutions.

In focusing its attack on the AMA, MCHR moved to consolidate an alternative position. In sharp contrast to the AMA, MCHR argued for universal prepaid health insurance, group practice, multidisciplinary health teams, community outreach, more professionals, and community control.

With the influx of a younger generation of medical and nursing students and housestaff, MCHR openly espoused political advocacy of nonmedical as well as medical issues. Beginning with the adoption of an antiwar resolution at the 1967 convention, antiwar activity displaced Civil Rights as the organization's main focus. In some chapters, MCHR was submerged in such groups as the Medical Committee to Aid Indo-China. Along with participation in antiwar activities and medical presence at antiwar demonstrations, MCHR began a nationwide draft counselling service. To health activists, the slogan, "Bring the War Back Home," meant questioning the relation between war spending and national health priorities as well as the political use of medical personnel and services by the military.[127] During this same period, local MCHR chapters examined repressive nonmilitary uses of medicine.[128]

MCHR also turned to service delivery, funding, supplying, and servicing a variety of community health clinics referred to generically as "free clinics." These clinics were both free of charge and free in the sense that they were not satellites of existing medical institutions. For a sense of the scope of MCHR's involvement, MCHR claimed to have supported the development of many of the 150 free clinics in the country as of 1971; in Chicago, MCHR had 40 to 100 volunteer physicians on duty at one time. The free clinics were, to varying degrees, attempts to come to grips with professionalism.[129]

In keeping with these changes and the tenor of the times. MCHR adopted a less formal organizational style. Initiative lay with the local chapters which varied greatly both in organization and activity. Not only was this a period of drift and floundering, but a period of experimentation and creativity at the local level. Some chapters worked with consumers, others with workers, still others on institutional projects which explored the political nature of medicine. The national office moved to someone's home and the governing council met in open discussion.

As the 1970s began, there was mounting criticism from within MCHR and the health Left of contradictory aspects of MCHR's behavior. The free clinics, to which a vast amount of MCHR's energy had been directed, were condemned for being ineffective and counterinsurgent, for treating the patients no one else wanted to treat and for channelling the energies of activist health workers.[130]

Emergent caucuses denounced MCHR for its racism, classism, sexism, and elitism. Clinics, for example, serviced white middle-class hippies as opposed to the "less attractive" and more difficult poverty community patients.[131] The draft counselling project was accused of being more readily available to white middle-class than minority draft eligibles and of having become a lucrative form of medical practice.[132] Draft deferment was itself a questionable strategy. Perhaps white, middle-class, antiwar activists should be drafted and not deferred because "these are just the ones we need to have in the service to bring about the collapse of military rule in this country."[133] Needless to say, this argument was in turn criticized as "elitist."

Sexism was a long smoldering issue that dated back to the voter registration project: the nurses said that while they did the "day-to-day nitty-gritty work" and received sustenance wages and little credit, the doctors flew back and forth from North to South basking in the limelight of fund-raising parties.[134] The East Coast Women's Caucus proposed to bring the leadership of the organization in line with the composition of its active membership by introducing women, minority members, and mid-level workers, by "stamping out male-doctor-domination," and by changing the hierarchical style of leadership.[135]

The generic question of "who we are and what we stand for" was discussed by local chapters and took two forms. The first, that

MCHR should extend itself to all parts of the expanding health movement, consumers as well as workers; the second, that in creating new projects and foci, MCHR had expanded too much already and lost touch with the strategic pulse of the health movement which was health workers in health institutions.

The Hampton's Family Paper, a critique of MCHR written by a health worker collective in Brooklyn in 1970 and submitted to the local chapters at the 1971 Annual Meeting, commented on the distance between the national organization and the local scene and the failure of the national organization to provide leadership to local groups "often caught between militant community demands and the rigidity of health institutions." The paper argued for a narrowed base and focus. MCHR needed to develop:

> a sense of its own proper role in these struggles, a clear understanding of who its constituency is (mid and upper level health workers), how to reach them, and in general . . . a strategy for challenging the health empires and their subsidiaries.[136]

The tension between being responsive to and inclusive of movement groups and developing a program for a narrowly defined, and perhaps middle-class professional and student constituency, was analyzed in a popular Left document of the times. In "Letter to the Movement," Nick Egleson focused upon what he described as the typically guilty identification of activists with other "usually more oppressed strata." He called instead for "self-transformation," the correct identification of the ways in which "oppressive mechanisms have been internalized into all classes," not only the lower classes.[137]

While the Left argued that MCHR had failed to politicize health adequately, liberal reformers found "hidden reactionary roles" in the politicization that had occurred. In a well-read article in *Social Policy*, Jack Geiger, an original member of MCHR said of MCHR's recent stance: "If diagnosis is put to this political or moral use, is there a distinction between the MCHR physician and a white Alabama physician who certifies for induction every warm Black body he can find, while overlooking whites."[138] Arguing that "all knowledge is not instantly transferable in the name of demystification," he presented a vision of "affluent radicals, rich in the options open to them and their families," recommending the return of less specialized family practitioners. Geiger's critique indicated the extent of disagreement between liberals and the health Left. An article on MCHR in *Science* magazine noted that "the conflict between professionalism and political advocacy has made the organization's steady movement to the left a continuously painful process" and has meant the loss of the more established doctors.[139]

MCHR as a Mass Membership Organization with a National Program

In response to the accumulating grievances and the general sense of drift, MCHR reorganized itself in 1971. The Eighth National Convention created a strong national office, a broader and more representative leadership, and a national program composed of task forces which centralized local projects and was capped by a National Health Crusade.[140] MCHR also stepped up its political commitments. Linking "international imperialism" to domestic oppression, the convention endorsed the People's Peace Treaty signed by United States, North Vietnamese and South Vietnamese students and proposed a military chapter for doctors and other health workers to focus antiwar activity within the military.

Within one year, MCHR grew from 31 to 74 chapters.[141] Within six months, it was clear that the National Health Crusade was a failure and within a year, strong criticism, particularly from older chapters in big cities, led to the creation of a radical caucus. By November 1972, the national organization was in crisis; its two staff members had quit; *Health Rights News* had ceased publication, and the national office, broke, moved again to somebody's home.

One of the objectives of the reorganization was to create a centralized organization with a unified program out of the network of local chapters. As a prime example of this effort, the National Health Crusade illustrated the national/local tensions stemming from a top-down strategy.

In 1971, MCHR developed a position paper on National Health Care. It was a five-point proposal which called for a neighborhood based, community and worker controlled, progressively financed, nondiscriminatory, and nonprofit health care system which provided comprehensive and preventive care.[142] The significance of the document was that it defined MCHR as "neither solely an anti-AMA group . . . nor merely a super extension of Knowles/Kennedy corporate rationalism and reform," but as the proponent of a new position, an alternative to the various national health insurance plans being promoted.[143] The document took the radical position that the health care crisis "lies at the roots of our economic system" and "solutions will require fundamental change." Furthermore, "MCHR does not expect an adequate health care system to be legislated from above"; that "decent health care can only be realized through action at the local level."

In line with this position, the National Health Crusade was envisioned as a "mass movement to alert people to the weaknesses of the current proposals for national health insurance," and to widen the "growing health legislation debate."[144] The Crusade was to consist of a publicity campaign of leaflets, petitions, and mass media coverage, along with coalition building among various groups— health professional organizations, health worker and consumer groups, health science students, Civil Rights associations, trade unions, and women's organizations. Health care would become the basis of a national movement predicated on restructuring the entire system.[145]

In reality, the National Health Crusade was soon criticized by local chapters as an overly idealistic strategy.

> Very few people in the United States have ever heard of National Health Insurance; fewer are looking for a radical alternative; MCHR as a white middle class professional and student organization is incapable of speaking to those consumer groups who might be turned on to the Crusade.[146]

It had an unrealistic image of how change occurred.

> To imagine those who control the wealth of this country quietly accepting progressive taxation is blind idealism. To think a large multinational corporation that reaps its gains at home and abroad from drugs or medical supplies will allow one of its greatest profit making parts to be socialized is idealism. Hospital costs in Maryland rose 14.5% last year and 30 out of 35 claimed profits. How can anyone think those who benefit will give that up because there is a better idea? None of the MCHR proposals lead us to organize or direct us to struggle for change.[147]

The Baltimore chapter argued that by ignoring power and conflict the National Health Crusade remained the sort of agenda that intellectuals formulated in isolation from the rest of society. The Crusade failed to provide a "political framework" for involving people as they work and live. Change, they argued, involved "class struggle" and happened from the bottom up.

A coalition strategy also had its dangers.

> We want MCHR to share its radical analysis of the health system with other groups but there are pitfalls in coalitions. Entering into a coalition can lead to a dilution of our message as only commonly held principles among all the organizations can be promulgated. [Furthermore], coali-

tions, particularly those concerned with national health issues may well be tempted to enter the legislative arena. It should be our position that our national health care plan cannot be legislated because it presupposes the socialist transformation of our entire society, and because liberal legislative reform has inevitably failed the people.[148]

Last, but not least, there was the sense that organization building had displaced the importance of local organization and substantive activities. Although MCHR's national magazine spoke of increased membership, new chapters, and successful projects, the rhetoric was at odds with the experience of those at the local level. Many of the new chapters consisted of only a handful of dues-paying members. The local chapters felt that in expanding MCHR's appeal and programs to suit all comers, MCHR became "a revolving door" in which many entered and few stayed. Many felt that in seeking to address the "country's 200 million consumers," the Crusade had diverted energy from MCHR's true base and the work it could most successfully do.

> MCHR members [must] organize their own sectors within health care institutions. . . . This type of organizing is necessary because MCHR can relate to their fellow professionals and students and because the seat of power in the health care system lies within such institutions as hospitals and medical schools.[149]

In addition to debates about organizational change and focus, MCHR also faced the continuing criticism that it lacked political clarity and consisted only of a string of projects from prison reform and occupational health to abortion and psychosurgery. This criticism intensified as the national leadership avoided political discussion for fear of alienating its now broadly defined constituency. The minutes of the North East Regional Caucus state,

> although MCHR literature describes many projects, there is little said as to why these projects are meaningful. We have been told that the National Health Crusade and Occupational Health were MCHR priorities, but many of us are still unclear as to how these priorities were established.

The minutes then record a discussion of occupational health in which "two distinct philosophies about dealing with unions emerged for the first time": that MCHR serve and support the unions because they are the expression of the working class, and that MCHR begin by working with unions for tactical reasons but not become totally identified with union leadership. This discussion raised a series of issues which "had their roots in deeper underlying differences over the entire political conception and role of MCHR."

A report from the Boston Chapter focused these concerns by questioning the MCHR slogan. "Health care is not a human right in the United States at this time . . . . Health care is a class privilege."[150] The report argued that MCHR had no idea of how to proceed because it had no analysis of why things were the way they were. The report suggested that a political analysis would enable the chapter to concretely examine the Boston situation in terms of conflicting interests and groups within the health care arena. This, in turn, would help them decide where and when to act. In contrast to a National Health Crusade, Boston argued for

> developing a concrete, non-rhetorical class analysis of how to change the health care system, an analysis that emerges from our past practice, and uses theory to guide our present and future practice. We are trying to get away from the 'coalition around crisis' mentality.[151]

There is an analogy between MCHR's situation and the demise of the Welfare Rights organization in the same year.[152] At the same time that health activists were trying to move beyond picketing the AMA, to confront the need to produce progressive alternatives to national health proposals, the changing economic and political climate—the break up of the New Left movement, the dismantling of War on Poverty programs, and the inflationary character of the health sector—made the passage of some form of health insurance highly unlikely. These events raised questions as to the economic and political viability of a national mass membership organization such as MCHR.

In addition to factionalism from within MCHR, the break up of the New Left in the late 1960s left a resurgent Communist Party and a variety of Left-Leninst groups on the political scene. These groups attempted to take over independent movement organizations such as MCHR.[153] Between 1972 and 1975, MCHR was challenged in Boston and New York, first by the Progressive Labor Party and then by the Revolutionary Union, in a manner that cost MCHR members and organizational allies. Although MCHR continued in a low-key fashion, it did not regain its earlier momentum. It became increasingly peripheral to health activism and ceased to function in 1980.

5

Empowering People

*Technical assistance is our style, not theirs. Thus the obligation
planners have to community people is to use it in ways that
will not impose it as a style upon them. We do not, in other
words, choose issues whose resolution depends on middle-class
technical skills which cannot be transferred.*
Urban Planning Aid
1970-1972 Files

*The Health Center should be directed to service, not political
organization and action. If the Center were to be involved in
political action, it might make it more difficult to continue to get
government funds and other funds. This would affect the
Center's ability to provide medical care.*
The NENA Health Committee
Minutes, August 7, 1969

Activists who turned from serving the poor to empowering them
focused on process—both as a means to more equal outcomes and as
an end in itself. The problem was not delinquent professions but
professionalism per se. Medicine and planning created and fostered
dependency among clients and helped maintain social control. Given
this analysis, the activist role was to mobilize communities to help
themselves and to democratize the delivery of services.

The politics of empowerment grew out of and reflected activists'
experience delivering services, as well as developments in the New
Left and Civil Rights movements, and federal programs and policies.
For example, the shift away from technical assistance as a strategy
was encouraged by OEO grants for advocacy projects geared to
"maximum participation." Between 1965 and 1969, federal funding

not only supported the expansion of professionally initiated projects such as SHO, UPA, and NHC, it also legitimized the ongoing direction of change toward greater community input, control of the experts, and the subordination of planning and medical care under a broader strategy of community organizing for social change.

Issues also changed. The existence of ongoing programs meant that activists and communities now had to deal with the implementation as well as the initiation of services. Problems related to rent control, housing code violations and health care delivery in local health centers required that communities mobilize to demand what was theirs rather than be given technical assistance. Changing federal policies and programs affected what activist organizations did, who they recruited, and how communities accepted them, as well as activists' own assessment of the political and personal viability of their work.

As the case studies of SHO and UPA show, many organizations which became politicized rejected delivery strategies and tried to adopt roles more congruent with their shifting analysis. But these efforts also proved to be difficult.

URBAN PLANNING AID:
FROM PLANNING TO ORGANIZING

UPA's second stage, marked by new leadership and OEO funding beginning in 1969, enabled the voluntary organization to expand to a full-time staff of 22 and was characterized by different aims, activities, organizational structure and identity.[1]

In contrast to its original goal of technical aid to unrepresented groups, UPA redefined its objective as the "maximization of participation in the public planning process by citizens and grass roots groups, especially those in low income communities." In contrast to UPA's past work, which consisted primarily of presenting professionally defined alternatives to community groups, UPA now described its brand of advocacy as "initiative"—getting into the community and developing issues from the ground up.[2] Although one could argue that the emphasis on participation was predictable given OEO guidelines, at this point in time, UPA's official face was a case of congruence of interest rather than cause and effect.

Along with the priority given to organizing, UPA called for a new breed of staff member—the "community organizer/planner." Most of the newly hired staff had no technical training. One member characterized UPA during this period as a dual organization of professionals and organizers with the organizers predominating.[3]

The need for planners as planners became even less apparent over time. As organizational objectives were redefined as "processual," it became increasingly clear to all involved that "alternative plans are beside the point."[4] An in-house proposal for the evaluation of UPA prior to the 1970-1971 grant activity recorded several shifts that moved UPA's focus even further away from technical assistance and toward organization and mobilization. Evaluating "transfer of skills," the memo indicated that technical and scientific aspects of planning were themselves part of the problem:

> Where there had originally been seen a rather formal idea of teaching map reading, drafting, principles of planning and the like, there developed over the course of work, an emphasis on helping community members overcome awe of professionalism, and develop the ability to question 'professional advice' and demand relevant explanations in place of technical language, and responsiveness from government agencies. To a greater extent than had been foreseen, this meant teaching professionals to communicate with community people rather than the other way around.[5]

The memo suggested substituting the following as a UPA objective: "Enabling community members to deal *effectively* with professionals and government officials in such a way as to assure that services affecting the community are responsive to the expressed desires and needs of the community." This sort of work could be done by nonprofessionals as well as professionals; it certainly did not require a planner.

Issues changed and in turn affected UPA's role. Rent control or housing code violations did not require the planning expertise required by housing rehabilitation or highway relocation. A second memo, which described the problems for which client organizations sought assistance, noted: "They are related to the actual execution stage of urban renewal." To reflect this new reality, the writers suggested deleting the word *planning* from the purpose of the grant.

A rift between organizational generations developed during this period and contributed to UPA's shifting focus. The founding members, who now composed UPA's board, rejected the subordination of professional work to political organizing and chose to retain their identity as professionals. Most of them had moved on to make careers in advocacy via academic or government appointments. The new director and his staff had their roots in the student movement and defined themselves as organizers with ties to the movement rather than as planners seeking to reform the planning profession. Most of the staff hired by the new director came to UPA without specific technical skills but often with activist experience. This "second generation" took issue with the higher salaries paid to architects and city planners and voted to allot salary in terms of need.

Although the staff still included and recruited professionals, UPA no longer consisted primarily of planners and architects. A lawyer, a medical doctor, and a graphic artist were members as well as community organizers. New policies, such as salary equalization and geographic decentralization, made it hard to recruit or keep professionals and several left. The experience of one doctor illustrates the dilemmas that professionals at UPA faced at this time. It was difficult to find an appropriate role. The doctor tried first to redefine housing problems in terms of health but in his words, "no one bought it." Then he became involved in the strike of a major local employer on the side of the union. This finally led to working with local unions on occupational health and health care delivery. Although he had succeeded in finding a viable health related issue, UPA's funding crises and the decision to equalize professional and nonprofessional pay scales proved to be the final straw. Not prepared to reduce his salary by one-half, he developed a professional interest in occupational health which he was able to parlay into a full-time job.

One issue that sparked great bitterness and debate between the more professionally oriented board and staff and the "organizers" during this period was UPA's structure and strategy. Adopting the cultural argument of the New Left— that the personal is political— and that a revolutionary lifestyle is a prerequisite for revolutionary work, the organizers opted for decentralization and participatory democracy. Participatory democracy was reflected in specific policies such as equal salaries, shared office work, and collective authorship, and in the general attempt to share decision making with clients and nonprofessional staff.

Decentralization meant "intensive organizing," a strategy that involved the geographic dispersal of staff from a central office to live in the community and become a staff organization for the community.[6] "Extensive organizing" was the reverse in that it meant a central office, a separation between issue and functional areas such as research and media, and an emphasis on coalition building as opposed to serving the community. By this time, spot technical assistance had entirely disappeared from the debate. The question for planners as planners was whether they should be relegated to short-term back-up units for community efforts or whether they should retain organizational independence and project initiative.

During 1969 and 1970 and under the impetus of the new director, UPA decentralized to three white working-class communities. At the same time, the organization moved toward participatory democracy with its staff and clients. The offices of secretary and director were abolished along with hierarchical authority. Even more dramatically, salaries were equalized. The composition and function of the board changed during this period: from professionals who oversaw technical aspects of work, to a combination of staff and individuals with community organizing experience whose primary concern was UPA's community relations.[7] Other examples of UPA's "greater democracy" were the use of rotating directors and SLUD, an allowance granted upon request to "spouse-like dependents."

Decentralization meant that instead of working "with groups in different areas around one or two issues . . . producing detailed reports and other technical ammunition to support local groups' activities," UPA was now involved "in trying to build a network of ideas and actions around groups [already] working on different issues related to services in a community."[8] This led UPA to reach out to new issues that were either popular or seemed to have organizing potential such as industrial health, educational curricula, day care, and public housing. This sort of intensive strategy required that media and research output be geared to the community, not to the organizational class as was the case with advocacy planning. Typical resource materials produced during this period were slide shows and "how to do it" manuals on topics such as tenants' rights and landlords.

As an organizational policy, decentralization drew opponents even among the more community inclined. A memo from the Somerville group illuminated the problems of intensive organizing. In lieu of a larger sustaining movement,

> we absolutely agree that work within one community is a waste of time because organizations which do not have allies eventually become either social clubs or lose their radical edge. . . .had there been a tenants movement, South End Tenants Council might not now have the reputation of being a management group for the BRA [Boston Redevelopment Authority].[9]

Their analysis continued, however.

> What makes people in a community ready to form alliances? Somebody has to suggest it, and that person has to suggest it in terms of political strategy, which means he or she must be someone who has thought about general political strategies. That probably means an organizer

and at this stage of the struggle, that probably means somebody being paid by a group like UPA. After a somewhat longer period of time this will not be necessary in any given community—but for the first, say three years, it is unduly optimistic to believe that people will be making this kind of political judgment themselves, without someone they trust to talk to.

Organizing was deemed necessary and someone had to do it, but they concluded, "it's not us." "The Somerville group is currently exhausted." The issue crystallized in a phrase of the times—being good to ourselves. This implied "trying to find work for people like us, rather than [first] defining the work that needs to be done, and hiring people that will do it."[10] This phrase characterized the tension that UPA and similar organizations experienced between serving movements and communities, and defining a work, a politics and a lifestyle more conducive to the staff's own needs.

To understand these tensions and changing directions, we must also note the emergence of Black Power and its message to white activists: to pull back from the black community and organize their own house. The search for strategies and issues appropriate to changing conditions led UPA to work with white working-class communities in contrast to the minority and welfare constituencies of Civil Rights and OEO guidelines and on issues such as industrial health and safety. It was at this point and over this shift in clients and issues that trouble with OEO began. In 1970, UPA faced the first of several defunding crises precipitated by working with "over income people" and organizing around housing.[11] Although UPA and OEO interests had converged or fit for a while, UPA now came into conflict with its funding source.

By 1968, the Student Health Organizations, which had started large-scale federally funded health advocacy projects, also entered a new phase. Medical activists rejected advocacy and creative federalism because they felt it contradicted a "medical politics." Between 1964 and 1968, SHO moved from a position of alliance with medical schools and the federal government, working for change within the system of health care, to a position to the left of the progressive coalition, critical of sponsoring universities, the federal government, and their own advocacy and reform efforts.

STUDENT HEALTH ORGANIZATIONS: PATIENT
ADVOCACY TO COMMUNITY ORGANIZING

During the summer of 1968, SHO members questioned the objectives of medical service as well as SHO's educational goals. They felt that health was not a major priority for the ghettos. It became a commonplace that "jobs, education and housing and the elimination of police brutality are certainly much more essential to improving the daily life" than health.[12]

> If all the health problems of the urban ghettos were solved tomorrow, the only significant change would be a lot of healthy people throwing bricks and bottles at policemen and firemen.[13]

This observation affected the choice of roles. Students moved away from one-to-one patient advocacy in clinical settings and even away from health. One medical student working in a low-income community in Brooklyn described his decision this way:

> The problems to be solved first are economic ones. . . . I recognized this at the beginning of the summer and chose to work with Youth in Action's education program rather than in health problem areas.[14]

Even where specific health problems were important priorities, patient advocacy and technical assistance were not always effective means for the given end. A medical student working in the Bronx explained why he shifted from patient advocacy to community organizing.

> After working as a patient advocate for four of the families in the building, I decided that an effort should be made to confront the landlord and to make him pay for his negligence.[15]

Comparing the relative merits of the two strategies, he said,

> These efforts may contribute more to the good health of the community than all of the screening, physicals, and referrals that could be made for this same neighborhood.

The summer of 1968 was marked by a general reevaluation of patient advocacy. Initially, it had been seen as valuable for both the health student and the community patient.

> The student learned about the different agencies that the poor must confront. This practical knowledge, which enables the health profes-

sional to give comprehensive care, cannot be learned any way other than by direct experience. . . . The patient was able to confront the bureaucratic institutions, whereas before he had been confused and discouraged.[16]

One student's final report summarized the thoughts of many.

My feelings toward the benefits of patient advocacy after last summer and at the beginning of this summer were very favorable. Now, at the conclusion of my second summer, I have quite different feelings. At this point, I am not sure whether either party benefits.[17]

In addition to being slow and ineffective, patient advocacy was accused of creating and enforcing dependency. People came to rely on advocates for services which ranged from transportation and shopping to translation and cutting through bureaucratic red tape. Furthermore, the patient advocacy effect was ephemeral: "Whenever anybody from SHO took somebody to the hospital they got better care that day, but the day that you couldn't be there, they got the same old run around."[18] Since the projects only lasted ten weeks and many of the multiple problem patients could not continue treatment on their own, the question also arose, whether "medical care without follow up is better than no medical care at all."[19] These critical observations led to a range of suggestions for changing SHO, from the need to transfer skills—"to restructure SHO so that it trains community people to do what medical students think they can do"[20]—to strategies that moved beyond technical skills and direct service entirely.

In my opinion, patient advocacy is a stop-gap service. The real problem lies with the system that causes the need for an advocate. I would like to see SHP's energy directed at the institutions.[21]

The history of the two successive summers that SHP worked at the Robert Taylor homes, a giant housing project in Chicago, illustrates SHO's reevaluation of health advocacy.[22] A student survey of health needs in 1967 had promoted the idea of a well-baby clinic to a group of local women. These women formed a committee to seek a clinic. They were opposed by the black doctors in the area who had not been consulted and who saw the clinic as another "University of Chicago infringement" on their turf. As a consequence, the clinic had difficulty finding local medical staff and became dependent upon SHO resources. At the start of the 1968 summer, a newly militant black youth organization told SHO to leave the clinic and began to repair the rifts within the local black community.

In their final report on this experience, the Chicago SHP stated that "the lessons of the Taylor story are classic." SHO blamed itself for failing to understand that "many of the black doctors had been attempting to improve the health conditions of their people for years" and were genuinely threatened by the medical school sponsored intrusion. Thus, SHO unwittingly promoted rifts in the already fragile black community by creating links with the women and bypassing the doctors. The final report also noted that the ladies health committee came to rely upon SHO for all sorts of technical and administrative jobs. This meant that

> black volunteers now working with the Taylor Committee to increase the power of the black community must now surmount an extra obstacle placed there unintentionally by white students . . . the dependency relation.

SHO's verdict was that through "naivety," "ignorance," and "personal bias" much subtle damage was done. "We treated a symptom rather than the cause." SHO reported that the clinic finally worked when it was under black control and when "everybody working in the clinic was a member of the black community." The Chicago organization concluded:

> Students do not need to organize in poor communities . . . to learn about the problems that affect the poor. Middle class whites are foreigners to the poor and always will be. The real problem lies in the white community and must be dealt with there.[23]

Although radicalized health science students moved toward community organizing and nonhealth related activities, these broader political roles, for the most part, were rejected by community organizations and by black caucuses within SHO. These groups demanded that outsiders to the community function within it in their more limited technical capacity and preferably upon request. The director of a child care organization said that the students were wanted as patient advocates and not "as poor strung out imitations of Caesar Chavez."[24] Another preceptor who directed a community action agency, wrote to the SHO codirector criticizing SHO's "abandonment of the problem of the medically underprivileged" for its newly politicized direction:

> Students who insist on a 10 week involvement in the complexities of community organization, end by interfering with the process of social change, at best, and may even destroy good work that has gone before

them. We don't hire 10-week organizers and we don't accept them as volunteers, not from VISTA, the Boy Scouts, or SHO.[25]

Patient feedback was equally critical and skeptical. In underdeveloped rural areas and in urban ghettos, the long hair and beards of the more politicized activists were experienced as alienating.[26] One medical student in Brooklyn summed up his experience, "I thought our involvement in hospital settings was best. . . . Recipients expect doctors to act like doctors . . . not as quasi-social workers or priests."[27]

At the final conference, the Black/Brown Caucus of the California SHP spoke out against another summer of "white paternalism" and listed several authentic roles "still available" to white students in black communities: "patient advocate in the context of white service institutions, catalyst and liaison for community groups seeking participation on boards and councils which control services, and research analysts." They concluded:

> Ultimately, those of you who are sincerely committed to social change must examine, confront, and expose those white institutions (hospitals, medical schools, welfare) which by their very structural nature insure and perpetuate oppression, racism, and deprivation. This is essentially the white radical position.[28]

While the Black/Brown Caucus criticized the liberal reform model and demanded a radical politics, it also criticized the movement of SHO toward political roles within SHP projects and argued, on political grounds, for more limited and technical roles. By the end of the summer, many SHP participants questioned the combination of medical service and activist roles.

> There just isn't time to split one's attention and energies between medical practice and medical politics. . . .We can no longer afford to keep winning the small skirmishes (for example, patient advocacy) while losing the war (for example, little or no change in the health care delivery institutions with which we worked this summer).[29]

Sponsors also reacted to SHO's new politics. SHO was attacked for its more critical stance to the health problems of the poor and because it had become a source of community conflict. This meant that SHO no longer provided good will for the medical centers or functioned as a social change agent for OEO. The dean of the University of Southern California Medical School warned the participants of the 1968 summer project:

The aims to which this project has been devoted are probably three-fold, and it would seem to me that if those aims are not kept paramount in your consideration this could well be the last year of your project. The purposes for which the government has been willing to finance these summer experiences are: (1) to help future doctors, nurses, dentists, social workers and others interested in the field of health to learn at first hand the present methods of the delivery of health care to the very poor; (2) to think about and discuss ways in which this could be improved; and (3) to show by their presence to these poor their interest in them and concern about their problems and through their efforts, still as students, to help correct them.[30]

The faculty director of the California project was equally explicit. In a statement entitled "Goals and Directions," S. Douglas Frasier, M. D., said:

Funding agencies do not write blank checks. Although considerable latitude has been given thus far for projects of the SHO, it is unlikely that this freedom can continue. A return on funds expended will be expected.

The final report of the Greater New York SHP concluded, "One could not work for long in the South Bronx without becoming critical of almost everything."[31] Increasingly aware of the failure of reform efforts, SHP's focus turned, most naturally, from the old villain—the bureaucratized medical establishment, to liberal reform—federal programs such as Medicaid, federally funded projects such as the Neighborhood Health Centers and to their own projects.

In New York City, six SHP fellows under the direction of Harry Becker undertook a study of the entire Medicaid program. They concluded:

Medicaid has aggravated . . . an inequitable distribution of health services, an acute manpower shortage, a definition of roles which prevents health professionals from realizing their full potential, a lack of public accountability.

This program perpetuates the two class delivery system by distinguishing Medicaid patients from non-Medicaid patients . . . and by limiting the patient's choice of physician to those doctors who are willing to accept Medicaid patients.[32]

SHO also found fault with the outreach or storefront clinics established by medical centers. SHO argued that the medical centers were interested in "generating funds through Medicare and Title XIX" and in their own research agendas. They were certainly not committed to patient service or to community control.[33]

Criticism intensified within SHO over the nature of the summer projects, SHO's linkage with university medical centers and with the federal government. SHO began to see itself functioning as "middle men between the service delivery establishment and the outcasts." This perspective made information gathering and service roles doubly suspect.[34] A major confrontation occurred in mid-summer 1968, between SHO and the Regional Medical Programs (RMP), a federal sponsor of the projects. RMP called a meeting of student directors and asked that the projects submit a "community inventory" listing and evaluating contact sources within the community.[35] The possibility that this information would be used against community groups raised the issue of SHP's counterinsurgent potential.

Health activists began to see medical services in the same light as information gathering. If the system was in need of basic change, then health advocacy constituted "mere patchwork." Advocacy also provided "good press" for uneasy medical centers, presenting an image of change to the community surrounding these expansive institutions, and fulfilling federal promises to ghetto inhabitants.[36] Speaking of the medical schools, Lambert King, an SHO leader in Chicago said,

> We want to divest ourselves of that connection, even at the cost of the money that's available through the schools. We don't feel that the schools have any real commitment to community power in the area of health care.[37]

In addition to its concern with information gathering and medical service strategies, SHO began to feel increasingly uncomfortable being defined solely by the summer projects. The summer projects consumed too much organizational time and tied up SHO's leadership. Lambert King described a seasonal ordeal:

> In the spring, everyone would get concerned about money and recruiting and negotiating with Washington. Often sites were too hurriedly arranged, badly planned or too widely dispersed. Here in Chicago last summer, we had about 125 health science students and 75 high school interns working at 41 sites. And then in the fall there was the report to write. The Chicago report alone is 296 pages long.[38]

The activists began to feel bought off; that their time and energy could be spent more creatively. The finale for the summer projects was the Democratic National Convention held in Chicago at the end of August 1968. Although SHO voted not to participate officially, many went to the convention which symbolized a final disenchantment with the liberal commitment to change.[39]

The Fourth National Assembly held in November 1968, labeled SHO's identity crisis one of "Rhetoric or Action." Caucus groups exposed male chauvinism and medical student chauvinism within the decision-making apparatus of SHO as well as in its "interdisciplinary teams." The conclusion seemed to be a failure of strategy based upon a failure of analysis. After this assembly, the decision on the part of most SHOs not to continue the summer projects came as no surprise.[40]

Along with attempts to reform existing institutions, went attempts to create new forms of decentralized service delivery. In the course of the decade, these ranged from OEO funded Neighborhood Health Centers, based upon concepts of community participation and control, to the volunteer-staffed and low-budgeted free clinics, concerned with demystifying and deprofessionalizing medical care.

Health activists who believed that the answer to the failure of medical care for minorities and the poor lay in community control, gravitated to the Neighborhood Health Centers (NHC) and the free clinics. The free clinics, with their roots in the counterculture and Black Power, reflected disillusionment with large-scale liberal reform efforts such as NHC as well as with more traditional providers. The free clinics grew rapidly during the early 1970s, exhibiting a great variety of sponsors and forms. Although the two movements differed in size, scope, and institutional support, they represent poles on a continuum rather than disparate phenomena. Both were strategies of decentralized, alternative service delivery. Both involved the energies of a generation of medical activists, and both were, in turn, criticized by these activists for their limitations and failures.

The model for the NHC was a health clinic in Mississippi, initiated by Dr. H. Jack Geiger in the summer of 1964 and sponsored by MCHR and Civil Rights groups.[41] OEO picked this clinic in 1965 as a political model for broad-based social change under the rubric of health.[42] Over and beyond improved health care, the idea was to coordinate existing fragmented local services, encourage community participation and organizational involvement and create new job opportunities.[43]

From their inception, these neighborhood health centers became magnets for medical activists seeking to implement a community controlled, comprehensive medicine. Desmond Callan, a doctor who

left Yale University to become associated with a neighborhood
health center described the movement in these words:

> The NHCs represent a response to the failure of the American health
> care system, to its collapse in the slums, ghettos, rural back stretches of
> Appalachia. They are also a response to the inability of the existing
> medical care system (private practice, hospital/institutional, federal
> government) to do anything about it. The large institutions in particular
> are losing their legitimacy: especially as they perpetuate a two class
> system of care and give primacy to teaching over service. . . .
>
> What is a NHC? In a technical sense: one-door policy; one class of care
> . . . family-based care; shift of focus of attention from hospital to office
> care and preventive medicine. . . . And in a social sense: NHCs respond
> to the slogan of 'let the people decide,' away from Big Brother and from
> distant, complacent and uncomprehending bureaucracy.[44]

The NHC were not all of a kind. For the most part, NHC were
initiated by medical centers and controlled by them. This led to
criticism from health activists as well as from the militant black
community. The North East Neighborhood Association (NENA)
Health Center in New York City, was one of the few health centers
initiated and controlled by the community and one that kept its
independence from university medical centers.[45] NENA was a favor-
ite of health activists and of the health movement press.

NENA was chosen as a case study both to understand what
made for its organizational independence and as the deviant case
which illustrates the general rule: the limits of even a community
initiated and controlled health center as a strategy for medical
activists. Toward that end, NENA will be compared with Dr. Martin
Luther King, Jr. Health Center in New York City—a medical school
initiated and controlled health center.

NENA HEALTH CENTER: COMMUNITY CONTROL
AND SOCIAL CHANGE

> Traditionally health services are conceived, planned and delivered by
> the medical profession through various kinds of medical institutions
> without users of services being involved at any stage of the planning.
> Only after the plan becomes operational, often when it is noticed that
> the community is not responding, some effort is made 'to reach the
> community' with an attitude of 'here we are,' come use this marvelous
> service we have designed for you.

For the first time in the history of health services, in this nation, a group of low income people, recipients of services, took the initiative and the leadership in direct planning for medical care and mobilized themselves to involve a major medical institution in their plans, thus reversing the trend.[46]

The idea of the NENA Health Center originated during a 1966 transit strike. Residents of Manhattan's Lower East Side were cut off from their closest medical service and an asthmatic child almost lost his life. A group of mothers turned to NENA, a coalition of 62 groups, to form a committee to explore the possibilities of establishing a local health center. The health committee first tried to work with a group at New York University Medical Center who were interested in creating satellite services in the community. But after developing and submitting plans to the dean, the health committee discovered that the university had dropped its commitment to the project. At this point, the health committee hired a professional community organizer and set out to obtain funding on its own.[47]

The struggle to obtain funding revolved around the nature of the strings attached. OEO grants required that a medical center administer the grant money and that care be restricted to the poor, two constraints the local health committee would not accept. The committee finally obtained Public Health Service funds which did not carry the OEO restrictions. This grant allowed NENA to balance its desire for institutional independence with the need for some sort of back-up arrangements, by affiliating with a small private hospital, the New York Infirmary.[48]

The well-discussed and carefully thought out objectives for the NENA Health Center reflected the health committee's desire "not to have another Bellevue." Instead, there would be quality health services available to all area residents. The health center would be free to low-income and welfare recipients and use a sliding scale of fees for others.[49] The center would be run by a board consisting of community representatives. Health care would be delivered by teams; it would be comprehensive, preventative, and not least important, delivered with courtesy. To avoid long waits, appointments would be required. Neighborhood people would be hired in as many capacities as possible, trained for their work, and given upgraded training programs to create career mobility. There would be a community education program oriented to widespread health problems such as drugs and venereal disease and the center would provide social services.[50]

The committee's proposal linked health care to the "downward spiral of the poverty syndrome" and presented a familiar War on Poverty analysis:

> The interventional influence of a quality health center will provide an additional major factor in the enabling of an economically poor but culturally rich community to strengthen its fabric of interlocking relationships.[51]

But it also represented a more radical agenda of "innovations in the field of medical practice . . . with political overtones and implications." Key among these were the "redefinition of the doctor-nurse-patient role, the training and recruitment of medical professionals and paraprofessionals, and public and professional acceptance of the concept of group practice and especially of multi-team practice."[52]

The NENA Health Center was funded in the summer of 1968 and opened its doors in September 1969 with a staff of seven physicians, four nurses and 40 paraprofessionals. Within five months, it had more than 2,000 registered families (more than 5,000 individuals), a staff of 78, and 40 patient visits per day.[53] Within 14 months, more than 4,000 families (15,000 individuals) were registered and there were in excess of 150 visits per day. At the three-year mark, there were 35,000 registered patients, a staff of 125, and 250 patient visits per day.[54]

Within one year of opening, strains and tensions between various groups at the center culminated in the board asking the director to resign.[55] The Health Council and the professional staff were at odds over the nature of services, the administration of the center and the "representativeness" of the Health Council itself. There were similar tensions among the broader NENA Board, the Health Council, and the staff over their division of labor regarding the center and the extent to which the center should take on broader social action or political roles; and between the Board and the Health Committee over control of the Center's funds.

Professional Staff: Radical Politics and Conservative Medicine

In line with the requirements of the grant, NENA's key medical and administrative staff, who had been selected before the grant was submitted, were committed to the principles of community control and social change.[56] They charged that the Health Committee did not represent the "community" and, instead, aligned themselves with militant black and Puerto Rican groups.[57] Originally elected by representatives of the community organizations that composed NENA, the Health Committee as of 1969, was controlled by a predominantly white Reform Democratic Club and had become self-perpetuating. The broader NENA Board, composed of the "stuffy social work establishment," was also not considered "representative." As a consequence, the more radical NENA staff and administration encouraged militant group representation on the board and power struggles among the different factions involved in the community health center.[58]

The professional staff held different conceptions of what the health center should do as well as who the community was. These views surfaced in a debate about what kind of social services the center should offer. Should there be patient advocacy and case work related to health problems, or medical presence and backup at such events as a school confrontation?[59] The more overtly political people wanted to use the health center as a base for community organizing; they assisted militant groups and printed leaflets listing NENA as their base of operations. This caused trouble for NENA with its funding agency. The NENA Health Committee, on the other hand, was quite explicit about the objectives of the health center. Its goal was medical care, not political action, and the committee felt that overt politics would endanger such care.

While radical in terms of overall objectives and community alliances, the professional staff tended to take more traditional—even conservative positions—in terms of health care or the administrative control of the center. For example, frustrated with broken appointments, with trying to make a team approach work, and with patients who wanted open-door crisis care, the doctors and administration wanted to shift NENA's policy from its original innovative preventative care model to more traditional episodic care.[60] They moved to close the family registration without consulting the Health Council. A NENA physician claimed, "It's either an increasingly thin bandaid for everyone, or continuous medical care for a limited number of people."[61] The community board resented not being consulted. They felt that the community only wanted episodic care because that was what they had been taught by the system and that it was the function of the health center to reeducate the community.

Another source of friction were the demands of community members of both the staff and the Health Committee. They placed more importance on job training and upgrading within the health center than did the professional staff. One issue was policy toward the center's expensive security guards. The staff association argued that the security guards be included (along with secretaries) in the medical training program and be used elsewhere in the center in medical as well as nonmedical capacities.[62]

An important medical and administrative issue was the referral system for pregnant women. Many felt that the doctors at NENA favored the more prestigious New York University (NYU) Medical Center with which some of them were personally affiliated. This undercut the community view that success was based on autonomy and that dependence on NYU would hurt the health center. They felt that if medical care was the issue, all but the most complicated cases should go to New York Infirmary.[63]

Finally, there were questions about the administration of the health center and the role of the Health Committee. Critics felt that the Health Committee should have left the day-to-day administration to the staff and moved on to take "the long-range view"—to build upon the Health Committee's "one time role as militant spokesman on health affairs for the community at nearby hospitals."[64] Instead, the Health Committee had "assumed the administrative prerogative," interviewing and approving all personnel, and superintending the daily operation of the center. In the words of one doctor, "They come traipsing into the center and visit and say or do anything to the staff."[65] The critics also charged the Health Committee with adopting a defensive posture toward the center, keeping meetings and minutes secret, and fearing to challenge the community with regard to a building site for expansion.

On the other hand, there was some feeling that the critics' charges, which ranged from defensiveness, conservatism and fear to incompetence, represented a traditional case of medical and professional personnel refusing to surrender authority to community groups. An outside advisory council of well-known professionals was originally designated to evaluate medical care at the center and report only to the board, but this plan was never implemented. Although the staff claimed that the advisory council represented "establishment people," many took this as an example of professional resistance to accountability and control. An evaluation study of the social service component at NENA called the health service "over-professionalized." It suggested that the NENA project director need not and should not be a medical doctor, and urged more emphasis be placed upon the training and upgrading of low-paid service workers.

> The doctors have too much to do with the way the agency is set up. Everything depends on the doctor. A doctor is a technician with superior judgment in his area of competence. . . .Like all specialists, he should be on tap, not on top.[66]

The community organizer who worked with the original Health Committee in formulating the proposal and getting the grant, defended the Health Committee's stance: "Our vision of the health committee was to be involved with day-to-day care, a watchdog. Health services were our primary concern. Not to have a Bellevue."[67] She noted that in terms of health care, "our original proposal was very advanced. We sat around and said, these are the problems in the community and worked out how to solve them." She added that one of the center's original goals was financial independence.

> We had a five year grant with the understanding at the start that we should become self-supporting. After I left, I contacted the unions about arranging with them for new patients and funds. But no one followed up on this. We also wanted to develop a group practice. . . .

Her conclusion underlined the disparity between the political objectives of the doctors and the medical objectives of the Health Committee. "The doctors weren't interested in this. Their politics distracted them from the real health work."

While there were further declines in the morale of the community staff and the Health Committee and a further erosion of the original model of continuous comprehensive care overtime, it began to be apparent that whether the NENA Health Committee was "representative" was of less importance than the constraints imposed by the larger economic and political context. By 1972, a formerly supportive health movement publication found NENA, "caught in a series of binds, basically not of its own making, that have often set one sector of the Health Center against another."[68]

For all of its success in becoming the first autonomous health center, NENA still remained a marginal institution in terms of medical care, dependent upon securing federal funds, an effort that required much of its time and energy. The very fact of success meant that people came to depend upon NENA for jobs and services. This made those involved less likely to endanger their grant by political activities. In the words of one observer,

> NENA became a job center, with all the factionalism that this engenders . . . the issues became employment and control over day-to-day operations. . . . They fell into the pettiness we were all trying to break out of.[69]

While radicals at NENA had learnt that "you can't use health as a cover institution" for radical social change,[70] NENA was also faulted for its failures as an incremental model.[71] Community con-

trolled health facilities came to be perceived as a trap which consumed the best community people. Without adequate resources, the
community could do little better than the city in operating the
facility, whether with regard to health care or employer relations.
According to one long-time staff member, one of the things that kept
NENA going so successfully through inflation and cutbacks was the
exploitation of its nonprofessional workers.

> When I got there, they were so passive and oppressed. In terms of
> salary and hours, they made less than city hospitals or even other
> health centers. Finally some political people got jobs at NENA and
> fueled the resentment.[72]

In 1978, after staging a month long walk-out over wage increases, 95
percent of the staff voted to unionize.[73]

In the long run, NENA's hard-won and "historic" autonomy
came to be seen more negatively both in terms of financial and
political consequences. In the words of a former staff member, "One
of the disasters of NENA was that it had no relation to Bellevue."
The use of New York Infirmary as an affiliated hospital meant that
fewer than 50 percent of NENA's patients could be hospitalized at
NENA since they had to have insurance policies. The rest went to
Bellevue.[74] Autonomy also foreclosed the possibility of political struggle against major institutions on the Lower East Side and at a time of
fiscal constraint, this meant that conflict turned in upon the health
center, rather than remained directed at appropriate external forces.

DR. MARTIN LUTHER KING, JR.
HEALTH CENTER

A comparison of NENA with a more typical health center, initiated
and controlled by a medical center, gives additional perspective on
the limitations of neighborhood health centers as models of health
radicalism and social change.

In both the community initiated and controlled as well as the
medical center initiated and controlled health center, community
staff members and boards became more concerned with job security,
training, and upgrading over the course of time than with either
health care or political objectives. Community control was often not
sought by the community for a variety of reasons.[75] Where it
occurred, it was linked to strong leadership such as was found at
NENA.[76] At Dr. Martin Luther King, Jr. Health Center (MLK), resistance to the community board becoming the fiscal agent for the

grant came from the community board and staff and reflected their fear of losing hard-won gains if the community could not manage the health center as well as Montefiore, the medical center.[77]

As at NENA, community control was not necessarily in the best interests of either the activists or the community. At MLK, where the community board had administered and managed the health center since 1974, full fiscal control meant the possibility of "the increased cost of malpractice *insurance* in the event of a split from Montefiore; the increased cost of insurance for the building and the possible unavailability of insurance because of the local neighborhood; and the need for an affiliation with a hospital to facilitate admissions of patients. . . ."[78] Although the issue was ostensibly power, for the community, control translated into concrete concerns regarding money and jobs. The community

> may be most comfortable with, in fact defensive about any possible infringement upon their very restricted locus of power even though it might be administered by a hospital who has a history of little self-initiated community orientation.[79]

In both health centers, conflict emerged between the community boards and the staff. At MLK, where the community board was initially convened as a legal necessity for funding purposes and was "benign" for the first two years, conflicts later arose over administrative control of the center and over patronage.[80] The first of a series of difficulties occurred over the firing of an administrator, as at NENA. The board felt it should have been consulted.[81] Thus, community control, with its vested interests in jobs and day-to-day administration, emerged as a threat to the medical center administration and to the traditional prerogatives of doctors whether they were activist or conservative.[82]

Both cases underline the low priority of health to communities which lack jobs, housing, and decent schools as well as the different meanings which these communities attached to health. At NENA, health initially meant a local facility not like Bellevue. At the first meeting between Montefiore staff and the local community to discuss MLK, Montefiore was "surprised" to hear that people were not interested in a health center with new approaches but in jobs.[83] Both liberals and radicals had different agendas than the communities they sought to serve and they both learned that community control does not necessarily fit with radical agendas let alone change. For activists, this raised the question of whether health care could serve as an institutional cover for social change.[84]

The health centers were also criticized by their medical staff for the quality of care they provided. This concern with quality was related to the increasingly bureaucratized working environment of the health centers and to the use of paraprofessional workers. MLK, "the premier flagship" of the NHCs in terms of innovative care in the 1960s, had a staff of more then 400 subdivided into four units and eight health care teams. Yet it was not at all horizontal like it was supposed to be. Over the years, lines had become centralized at the top and it was hard to get things done. "Records are in one central file and if I get a phone call I can't reach for the file. . . . Lab work takes forever." Community workers were less efficient. "Most people here have only one skill. Nine-tenths of the tasks which are done in a doctor's office by one person, are done here, less well by nine or ten different people."[85] This criticism of the deprofessionalized model of health care delivery pioneered by health centers such as MLK, by a doctor who had worked at several neighborhood health centers throughout the decade, suggested that the objectives of innovative quality medicine conflicted with those of job creation.

Doctors at the health center were also concerned with the continuing stigma of community medicine. In addition to being penalized for Medicaid's low reimbursement rates, they felt that they took on the attributes of their low-income patients and were treated as second-class citizens when they tried to get work done at other hospitals such as Montefiore. Poverty work was also draining.

> Too many people here can't make the change in their life circumstances which would help them deal with disease. . . .You get burnt out working with the poor.[86]

Low status and low pay made for low morale and, in turn, made staff recruitment difficult. In the late 1970s, most of the doctors at the center were foreign-born and/or foreign-trained, raising the question of whether the center helped perpetuate the second-class medicine it set out to change.

As with NENA, MLK's experience over the course of a decade confirmed the importance of the larger political and economic environment. Some observers felt the major problem was that the basic ground rules changed—from delivering innovative services in the 1960s to financial viability in the 1970s.[87] This shift from a broad definition of health, which included social change, to a narrow medical definition, marked the dismantling of OEO. As with NENA, the narrowed criteria and budget cuts supported the ongoing retreat from a more innovative comprehensive team medicine, to a more traditional physician dominated model.

> When the cuts come, they won't part with the M.D.s. If they were willing to hold on to and fight for the community projects, while not immediately beneficial to the community, it would make a difference.[88]

Cuts in the broad range of social services and job training programs further hurt morale. Many feared that MLK would become another Medicaid center serving only the reimbursable poor. But as with NENA, shifting federal policy and support encouraged but did not create these trends. In addition to the community/professional staff dynamics, the larger picture must include demographic trends and their economic implications. During the same period, MLK saw a welfare population replace a working-class population. This made for competition between public and private hospitals for reimbursable clients.

How did community control deal with the medical center presence, both in daily hospital work and policy decisions such as investing in new technology? Experience at MLK and elsewhere suggests that community control faltered before technology and that, for a variety of reasons, decision making reverted to experts whether they were in the medical centers or at the satellite clinics. Community boards remained in awe of the expertise implicit in medicine and were overwhelmed by the complexity of large clinics. An executive director at MLK, an institution which prided itself on advancing community people to top administrative and management positions, said of further extensions of community control:

> This community does not have the skills or the time to run a program . . . they can barely deal with the struggles in their own lives. . . .Power is not in the community. The power is in the technology: the doctors, the nurses, the technicians.[89]

At NENA, despite autonomy from a large medical center, the Health Committee did not control the health center. One doctor noted:

> By the time I arrived, five years ago, the community board played no role in the Center. Not only can't you control NYU, you can't control a medical center on the block unless you are there everyday.[90]

This doctor felt that experiments such as NENA represented the failure of the Left model of people learning through experience. In addition to the difficulty of restricting medical professionals to strictly medical decision making or of increasing community input into technical matters, community boards themselves favored technology which they equated with "better medical care." The irony was that support for technology gave power to the technicians and confirmed a hospital based model of care.

By the late 1970s, many activists felt that neighborhood health centers as a battleground for community control and social change had coopted the best members of the community and proved a stalemate for innovative change. Placed on boards as consumer/providers, community leaders became dependent on uncertain federal resources, scapegoated for federal policies, and torn by internal conflict over these same issues. Finally, they were up against a technical model which they either wanted to emulate or could not fight. One observer said of NENA and MLK, "They've arrived at the same point. Both are now part of the problem."[91]

THE FREE CLINIC MOVEMENT AS A RADICAL HEALTH ALTERNATIVE

While activists' hopes for the large-scale federally funded neighborhood health centers focused on community control to reorder priorities, the aspirations for the numerous small-scale, voluntarily staffed, free clinics were for resocialization, a revolution from within combining democratized service and political education. The image of social change was of bureaucratic institutions withering away when disaffected workers refused to work in them and patients refused to use them.

The turn to alternative institutions as a strategy for change reflected several developments in the mid-1960s—the disillusionment with liberal reform, the emergence of minority and women's politics, and of a counterculture. For those who were disaffected with the politics of the 1960s, the clinics represented unaffiliated or "free" efforts, small enough to be locally controlled and responsive to community input. Minority and women's groups flocked to sponsor these clinics because they felt that health clinics had a base-building potential and that health care was something they could offer their constituencies.

The counterculture was at the center of the free clinic movement. First, it created demand—a class of drug-taking youths for whom no facilities existed. Second, countercultural ideas and values encouraged experimentation with democratic forms of organization, decision making and delivery, including the transfer of medical skills to nonprofessional staff and to patients. Based on many of the same assumptions about health care as the SHO projects and the NHC—"health care is a right and should be free at the point of delivery. . . health services should be comprehensive, unfragmented and decentralized . . . medicine should be demystified . . . community-worker control of health institutions should be instituted"—the free clinics represented a radical populist version of the NHCs.[92]

Given its do-it-yourself quality and antiestablishment stance, the free clinic movement spread rapidly. Any group could set up a storefront clinic. The staff were volunteers, the funds were donations from multiple sources, and the supplies, begged, borrowed, or stolen from local institutions. In terms of sponsors and clients, these clinics ran the gamut from clinics for hippies and street people to community sponsored and controlled clinics in areas without services, to politically motivated clinics run by groups such as the Black Panthers or the Young Lords. MCHR sponsored the development of many of these clinics and its local chapter members funded, supplied, and serviced the local storefronts.[93] In 1970, a National Free Clinic Council (NFCC) appointed itself representative of the nation's free clinics. This controversial organization, whose board was composed of doctors and representatives of major drug companies, sought and received a $1 million grant from the Nixon administration for drug abuse clinics.[94]

By 1971, the free clinics began to come under strong criticism from the health Left, both because of their inability to give quality day-to-day care and their function within the system as a whole (the direct cooptation of the movement by the NFCC).[95] In terms of day-to-day care, the clinics were criticized for being as ineffective as hospital out-patient departments—the types of establishment institutions they sought to replace. Dependent upon doctors and limited resources, they were often unable to provide more than first-aid. This meant that they faced a typical bind: either they supplied "humanistic care" to a few or more impersonal "institutional style care" to a greater number of patients.[96] Similarly, although worker/community control was an ideal, it proved difficult to realize given the lack of interest of patients and communities and the exhausting hours of the clinic staff.[97]

The critics argued that the free clinic, as a model, could not escape the constraints imposed upon the established medical system by the larger political economy and that free clinics replicated the established system in miniature. Looked at as a whole, they concluded that free clinics were "bad politics." The clinics channelled the radical energy of medical activists and served as a safety valve for hospitals and health centers by caring for the medically disen-franchised, the patients the established institutions either did not want to treat or could not profitably treat. The NFCC's role in gaining support from drug companies and the federal administration amounted to further proof of its "counterinsurgent function."[98]

As the 1970s began, health activists argued that rather than remain service projects as most had been, free clinics must become politically directed instruments of change along the lines of a few Hispanic and black clinics; that they must fight to gain resources from wealthy medical centers, recruit workers from the same hos-pitals where the clinics referred their patients, and keep their gaze focused upon the health care responsibilities of established medical institutions.

6

Transforming the Workplace: Professionals as Workers

As public employees providing care predominantly to the poor and lower class patients, we occupy a unique position in the United States health system. Our experience forces upon us an understanding of municipal institutions which is not shared by any other segments of organized medicine. It therefore becomes our responsibility to take a more aggressive role as advocates for our patients and contribute our share to political and scientific battles being fought within the profession.
Richard Cooper M.D.,
CIR *Bulletin* 2:5, 1973

Believing that the staff [Department of City Planning] work for them, the Commissioners, the Executive Director and the Chairman have asked the staff to do things which many on the staff feel violate their rights as persons and workers. We have been asked to violate our personal integrity by justifying decisions to the public on a technical basis when they were made on a political level in the Mayor's office; we have been asked to conceal information which should be available to the public. For these reasons I have come here today to testify.
Lynne Aston, *Urban Underground Resurfaces*, public hearings of the
New York City Planning Commission,
February 19, 1969

What I do from 9 to 5 is more important than what I do from 5 to 9.
T. Sachs, Boston SHO, quoted by
Dr. Ken Rosenberg

An ideological belief in the possibility of social transformation mark- ed the turn to socialist strategy. Activists now emphasized the functions of medicine and planning for the economic and political needs of capitalist society. If the professions were key agencies of a class state, redistribution of services could not occur without political movements for systemwide change. The activist solution: to build political movements based on restructuring medicine and planning.

Two somewhat differing strategies emerged within the socialist perspective: professionals as workers and professionals as political vanguards. Each projected a different role for insurgent professionals. For the former, planners and doctors were part of a changing class structure—public sector workers becoming proletarianized and there- fore potential agents of class struggle. The activist role was to organize other professionals to reshape the workplace and to link up with clients against the corporate state.[1] For the latter, because professions performed increasingly central functions in a class state, the crucial activist role was to demystify professional knowledge.

Whether as class-conscious workers or as an intellectual and political vanguard, activists believed that theoretically based analysis must inform action; hence the popularity of study groups. Compared to empowerment strategies which viewed planning and health pri- marily as a means to political consciousness, planning and health now became strategic sites for the achievement of institutional and social change.

Although these strategies developed partly as an attempt to escape the dilemmas of other political strategies, they exhibit their own strains and contradictions along both ideological and structural axes. I look first at workplace organizing, and in the following chapter, at vanguard groups.

The shift to institutional sites and professional constituencies took place in the context of the changing opportunity structure for activists—the pullback of federal funds for community action pro- grams—and coincided with the matriculation of a generation of activists from training programs to institutional settings. Attention to organizing professionals in the late 1960s owed much to a branch of the New Left, the Movement for Democratic Society (MDS) (see Chapter 2). Adopting the perspective of theorists of the "new work- ing class," MDS emphasized that professionals were a source of discontent and change because of their membership in the labor force, not only their sympathetic identification with minorities and the poor.[2] This meant redirecting attention from the distribution of the social product to the work process—from consumers as active agents of change to educated workers in government bureaucracies.

In using the term *institutions* I am adopting the phrase used by activists to describe their activities in mainstream as opposed to alternative settings such as free clinics or community advocacy groups.

Institutionally based action took the form of collectives and unions. Although these efforts differed, they shared the belief that professionals could join with other workers and clients to bring about institutional change. But in the course of action, institutions proved resistant to change and differences of interest arose between professional and nonprofessional workers as well as between workers and community clients.

THE URBAN UNDERGROUND: INSTITUTIONAL COMPLICITY AND INSTITUTIONAL ORGANIZING

The Urban Underground (UU) was one of the most active and successful MDS groups that organized among professionals in the late 1960s. This group of planners and architects addressed the planning profession in general and New York City's planning bureaucracy in particular. Located primarily in the Department of City Planning, they recruited other "insiders" and formed study groups which took up work related topics such as "who decides your schedule?" and "whom do you work for?"[3]

In existence from 1967 to 1973, the UU's most effective actions took place between 1967 and 1970. These were a description of typical planning jobs entitled "Letting the Cat out of the City Planning Bag" (n.d.); a demonstration at the new General Motors building attacking the auto industry for its contribution to the destruction of cities and calling for a ban on cars in Manhattan (1968); and public testimony on the City Planning Commission's plan to "upzone" the Lower East Side of Manhattan (1969). These actions constituted a critique of the "myths" of professionalism and meaningful social change for planners and planning.

Comparing detailed analyses of what planners "really do" with typical job descriptions, the UU documented an abundance of "makework studies and statistics," "mechanical and clerical type activity" and "dead time." This held true for both senior and junior level planners. Analysis of actual job content led to a more general questioning of the expectations created during professional training. In what ways was planning a "profession?" And did the disparity between the expectations and the actual practice of planning make for an "emperor's new clothes syndrome" in which planners, their expectations dashed, pretended to be busy with meaningful work.[4]

Summarizing the results of their analysis of actual planning jobs, UU concluded that although "planning has recently moved to encompass social planning . . . and although the words *physical* and *social* may be different, the results for people are not." Planners who wanted to effect change remained "frustrated in their work situation and powerless to carry out ideas." Solutions such as the "advocate approach" of some firms, created their own contradictions: the planner could be "paid by the government" and "working for a community whose views he doesn't share." There was little grass roots participation. "Social planning has not given people power over the decisions that affect their environment." In fact,

> by being intimately involved in the planning process to change their community, a change which eventually removes them from the scene, people have helped dig their own graves. Again this leads to the sense that I as the planner am being used to manipulate community people.[5]

The brunt of criticism was directed at first generation advocacy efforts. Since attempts to aid minorities and the poor by means of new roles, organizations, and services—often state-funded—had been compromised or had worked to state advantage, UU called for a new strategy. Activist planners should educate, organize, and attack within the work place—not the academic establishment nor the national professional associations, but the governmental planning bodies where the majority of planners were employed, and where the "most damage is done."

UU flyers insisted that planners "analyze every program and project and ask, who it serves. Does it serve the people or private profit?" This query raised the issue of the individual responsibility of professionals in bureaucracies. The flyers also broadened the field of reference for planners beyond such immediately relevant institutions as the city planning establishment by linking military and defense spending and corporate priorities to the lack of low-income housing, to unmet transportation needs and to the problems of cities in general.

UU's criticism of the City Planning Commission's proposals to rezone the Lower East Side of Manhattan went right to the heart of many of these issues and it was in this action that work content, "in whose interests," and institutional complicity, came successfully together. Asked by the Cooper Square community to help halt the rezoning of lower Manhattan, UU members on the staff of the Department of City Planning testified at the public hearings of the New York City Planning Commission in February 1969. They stated that staff recommendations had been ignored and hidden from the public:

> Their [City Planning Commission's] own studies, memorandums and stated policies argue that there is sufficient land currently zoned R10, that private developers can operate economically on R7 land, and that such land ought to be preserved for low-income housing. My own office compiled a listing of 204 desirable sites currently zoned R10 which are available for development.[6]

The activists were explicit as to why this was done:

> The city is indeed being planned, but not by the public agency. Decisions are actually being made by banks, big corporations, and real estate developers. The administration, through the City Planning Commission, only ratifies those decisions.[7]

Because the operative interests were real estate, activists felt that rezoning would "spur the development of luxury housing."[8]

The activists criticized the Department of City Planning and city planners in general for providing rationalization after the fact:

> The rezoning proposals before the Commission are presented to the public as resulting from technical, and thus politically neutral, expertise. In fact, they result from high level political decisions, in response to pressure from real estate speculators. They contravene the recommendations of city planning staff. They were made without consultation with the public. And they contradict previously stated policy. . . .
>
> By rezoning areas of the city in which poor and middle income people live and work so that speculative builders can move in and construct luxury rent housing, the City Planning Commission is serving as a kind of fig leaf, covering the naked power of big corporations, banks, and the real estate speculators. Not only are people like ourselves powerless to prevent this from happening; we are also being used as part of a liberal facade. We talk to community groups, we make surveys and studies (using our technical skills), we make recommendations, and we are on the firing line having to justify to the community whatever happens.[9]

The planners had come to see themselves as agents of social control, manipulating the public for the benefit of private interests. In the wake of the hearings which received much publicity, more than 100 city planners signed a petition against R10, the rezoning was not accomplished, and interest in UU was generated among the city planning staff.[10]

While the combination of worker and community protest had stalemated the rezoning, the UU had less success with other actions. With the start of New York City's much publicized fiscal crisis, UU attempted to organize around employee layoffs in the Department of City Planning. But these efforts were ineffective. One planner commented:

> They were worker issues. The community can't relate to worker issues . . . and planners can't be effective without the community's political support.[11]

Some of the more radical city planners were among the first to be laid off and others left, frustrated with their work or with agency harassment. Efforts to organize around the events in Cambodia in 1973 also failed. With the "collective spirit gone," activists turned to local actions which felt "more satisfying," like "community organizing around squatters and other housing struggles."[12]

Although the response to MDS was countrywide and spontaneous, "the timing was poor."[13] "It was the beginning of something that didn't get a chance, that happened too early to grow."[14] The UU lasted well beyond MDS and the movement of some MDS groups into the Weather Underground, but could not recapitulate the success of the 1969 hearings of the New York City Planning Commission.

The Urban Underground did not survive the falling apart of the New Left movement nor the impact of the fiscal crisis on public workers in the 1970s. While discontent and responsive to organizing, this study illustrates both the conservatism and vulnerability of publicly employed planners in hard times. With layoffs, the issues became bread-and-butter issues. In contrast to the rezoning case which linked professional and community concerns, planners who organized around the narrower job actions, could not gain community support. Thus they lost political clout as well as their sense of legitimacy. This plus the failure of the larger political movement left them at the mercy of the organizational environment where, unlike teachers or doctors whose "skill gave them the power to stop the economy," activist planners did not have equivalent organizational threat power.[15] Although MDS collapsed with the demise of the movement and the recessionary economy, the vision of professionals including planners, as part of a changing class structure, remains a contribution of this strand of the New Left and a recurrent line of critical analysis and action on into the 1980s.

Another example of planners' workbased activism was the attempt to politicize a municipal civil service union in New York City, a union which was composed primarily of city planners and engineers.

PLANNERS IN UNIONS: THE TECHNICAL GUILD OF A CIVIL SERVICE UNION

Beginning in 1978, activist planners attempted to "takeover" New York City's Civil Service Technical Guild. Before the city's planning agencies expanded in the 1960s, the Technical Guild was dominated by engineers, but as the recruitment and actual numbers of planners increased, their attention turned toward the Guild.

Prior to activist involvement, the Guild, run by "the old team," functioned as a self-interest association. It fought for contracts and health benefits. It never fought departmental policy or reached out to other unions.[16] One planner described the Guild's position at the time of the Urban Underground: "We'd try to get the union to support us. Many of us were threatened with job layoffs because we were on special contracts, not the civil service. But it was impossible to get it to move. It was just dead weight."

Younger union members gradually started to vote different officials into office but the process was slow and disheartening, and took its toll on activists. Recounting how the first radical elected as vice president "failed us," one planner emphasized the milieu: "It was hard to dissent, to constantly say no. Now he [the radical] just does the right thing, gets promoted and gets the good assignments." Another factor was the other large membership group of engineers. Predominantly conservative, working against their traditions further blunted forward motion and increased the frustration of the planning activists.

Change came with the city's fiscal crisis and with increasing attacks upon the planning agency and the union. Civil service exams, for example, had not been given for more than five years and work pressure increased as did attempts to harass and intimidate individuals. The planners "sharpened themselves" in the face of "political attacks," forming study groups and making contact with other activists across the union.

An activist slate took over the city planning chapter in 1978 but found themselves ineffective before the old team's recalcitrance. The new chapter head coalesced with other dissenting groups across departments to lead a successful rank and file opposition at the local level under the slogan "bring the union back to the people."[17] But one year after the "takeover,"not much had changed. While the percentage of city planning staff in the union had risen sharply (from 75 to 95 percent), the planners remained basically apathetic to the union's efforts and few turned out for meetings. Of the 200 planners in the Department of City Planning only 10 to 15 typically came. The explanations that were given stressed "our low professional self-esteem" and "lack of control over our work," the same sorts of generic planning attitudes reported by recurrent surveys of planners in bureaucracies.[18]

Another problem for the union was that its planning staff had different contractual statuses which made for differing interests. Provisional workers, for example, pressed the union to fight for the right to take the civil service exam while the civil servants wanted to protect the status quo. Although the union tried to tred carefully between the fears of both these groups, this issue made cohesion and mobilization more difficult than it would otherwise have been.[19]

The new team pressed more aggressively against "contracting out"—the Guild's central workers rights issue, and for greater community involvement—a long-standing activist concern—although not as strongly as most wished.[20] The major gains, however, were bread-and-butter issues such as member services. More radical items such as the introduction of political resolutions directed at the international political arena or support for specific political candidates were dismissed as inappropriate or "communistic."[21] Thus while the Guild became a better run and more responsive union, the price of success for activists was a reform mandate.

The net result was that most of the activists moved out of city agencies for situations like the environmental movement, which seemed to be at the "forefront of change," and where an activist planner could work with mobilized communities and consumer groups. Some blamed the planners, arguing that "If even 50 percent of the staff at the planning department were committed and progressive, they could reach out to other agencies or to universities on issues like the South Bronx and Logue, and not always have to go through the community or through housing co-ops."[22]

One activist who had worked as a community liaison also expressed having been "let down" by the communities which advocates had served since the 1960s. He argued, "City planners must be supported by communities but they are not there. Where are the ethnic groups? Where is the Upper West Side or Brooklyn Heights?"[23] In the absence of both constituency and community support, activism was not viable.

Although fiscal crisis and city attack mobilized some planners to press for a more political agenda, activist objectives were ultimately constrained by the general lack of support on the part of planners as well as engineers. One activist put it this way:

> The union's first line right now is to protect the worker, if we can do this. We can't do anything at all to influence policy without the community behind us. I can't see a real political progression over time unless we could create a new type of person and make him a planner.[24]

BUREAUCRATIC REFORM AND INSTITUTIONAL ORGANIZING

A comparison of bureaucratically induced forms of activism provides further insights into the possibilities and limits of institutionally based strategies for planners.[25] In a 1976 survey of planning in 27 cities, Susskind and Aylward documented a shift from comprehensive Master Planning to decentralized and participatory planning.[26] They offered several hypotheses as to the conditions under which these top-down innovations occurred. Neither closer linkage nor positions directly within city government ensured the implementation of plans. Rather, planning departments felt the need to create a "constituency" for planning and were "prepared to go to the public to get as many people as possible involved and committed so that the policy-maker will have no choice but to adopt the plans that are produced."[27]

The study emphasized the importance of the planner, not the plan. The link between "planning and regulation" was not zoning "as it was originally conceived":

> Market forces as well as the political clout of many private land interests tend to supersede the power of the zoning ordinance. Since planning is, whether we like to admit it or not, a political process, it makes more sense to focus on the role of the planner in personal terms (as a facilitator or catalyst of public action) than it does to count on legalistic documents. . . . The strategic linkage . . . must be viewed primarily in terms of the personal ties that the planning staff is able to establish with operating agencies and the credibility that planning departments are able to establish by staying one step ahead of the game.[28]

New roles required new skills. Called upon to be a mediator, educator, and facilitator—not expert—"much of the planner's stock-in-trade was virtually meaningless" or reduced to one of many roles in the planning repertory.[29]

Susskind and Aylward found that "neighborhood-up planning" tended to be characteristic of "central cities which had been abandoned in part, by real estate interests and which had come increasingly under the control of minority groups traditionally out of power."[30] This was also true for short-term, middle-range planning and the "more policy-oriented approaches." They reported that "the rationale for comprehensive planning is shifting, partly in response to the realization that mature central cities are no longer growing, and partly in response to the urging of the no-growth and slow-growth advocates." Thus, innovation in planning bureaucracies was correlated with declining urban areas, shifting populations, and interest groups.

One of the most forward looking planning documents, the revised city plan of the Cleveland City Planning Commission, illustrated these findings. In 1970, the Cleveland City Planning Commission began to revise the general city plan to coincide with a new reality—an older city and "a host of new problems that cannot be addressed by traditional tools."[31]

Revision led to a redefinition of the objectives and strategies of planning and the role of the planner. The plan put the aspirational norms of the AIP Code of Social Responsibility into action, specifying, "priority attention to . . . promoting a wider range of choices." The plan was also a social policy.

> a catalog of recommendations for solving or ameliorating some of the more pressing problems of Cleveland and its people . . . unemployment, neighborhood deterioration and abandonment, crime, inadequate mobility.

It emphasized implementation:

> If the Commission's goals and policies are to move from the printed word to the society to which they refer, the Commission cannot rest with the publication of a Policy Planning Report.

Instead, planners must "become activists prepared for protracted participation and vocal intervention in the decision making process." Agencies must also act. Given the importance of the cast of characters,

> the Mayor, City Council, HUD, the business community, the news media, or a host of others who figured powerfully in decision-making . . .

an agency that wished to influence decisions must often take the initiative. It must seize upon important issues and develop recommendations without prior invitation. And, in order to articulate issues, organize supporting data, and make meaningful recommendations, the agency must have goals and objectives.

In this scenario, the planning process became a combination of advocacy and policy planning, a "protracted lobbying for the positions the agency wishes to see implemented." The Cleveland Planning Report then described how these objectives had been applied over several years in specific areas such as transportation and housing.

An AIP Journal forum appeared along with the published report and moved the discussion from reform to a debate about the "meaning of reform."[32] Some viewed the Cleveland Planning Report as an example of a potentially "radical change in American planning thought and practice;"[33] "the model that will guide all planning that aims to deal effectively with the root causes of urban problems."[34] A more critical paper questioned not only the efficacy of the plan or the survival of the Cleveland planners, but the timing and motorforce behind the change. According to Piven, if there was a "new professional consciousness" it was because "many of the cities in which we ply our trade have changed."[35] Shifts of private capital out of the central cities make it possible and even necessary to give attention to class and race. Where others found cause for celebration, Piven suggested less optimistically that "we [planners] have arrived at this scene of struggle very late indeed."[36]

Other observers became equally explicit about the control functions of innovations and reforms. In a review of the decentralization literature, Kasperson and Breitbart noted that by 1971, one in three cities with populations of over 25,000 had adopted some method of decentralization.[37] These mechanisms ranged from complaint bureaus, to ombudsmen, to neighborhood councils and little City Halls. Like participation, decentralization indicated a wide range of phenomena and meant different things to different people.[38] Examining both the case reports and the underlying assumptions, Kasperson and Breitbart suggested that much that occurred in its name referred to "deconcentration"—a dispersal of facilities or functions without delegation of significant decision making or discretionary powers. They concluded that structural changes which increased visibility while dispersing little real power were a form of centralization or "penetration—bringing the periphery under the more direct control of the center by means of a set of professional "field officers."[39]

A further understanding of the political significance of these reforms is found in Needleman and Needleman's study of community planners within the planning agencies of nine mid-large cities.[40] They found that more than 75 percent of these decentralized community planners were acting as guerrillas or insurgents within their agencies. Given community pressure for action and the lack of real resources and power, all that the community planners could give was information. Labeling these activist roles "structurally induced," they pessimistically concluded that the activists served symbolic functions for the planning department as a whole. As financial conditions worsened, decentralized planning was "one of the most attractive options available" to beleaguered city governments, a form of "bureaucratic enfranchisement" for demanding community groups.[41] But for the planners, community planning was a destructive role, exposing them to contradictory demands and "burning them out."

The planners' lack of organizational strength and community support—the same factors which made institutionally based action ineffective—also made bureaucratic reform an attractive and cooptive strategy.

As with planners, many social, political, and experiential factors underlined the redirection of health activists' efforts to the heart of the system—to the hospitals which treated the poor and to hospital workers as well as patients. In medicine, institutionally based organizing was a chronological as well as a politically logical next step for a generation of SHO activists. After medical school, activists, along with the other new graduates, became housestaff in hospitals. Assigned on the basis of specialty and achievement, activists were isolated from each other and subjected to intensive work demands. They needed strategies that fit this stage of training.[42]

Institutionally based activism took two forms: work place collectives and housestaff unions. I look first at one of the most publicized collectives, the Lincoln Collective, and then at the Committee of Interns and Residents, the oldest and largest housestaff union.

THE LINCOLN COLLECTIVE: AN EXPERIMENT IN "CRITICAL MASS"

The Community Pediatrics Program at New York City's Lincoln Hospital was designed to be the first medical program with a "political element." Its goal was to change the system for the delivery of medical care in the South Bronx.[43]

Lincoln Hospital was a natural site for collective efforts for several reasons. The only hospital and source of medical care for the 400,000 Puerto Rican and black people in the area, Lincoln, with one of the busiest emergency rooms in the city, was over 100 years old, understaffed, and undersupplied. Lincoln's affiliation with the Albert Einstein College of Medicine in the 1950s had not stopped the downhill drift of both service and staffing. By 1969, the housestaff were almost all foreign medical graduates, and Lincoln was known as the worst of the "butchershops" in the city system.[44]

The stage was also set for action at Lincoln with community and worker groups mobilized over the provision and control of services. In April 1969, an OEO funded model mental health center, which was attached to Lincoln and which trained indigenous "new careers" people, had become the site of the first revolt of health workers in the name of community control.[45] In February 1970, the Community Advisory Board successfully challenged the City Department of Hospitals' choice of a new administrator for Lincoln. And in June 1970, shortly before the Lincoln Collective came into being, a combination of radical community groups presented several demands to the administration including an end to cutbacks, the establishment of a permanent grievance table, and community/worker control of all health services.[46] Thus, the Collective did not begin political activity at Lincoln, but came in its midst.[47]

Lincoln's pediatrics department also seemed to be receptive. The proposal for a Community Pediatrics Program, initiated by two former SHO leaders, was welcomed by the chief of the pediatric service who saw it as a chance to upgrade his department by introducing American trained housestaff.

The medical and political thinking behind the program was set forth in a preliminary statement of purpose and a housestaff recruitment brochure. At the heart of the strategy was the concept of "critical mass," a response to the plight of the isolated activist who must struggle to survive personally and politically in a large training institution:

> By concentrating a significant number of people with a socially conscious orientation in one hospital and one work situation, we hope to create a critical mass of people which will be able to change rather than merely adapt to what is admittedly a difficult working situation.[48]

To build community "among people working together," the hierarchical and authoritarian aspects of the medical system had to be

refashioned so that despite different technical skills, there was "functional equality of people in terms of decision-making about the
program." There were also medical objectives. The Collective reform-
ulated its pediatric services to give priority to general versus specialized pediatric medicine and to primary, preventative, and ambulatory
care. They introduced continuity of care, a team approach, and the
problem-list method of recordkeeping—a method which "demysti-
fies the medical care process." They broadened the physician's role
to include "time outside the walls"—elective time to work with
community, block, or regional groups "disseminating practical knowledge" and "transferring technical skills."
       Underlying the proposal was

> a health empire analysis which locates blame for the medical care that
> minorities and the poor receive in the public hospitals, with the private
> sector, and the ineffective and supportive city bureaucracy. Priorities
> have become teaching and research agendas—not patient care.

According to Fitzhugh Mullan, one of the founding members, the
image of change for Lincoln was the romantic notion of a community
in revolt, and a hospital ready for reform.[49] In this scenario, "a
medical cadre" was key to the hospital part of the equation.[50]
Activists assumed that housestaff would be able to surmount their
own class backgrounds and professional socialization to relate to
other hospital personnel and activist community groups. The adoption of collective working/living styles reflected a New Left politics
in which individual cultural change was viewed as a necessary
concomitant to system level change.[51] Activist doctors, hospital
workers, and communities would fight for community/worker control of Lincoln as a means to reorder the hospital's priorities and
change delivery of health care in the South Bronx.
       The Community Pediatrics Program began in July 1970 with the
recruitment of 32 socially committed housestaff, nurses, and ancillary
staff.[52] Within a year, Lincoln was known as the "vanguard of social
action in health."[53] The pediatrics staff had constituted themselves a
collective, aligned themselves with radical community groups, and
waged and won a battle for virtual control over their department.
The original chief of service was out by the end of the year and
replaced by a more sympathetic Puerto Rican physician. A wide
variety of programmatic innovations were also in place, but participants experienced disillusionment and a sense of political failure.[54]
There was a huge attrition rate—more than one-half of the housestaff left after the first year. By 1973, recruitment again yielded

predominantly foreign medical graduates and the locus of the Collective shifted to the Department of Medicine where it took on a more narrowly medical oriented focus. And by 1974,

> Pediatrics looked much as it had five years before, foreign medical graduates filling almost all positions. Some of the patient-care innovations begun by the Collective remained intact and the department continued to enjoy good leadership. . . .But collectivism, community control and worker democracy had ceased to be issues.[55]

By 1975, the Collective was declared "functionally irrelevant" to ongoing work.[56]

To understand this trajectory, we must look at the Collective's relations with community groups, medical staff, and other workers, both in the Collective and the larger hospital setting.

Community/Worker Control and Professional Accountability

Launched at a time when radical community groups were confronting the Lincoln administration in the name of community/worker control, the Collective supported these groups and their demands. In so doing, it stepped into the midst of an escalating political controversy that within two months polarized the medical staff and branded the Collective "a source of trouble" and "Communist."[57]

Up until the abortion death of patient Carmen Rodriguez (July 17, 1970), community/worker demands had focused upon input into and control over administrative decisions. Administrative offices were taken over, but there had been no disruption of patient care, and many housestaff were at least sympathetic to some of the community/worker demands.[58] But with the death of Carmen Rodriguez, demands escalated. The Think Lincoln Committee felt that the death—ascribed to professional malpractice—illustrated the inadequacy of the abortion program and moved to challenge professional power as well as administrative control. They demanded the resignation of the Chief of Obstetrics and Gynecology, a community/worker watchdog committee to monitor the abortion program, and damages for the Rodriguez family. The Collective was heavily involved in this event. Members of the Collective helped document and expose the medical details of the Rodriguez death in an unique public meeting—the "First People's Clinical Pathology Conference."[59] This conference violated prevailing medical norms on two counts: by discussing professional matters before lay bodies and by publicly exposing the mistakes of colleagues. In response, housestaff in the Departments of Obstetrics and Surgery threatened to leave and 10 foreign medical graduates in the Department of Pediatrics actually did leave without giving notice.[60]

The resignation of one-fourth of the Pediatrics house staff crippled the department and made it impossible to carry out some of its innovative programs. The affair as a whole pointed out the dependence of institutional strategies on their key actors, who must be placated if not actually won over, and suggested that challenges to professional control over medical matters set limits to any community/worker alliance. Although the hospital administration ultimately got an injunction prohibiting future political activity, the housestaff response was far more prejudicial to the outcome.

Beyond demands for community/worker control, other issues spilt and re-split the staff. The Collective was itself a source of conflict and disillusionment to those involved. First, there was the question of its identity. At the start, the Collective saw itself as a community of staff: male, female, professional, paraprofessional, white and minority.

> A unique aspect of the program is the collective atmosphere. There is a conscious effort to break down the artificial elitist barriers that exist among nurses, residents, interns, aides and other health workers.[61]

But from the start it failed in its attempts to recruit nurses or other workers or to reflect their interests. Female physicians, for example, soon dropped out. Reflecting upon the first six months of weekly meetings, one member said,

> The Collective and, particularly, its meetings were stigmatized much more than we ever realized. We were, I think, earnest and reasonable representatives of what we were—white, American, male, predominantly physicians from comfortable backgrounds. . . .Our meetings reflected our background and our bias. They were rambling, contentious, and ambitious of agenda but weak on resolution. The result was that community representatives, hospital workers, and even nurses who came to the meetings tended to be bored and to feel excluded.[62]

Under attack, the Collective withdrew, inviting only those groups with "common interests" to send representatives to the meetings.[63]

In its dealings with other groups within the Department, the Collective was accused of similarly elitist behavior. The nurses and the drug program were one example. Lincoln had no drug programs although drugs were a large problem in the community. The Collective supported a community detoxification program which moved onto a floor in the nurses' residence. The nurses, who had not been consulted, were frightened by wandering drug addicts and angry at the Collective's failure to take their interests into account.[64] The Collective's treatment of foreign medical graduates who comprised one-fourth of the Pediatrics housestaff and who were the majority of housestaff in other departments at Lincoln became another issue. No attempt had been made to explain the objectives of the Collective to these doctors or to invite their participation; they were even baited. One *Think Lincoln* brochure referred to them as the "foreign mercenary doctors."[65]

Another source of friction was the Collective's adoption of the cultural politics of the New Left. By departing from traditional image and wearing sandals, beads, and long hair, members of the Collective antagonized staff—particularly minority nurses—as well as patients and paraprofessionals.[66] To inspire confidence, the Pediatrics Department had to resort to posters which showed children (and their parents) that doctors came with all lengths of hair.

Along with the "hip" style went a casual attitude to the training experience and to medicine itself. According to one of the Collective members,

> For the most part, the interns and residents hoped to get their work done as efficiently and as well as possible so that they could move on to the many problems generated by the political situation at Lincoln. . . . The Collective was simply not a very academic group of physicians in training.[67]

Rebellion extended to academic medicine and to hierarchical authority. Interns and residents refused to attend chief of service Dr. Einhorn's teaching sessions. This made for additional strain between the Collective, Dr. Einhorn, and the foreign medical graduates who were at Lincoln for the best conventional American medical training they could receive. The teaching program disintegrated over the fall with the chief essentially withdrawing from the confrontations of the service. Finally, the Collective produced a leaflet demanding that the chief resign, and that staff participate in the selection of a new director, sympathetic with the social and political objectives of the program.[68]

The Collective won its battle for departmental control, but in the words of one of the Collective's members, "as usual at Lincoln, there was no real winner."[69] The abrupt resignation of one-fourth of the departmental housestaff meant that despite the appointment of a chief of service who supported genuine community electives and outreach, there was, ironically, no time for such programs. Housestaff also felt the negative effect of having spent so much time and energy in political controversy. "Tested politically" before medically, many were, in fact, burnt out for further work.[70]

Community/Worker Relations: Taking Leadership from the People

Relations with community groups were also problematic for the Collective. Who was the community? At the start, the Collective found not one community but an ethnically and racially diverse population in which "countless factions competed for power and purported to represent the people" but had their own interests at heart.[71]

The Collective aligned itself with radical political groups, already involved with Lincoln, for whom health was a means to political change—Think Lincoln, Young Lords, and the Health Revolutionary Unity Movement (HRUM). For these groups, white politics precluded leadership roles.

> Their [the doctors] role is to serve the people with their technical skills in a human way. We know what class they're coming from. They must understand that they are the weakest link.[72]

HRUM, a radical alliance of third world and black hospital workers in the city hospital system, supplied political guidance to the Collective during its first year.[73] In 1971, rather than deal directly with the white professionals, HRUM set up Health Revolutionary Alliance (HRA), a white intermediary which, in the words of a member of the collective, "took leadership" from HRUM and, in turn, "gave leadership" to us.[74]

According to members and observers, this relationship was based on a politics of guilt. The Collective tithed itself and gave monthly sums of money to third world groups without gaining in return any say in organization, activity, or any security, for that matter, as to what the money would really be spent on. The Collective also responded to demands for services from these groups, such as helping staff Black Panther clinics or giving physical exams to addicts in the detoxification program.[75] Some felt the service and support position reflected the failure to develop a politics of their own.

> We are a set up for anyone with radical rhetoric or affiliation with community groups. . . .We had difficulty distinguishing between appro-

priate requests and unreasonable demands . . . we had no tools to separate the correctness of their position from the inappropriateness of their presentation. . . .[76]

When HRUM revised its political line in 1971 and 1972 and chose to disband and work for reform through the unions, the Collective was left without a political perspective or leadership of its own.

The nature of social change in the South Bronx. The departmental take-over and the replacement of the chief of service marked the end of a first phase of political confrontation.[77] But other obstacles emerged as activists tried to implement a community medicine. With the Pediatrics Department under Collective control and a sympathetic chief of service in place, it became abundantly clear to members of the Collective that departmental control was not the solution to changing delivery of services in the South Bronx. Several examples illustrate the difficulties.

A long-standing desire to organize a parents group for Pediatrics was activated by the threat of budget cuts for 1973. Prior to the cuts, attempts had been made to establish a continuous relation, but according to one doctor, "for them medicine is a sometimes affair and a mystique."[78] The issue of the budget cuts enabled the staff to break through the usual patient apathy. The newly formed Pediatrics Parents Association collected 2,000 signatures from the community to stop cuts that would affect staffing and services and, together with community representatives and the Collective, presented these signatures at the New York City Health and Hospitals Corporation. The petition, however, received little more than press coverage. The Health and Hospitals Corporation ignored the community demands, and the Pediatrics Parents Association lapsed into apathy.

In another response to the threat of budget cuts, the Collective started a job action to hold back reimbursement sheets for Medicare and Medicaid. This was thought to be an excellent strategy in that it threatened the medical center without interfering with patient care. More than $1 million was withheld, but as with the petition to the Health and Hospitals Corporation, the administration found it could hold out and that with time, insurgent activity would die down.

The Community Medical Corps was one of the Collective's most "truly revolutionary efforts." According to Dr. Charlotte Fein, the Corps represented the carrying out of the original plan of the Collective.

This was a true attempt at demystification . . . a true barefoot doctors program with eight workers indigenous to the neighborhood.[79]

The program was an independent work unit operating out of a storefront. Dr. Rodriguez-Trias assigned Dr. Charolette Fein, one of the initiators of the Community Pediatrics Program, to work with community people to develop a medical training program and a program for door-to-door comprehensive screening and primary care. But although the program was revolutionary, it was also contradictory. Community workers found that training without credentials did not lead anywhere, and although the staff tried to credential the program through a community college, this proved to be unsuccessful. The unit's paraprofessionals were affiliated with HRUM and their demands changed along with HRUM's political thinking. Initially they wanted control of their own unit but later wanted to become part of the regular hospital staff, to the dismay of the innovators. Finally, the program faced financial difficulties. Funded first by the city in response to publicity about lead poisoning, it was defunded in 1973 when lead was no longer an isssue and Lincoln was quiet.

Efforts to democratize work relations along the lines of the original proposal also ran into difficulties. Initially, most felt that the difference between the work of interns and residents was artificial. This led to the decision to ignore differences in experience and to give housestaff a random choice of jobs and an equal number of nights. But in the face of the intense pressure of hospital work these efforts proved unrealistic and "collapsed quickly of their own weight."[80] Attempts to democratize work up and down the range of staff and to share departmental decision making among all ranks of workers were also unsuccessful. According to the director of the program at the time, the nonmedical staff were actually hostile to attempts to offer them a bigger role in departmental meetings. They did not want more control but job mobility and career opportunity.[81]

Medical innovations such as continuity of care in clinics, the problem-list method of recordkeeping, and night float, were institutionalized under the new director, but to the activists at the time, represented a relatively benign degree of change. There was growing frustration at the inability of the Collective to produce "quantifiable change in the hospital or community."[82] It became a commonplace among activists that the hospital simply absorbed the demands of its workers and activist groups.[83]

Looking back, several felt that the sense of political failure reflected the "grandiose" and unrealistic expectations of the original Collective—that they could effect change in medical care in the South Bronx in the course of intense working days. Part of the frustration lay in the fact that being a "political physician" at Lincoln was exhausting, leading to burn-out.

> After a year at Lincoln many interns found themselves wanting to work
> in a setting where they could 'get it together personally'; that is, spend
> time with family and friends. . . .Many Collective members began to
> question the degree of commitment that Lincoln required. . . .When
> medical work was completed there were meetings to be attended,
> flyers to be distributed, readings to be done, and street clinics to be
> staffed. Even standard house officerships seemed undemanding in
> comparison to being a political physician at Lincoln.[84]

With the budget cuts, it became increasingly clear to activists
that Lincoln's problems lay outside Lincoln. The Collective might
control the Pediatrics Department, but control of the hospital's
budget or staffing lay outside the South Bronx with the city administration and the affiliated medical center.

The Collective's Last Phase: Medical Reform and Worker Control

During the Collective's last phase (1973-1975), it narrowed its objectives and constituency—to improve in-patient medical care and to
work with middle-class, white male physicians. This strategy enabled
them to avoid the demoralizing "tailest" position of serving black
and third world groups.[85] Socialism was part of the emerging identity
of the Collective although the term was loosely applied and remained undefined. Members felt that a political framework would
structure group efforts and help to avoid prior patterns of guilt at
being part of the system they were trying to reform.

The Collective's publication, *Temperature Rising*, articulates its
politics at this time. The goal of "improving patient care at Lincoln"
was set within the larger task of "changing the entire health system
so that it serves the needs of people rather than the needs of
corporations or doctors."[86] Other objectives were: specific projects to
call attention to problem areas of health care at Lincoln; such as
patients rights, education, and outreach; to politically educate its
members by linking the plight of Lincoln to the larger city hospital
system. In contrast to its earlier isolation, the Collective wanted to
"communicate with people who have left Lincoln to work elsewhere" and to function as a support structure for the doctors.[87]
According to a new member,

> The days grow longer at Lincoln and the work which when taken
> piecemeal is rewarding, has a cumulative stultifying effect. There is a
> certain phrase, 'wouldn't it be better if . . .' that begins to die on one's

lips. The Collective represents a way of sharing the grievances, not to make them bearable, but to keep that phrase alive. It helps me see another worker's position; there are two sides to each unreturned lab slip, lost x-ray or failed appointment. It places the problems of Lincoln in the larger context of a malevolent social structure.[88]

Between 1974 and 1975, budget cuts and layoffs increasingly became the focus for the Collective's actions. The attacks and responses raised the political consciousness of hospital personnel. In a 1975 article in *Temperature Rising* entitled "What's Wrong with Lincoln," the authors pointed out that although there was an attempt to blame hospital personnel—goof-off workers or radicals—for Lincoln's many problems, the "problems lie with the Health and Hospitals Corporation, with administration, government and the big business interests behind them."[89]

In the face of budget cuts and the deepening New York City fiscal crisis, the old strategy of attacking Lincoln to improve it, became risky. When activists testified before the Joint Commission on the Accreditation of Hospitals (JCAH) and Lincoln was disaccredited, there was much questioning of a strategy which could result in cutting off Medicaid and Medicare funds as well as the supply of interns and residents.[90] The growing attack upon the city hospitals put activists on the defensive, forcing them to preserve what they were trying to improve, and making strategy difficult.

Although there was increased worker unity in the face of budget cuts and general fiscal crisis, community support for the Collective never emerged. In the words of one doctor, "the people here are too poor to put together any real support for Lincoln."[91] Furthermore, conflicts of interest between lower and higher echelon workers, para-professionals and professional workers, and workers and patients, did not disappear. Even writing a patient rights handbook in 1973 raised a number of issues for the Collective. Did they as professionals have the right to put out such a publication when hospital workers might become the scapegoats? How could they make certain that anger would be redirected to the correct source? Who should print and distribute the handbook—administration or staff? Without actual grievance procedures, would the handbook have more than symbolic value.[92]

Finally, although there was basic agreement on the need for a political analysis and on a socialist perspective, the emergence of a variety of warring socialist sects during this period led to debates within the Collective on theory and strategy. One group, for example, wanted to fight cuts by slowdown and sit-ins, but this strategy antagonized patients and burdened already overworked workers. No one viewpoint was able to dominate.[93] It was in this context that housestaff unions emerged as vehicles for political struggle. It was through the unions that Lincoln housestaff held public hearings on accreditation and took action on cutbacks in on-call rooms.[94]

By 1972, the health Left had begun to criticize the "critical mass" strategy based on the experience at Lincoln and San Francisco General Hospital.[95] It was deemed "irrational" to attempt to build a struggle with housestaff given the time commitments of internship and residency. Too many activists who had been through Lincoln and San Francisco General Hospital had burned out and became "lost to the movement."[96]

Reflecting back on the collective experience, one Lincoln "graduate" commented.

> The outcome could have been predicted if a broad structural analysis existed. It was obvious that we had no base for community struggles . . . we needed a socialist analysis of the system in which the limits of change is the public hospital set in capitalism—not community control.[97]

By 1975, community was out of the activist equation and for those interested in institutional organizing, the organizational context became the housestaff union.

With the advent of New York's fiscal crisis and the accelerated attack on the public hospital system, health activists needed a citywide unit. Many turned to the housestaff unions, which they had formerly dismissed as inherently conservative, and struggled to give them political content.

Housestaff organizing surfaced among public hospital staff in New York in the late 1950s over wage issues. By the early 1960s, there were housestaff associations across the country in a variety of institutions, holding "heal-ins" and other job related actions to force pay raises.[98] Beginning in the late 1960s and the early 1970s, housestaff demands broadened to include due process for housestaff, improved work conditions, and improved patient care. These demands culminated in several major strikes by housestaff associations during 1975 on predominantly nonwage issues.[99]

Spurred on by the competitive interest in housestaff shown by the AMA, the Physicians National Housestaff Association (PNHA) was established in 1972 to give national coherence to the housestaff movement. In 1975, PNHA voted to reorganize itself as a national labor organization.[100]

Along with doctors' traditional antipathy to trade unions as a working-class format and to the societal view that collective action by doctors was unethical and illegal,[101] housestaff have faced specific organizational and legal obstacles to unionization. Unlike other doctors, housestaff are not yet fully credentialed; they also undergo rapid turnover with about one-third of housestaff in a given hospital being replaced each year. This means that despite the fact that housestaff are M.D.'s, their internship and residency programs are subject to hospital certification, and they are vulnerable in strike actions to both threats and disciplinary measures from hospital administration. These complications have led to a dispute over the legal status of housestaff—are they students or employees?

The legal status of housestaff is further complicated by distinctions between public and private hospitals and differences between state and national labor legislation. For example, prior to 1974, housestaff were not included in national labor legislation: they could legally organize collective bargaining units in the public and private sector where not prohibited (or where expressly permitted) by state law.[102] A 1974 amendment to the National Labor Relations Act (NLRA) extended collective bargaining to voluntary nonprofit hospitals across the nation, but this procedure required housestaff associations to file costly and time-consuming petitions with the National Labor Relations Board (NLRB). A 1976 NLRB decision effectively overturned this amendment, through a ruling that housestaff were "primarily students" not employees, and in 1981, the U. S. Supreme Court refused to review this NLRB decision. This has meant that while housestaff can organize for collective bargaining in nonprofit hospitals, they cannot invoke the NLRB to protect their organizing activities;[103] as a result, existing unions have been loathe to organize housestaff for legal as well as professional reasons.

Over time, there have been two trends among housestaff associations. The first, a growing acceptance of collective bargaining and of unions as appropriate organizational frameworks for doctors. The second trend has been a shift from narrower economic issues to broader political concerns symbolized by demands for better patient care. Although these trends are related, I focus on the latter and define *patient care demands* as collective bargaining demands related to patient care. These range from out-of-title work and hours, to requests for increased nursing and clerical staff, translators, equipment such as EKG machines and crash carts, and laboratory services and consulting rooms.[104]

Patient care demands go beyond the traditional collective bargaining/trade-union emphasis on wages and benefits. I look at patient care from the perspective of the health activist agenda— significant change benefiting minorities and the poor. How compatible was patient care with collective bargaining strategies? Under what conditions did housestaff unions become vehicles for such demands as opposed to, or in addition to, self-interest? What are the problems and limitations of a trade-union approach to health activist goals?

For the experience of activists in housestaff unions, I have selected New York City's Committee of Interns and Residents (CIR). One of the oldest and largest housestaff associations, CIR moved to a more activist position in the mid-1970s. I also compare CIR to two other politically active housestaff associations: Los Angeles County Joint Council of Interns and Residents and Cook County Housestaff Association in Chicago. For the housestaff movement as a whole, the Physicians National Housestaff Association illustrates the range of political views among the diverse regional associations and their relation to the national organization, to organized medicine, and to organized labor.

NEW YORK CITY'S COMMITTEE OF INTERNS AND RESIDENTS: FROM WAGES AND BENEFITS TO PATIENT CARE

Housestaff in New York City's public hospitals were mobilized by the threat of large social security deductions from their already marginal wages. They formed the CIR in 1958 and hired a labor lawyer to protect their economic interests. A successful track record negotiating wages and benefits continued to attract members and by 1960, CIR was contracting with groups of hospitals—municipals through the Health and Hospitals Corporation, voluntary hospitals in the League of Voluntary Hospitals, and independent institutions by means of separate individual agreements.[105]

The matriculation of a generation of SHO activists into internship and residency positions in the late 1960s marked the beginning of an attempt to redirect CIR from its wages and benefits focus. "Less tolerant of deteriorating conditions, shoddy treatment of patients and foreign medical graduates," they were more assertive and themselves identified with minorities and the poor.[106] Fitzhugh Mullan wrote that he took his election to CIR presidency in 1970 as a mandate to make the union "a vehicle for change in the city hospitals . . . . a force in the debates surrounding patient care and hospital conditions."[107] Under his leadership, there was an attempt to write patient care demands into the contract and keep a "registry of abuse" to list mishaps caused by inadequate staff and equipment. But activist efforts were blunted and delayed by CIR's well-defined collective bargaining tradition. CIR's counsel, a labor lawyer, spoke out against introducing "management issues" into the contract and when negotiations started, the majority voted with him to drop the patient care demands and to settle for a wage increment. The housestaff were similarly loath to collect and report medical abuses. The judgment of activists at the time was that CIR was intrinsically "elitist" and would neither link up with other workers nor hold out for patient care gains.[108]

Looking back on the rise of activism that culminated in CIR's 1975 strike, Mullan later wrote: "The philosophy governing the effort comes not from the SDS or the SHO but from a blend of sound labor practice, liberal politics, and an agonizing first-hand familiarity with the crisis state of our medical care system."[109] Between 1970, when patient care demands were dropped by members in the course of negotiations for a wage settlement, and 1975, when despite agreement over wages and benefits, CIR voted to go on strike over working conditions and patient care demands, these issues had obviously gained credibility and support. In the face of increasing fiscal pressure on hospitals, the dominant CIR strategy was to argue for the inclusion of patient care items in contract negotiations. This meant broadening the content of contract negotiations to include such issues as hours-of-duty, out-of-title work, minimum standards for training and translators.

These new demands departed from the traditional arena of collective bargaining and were a source of tension between CIR and the hospitals as well as within CIR, for its labor-oriented lawyer and for housestaff for whom traditional professional norms dictated unlimited work assignments. To fight for the same sort of control over conditions and hours that blue-collar workers had won involved a reversal of deep-seated professional norms. Compared to a direct patient care benefit such as translators, it required convincing the doctors of the justice of the issue as well as the antagonist hospitals. Similarly, it was difficult to convince housestaff to codify abuses that affected patient care as this contradicted norms of nondisclosure to outsiders.[110]

Housestaff as doctors for the poor.   Although mounting fiscal pressures marked this period and served, as Mullan suggests, as a catalyst for CIR's politicization, leadership was also important. Editorial comment and analysis in CIR publications moved beyond criticizing hospital exploitation of interns and residents to link the interests of housestaff with their poor and minority patients and with issues of availability and quality of care in the public hospital system. Dr. Richard Cooper's statement which prefaced this chapter and appeared in one of a series of reports on problems "of particular importance to patients of city hospitals," reflects the growing identification of housestaff—who occupy a "unique position in the United States health system"—with their poor patients.[111]

The arguments put forward in CIR publications provided a particularly persuasive combination of medical ideals and professional self-interest: Budget cuts lead to job freezes and thus to job loss by attrition. Shortages of staff and technical services mean more work and less training for housestaff who are "the one uniformed service that always takes up the slack."[112] Shortages also mean deteriorating care which in some cases leads to disaccreditation, a direct threat to housestaff training. Deteriorating hospital care constitutes a form of "double jeopardy"; not only do housestaff suffer in terms of training and work conditions, but they are blamed by administrators for causing the decline.[113] Finally, budget cuts constitute direct threats to housestaff positions when there is talk of unit and hospital closings as in 1974 and 1975.[114]

In linking the interests of housestaff with their patients and with public sector care, CIR editorials raised political consciousness. Detailed chronicling of the systemwide consequences of cutbacks put the experience of individual doctors in particular hospitals into a larger context. These accounts turned attention to the comparative gains and losses of public and private sectors and to the roles of different political actors. One doctor put it this way: "I don't have much time to read. I see it happening in the hospital but they put it together."[115]

CIR was transformed, during this period, from an "organization which negotiates wage contracts for housestaff" to one which "identifies and speaks out on health care matters."[116] CIR became a political voice for housestaff on a wide spectrum of issues and at several levels: with city, state, and county medical societies, and nationally with the PNHA and the AMA. While an important factor in CIR's strength was its use of lawyers, CIR began to increase doctor input into the organization, "to put housestaff out front and make the lawyer, a second man on the team."[117]

Organizational changes also made CIR more politically effective; CIR increased its full-time staff and reorganized its constitution. The wider political context also encouraged CIR's politicization. During this period there was an increase in labor legislation and in collective bargaining in the public sector;[118] also a series of attacks on housestaff by organized medicine. Thus, at the same time that unionization became more possible, it became more attractive to housestaff as a necessary defense.[119]

The outcomes of a historic strike.   The immediate precipitant of CIR's 1975 strike was the League of Voluntary Hospitals' refusal to submit the issues of excessive hours and out-of-title work to arbitration. In response, CIR struck against all 11 members of the League as well as the municipal hospitals which had staff under affiliation agreements with the voluntary hospitals. The strike, which lasted four days (March 17-20), was considered a success on a number of grounds: it received considerable housestaff support—more than 2,100 members in 21 institutions participated;[120] favorable press and media coverage—*The New York Times* issued editorial support for CIR's position as early as one month before the strike; and the strike was endorsed by the AMA.[121] Finally, the strike ended in an agreement to limit hours—the first over-all limit on hours ever reached by hospitals in collective bargaining.[122] The new League contract established Joint Housestaff/Attendings Standards and Grievance Committees to set hours and deal with out-of-title work within each hospital.

The verdict is less clear if both the strike and its long term outcomes are studied. Many participants felt that the collective bargaining structure imposed a "narrow framework" and that CIR had to throw out many of its demands to have a legal strike.[123] In line with its trade-union orientation, CIR promoted a more conservative version of patient care, focusing upon protecting its members from overly long hours and "scut-work" as opposed to the more direct third-party benefits such as consulting rooms and equipment pioneered in Los Angeles and Chicago.[124] On the other hand, critics also acknowledged that working within the structure of labor law ensured membership as well as public support. When CIR went on strike in the winter of 1978-79, on similar grounds but without labor law protection, the press editorialized against the union.[125]

Housestaff behavior during the strike made for contradictions between CIR's policy of support for the public system and its members' personal interests. Support for CIR was strongest in the public hospitals and weakest in elite teaching institutions, where, as one observer put it, housestaff are "proud" to run up and down ten flights of stairs."[126] Although the union struck in the private hospitals under the NLRA and although CIR policy was to "try not to strike the city," housestaff were, in fact, more ready and more likely to strike in affiliated public hospitals than in private hospitals where they felt more intimidated and feared professional consequences.[127] Their concern was supported by reports of poststrike harassment in all cities which had major strikes in 1975.[128]

More serious than individual harassment, however, was a pattern of erosion of contract gains over time. Although mechanisims were established to give housestaff a voice in decisions regarding hours and out-of-title work, these provisions required housestaff follow through to be effective. In some hospitals the committees never started; in others they started and petered out.[129]

Finally, the strike by the CIR, followed in short order by similar actions in Los Angeles and Cook County, Illinois, produced a backlash. The NLRB decision, one year later, which stated that housestaff were students not employees, threw CIR into disarray. Hospitals refused to honor contracts; the League refused to bargain with CIR; and housestaff were forced, once again, to sign individual contracts. Although CIR lost member hospitals and became involved in a maze of costly and time-consuming legal proceedings subsequent to the NLRB decision, by 1977 the organization felt it had "survived" the attack and by 1978, membership rolls were up again.[130]

After the 1975 strike, a dynamic issue for CIR has been threats to the municipal hospital system posed by New York City's policy of economic retrenchment. As the nature of the threat escalated from care within one hospital to saving the public sector per se,[131] CIR changed its strategies, moving away from contracts toward extralegal and illegal job actions, political mobilization and coalition building, and health planning advocacy.

CIR's initial strategies to save staff, equipment, and services in the public hospitals leaned heavily on legal means of redress, but legal strategies were deemed slow and ineffective. One CIR editorial noted that "even if fast, they wouldn't have an impact on the city's plan to end financial commitment to municipal health care."[132] The general feeling was that laws only served to keep CIR from striking legally at the city system. Abandoning the legal route, CIR held a one-day strike in the city hospitals in January 1979 and a longer strike during March 1981.[133] In another departure, CIR's review committee on malpractice policy decided to "encourage victims of malpractice and their families to seek court action." The committee stated that because the "majority of malpractice cases were generated by tragic shortages of medical equipment, physicians, nurses and other medical support in municipal hospitals . . . we'll give them the information they need to build a case on, even if it means implicating ourselves."[134]

With increasing economic pressure on city hospitals, the need to mobilize broad based political support to prevent cuts and closings also became apparent. As early as 1975, CIR called for a coalition strategy, arguing:

CIR will not be strong enough to mount the kind of counter offensive necessary to bring about changes in New York City's health system of the kind demanded by the crises.[135]

However, it was not until the proposal to close one-half of the municipal system in the winter of 1978-79 that a coalition strategy really got moving. CIR was then instrumental in organizing a city-wide coalition that included labor unions and community groups and that won the support of the NAACP.[136] The call for a rational health policy for New York City and for CIR's involvement in "other aspects of health care—especially planning and financing," invoked the legislative framework of the 1974 National Health Planning and Resources Development Act, which set among its priorities, primary preventative care for "medically underserved populations."[137] By calling for planning, CIR hoped to move beyond such impasses as its fall 1978 negotiations, when the city refused to negotiate patient care claiming it lacked funds. Strategically, a call for health planning was a shift from defense to offense—from defending the public sector to planning a more equitable health care system. It was also a call for worker management, an attack on decision making by "remote bureaucracies as opposed to the medical team on the scene."[138]

Health planning reflected a changing analysis. Although the health empires model of a private sector consuming the public sector still carried explanatory weight, it was being modified by events and activists wanted "research to dispel myths."[139] For example, the continuing analysis of the hospital system revealed that certain voluntaries were in trouble along with public hospitals. This suggested that the problem lay with reimbursement mechanisms or in the underlying medical model and led CIR to call for national level solutions such as a National Health Service.[140]

LOS ANGELES COUNTY INTERNS AND RESIDENTS: THE PATIENT CARE FUND

In Los Angeles, the movement for patient care reflected and continued the earlier reformist impulse of the SHOs which began in this area. After initial wage gains in 1965 brought housestaff salaries up to a "living wage," housestaff activity at the three county hospitals turned to issues of patient care, overcrowding, work loads, and staff shortages.[141] Fueled by a strong history of medical student activism and supported by legislation which gave county employees the right to bargain collectively, the Los Angeles housestaff used two strategies to improve patient care: the specification of patient care items in the contract and a patient care fund controlled by housestaff.

Following the CIR strike in May 1975, 1,200 members of the Los Angeles Joint Council struck. At one of the affiliated hospitals, housestaff held out for and won a $1.1 million patient care fund from the county. Although this sum represented the turnback of one-half of the scheduled housestaff salary increase and, thus, minimal county money, the fund set a precedent. It represented the first instance of housestaff control over budgetary matters.[142] Administered by a committee controlled by housestaff, the fund was used to pay for needed equipment and staff.

In addition to obtaining the patient care fund, housestaff arbitrated specific contract provisions. In 1976, housestaff at Harbour General Hospital won additional crash carts under binding arbitration. This was the first time that a patient care item covered under working conditions was tested under binding arbitration and a third-party right in the contract upheld.[143] Los Angeles housestaff also introduced "adequate ancillary help" into the contract under working conditions and arbitrated this item successfully because a state statute required equivalent nurse ratios at public and private hospitals.[144]

Maintaining and increasing the patient care fund, however, proved "there is no such thing as an easy victory."[145] The medical school deans were able to keep the fund out of the next contract at the urging of the American Association of Medical Colleges (AAMC) who saw it as a dangerous precedent. The hospital demanded that the county drop the fund in 1976. They felt it undercut the authority of service chiefs as well as academic authority. To save the fund, housestaff organized a three-day walkout. The fund remained, although it was reduced to $750,000 and more consequently, its management enlarged to include county representatives.

In 1977, the patient care fund was again attacked by the deans. The housestaff association responded by lobbying legislative, patient, and community groups. They also commissioned a study of the hospital's fiscal problems to show how "irrational" cuts ended up costing the hospital millions of dollars in lost billings.[146] The housestaff managed to keep the fund and restore it to its original $1 million level. Ironically, a key factor in this victory was "the tacit support" from hospital administration and medical facilties. In the face of cutbacks resulting from the shrinking reimbursements from state and federal governments, the same administration and staff who had put forward the AAMC argument the year before now wanted to form their own collective bargaining unit.[147] A hiring freeze, for example, created serious staff shortages which led to the provisional accreditation of one department of medicine and to the closing of an intensive care unit. This made for a convergence of interest among administrators, the medical faculty and the housestaff; all wanted to get more money for the hospitals.

The move to turn one-half of a negotiated wage increase into a patient care fund showed that innovative and progressive action on behalf of patients could originate with housestaff associations. It also suggests that such actions might be somewhat restricted by a collective bargaining mentality. Unlike New York's CIR, the Los Angeles Joint Council had a strong history of medical student organization and activity around patient care and medical education. The legal and political climates also differed. Fiscal retrenchment was less severe and public hospitals represented a smaller part of all medical care and of the public sector. The Los Angeles experience also underlines the power of patient care, as distinct from self-benefit, to mobilize housestaff. This suggests, somewhat ironically, that patient care may be more compatible with traditional medical idealism than with either union ideology or structure.

However, the patient care fund was of considerably more symbolic than material consequence. It was difficult to maintain or increase, and eventually housestaff lost control.[148] In Los Angeles, as elsewhere, specific contract gains were conditional upon implementation and were undercut by noncompliance and by economic retrenchment. For example, the $5.5 million patient care fund, won from the County Board of Supervisors, was subsequently cut directly from hospital departments as an overall 3.5 percent budget cut, leading the head of the Joint Council to say: "They're taking the money from the hospitals to give to us, and we end up right where we started."[149]

COOK COUNTY HOSPITAL:
THE POLITICAL ACTIVISTS

At a workshop on patient care tactics at the 1978 PNHA Conference, a Cook County housestaff representative rejected the patient care fund on both political and theoretical grounds. "We don't want a patient care fund. It's the old charity image . . . we want to make them [the hospital administration] do their job in keeping the hospital staffed and equipped."[150]

Chicago's Cook County Housestaff Association was the most politically developed housestaff organization for a number of reasons. From the start, a majority of its members recognized the need to separate patient care from self-interest so as to establish credibility with community groups and patients.[151] The early politicization of this association resulted from the convergence of several factors particular to Cook County Hospital and to Chicago. First, there was the presence of medical activists who had been politically active in Left politics in the 1960s.[152] Second, as the only public hospital in Chicago, Cook County was a giant institution used by several medical schools. This meant that it functioned as a meeting place for medical students from all over Chicago and was also a center for community groups and their demands. Thus, social consciousness regarding class and race was heightened among both professional and nonprofessional workers, as well as among patients.[153] Finally, housestaff politicization was a response to Chicago's own political centralization, reflected in the direct political control of Cook County Hospital by the Daley machine.

The first wave of housestaff activity, in 1971, was directed at taking control of the hospital away from the politicians who used it for patronage. This issue united many segments of the hospital community. At the time, Cook County was on probational accreditation. The Residents and Interns Association formed a coalition with nurses, attending staff and nonprofessional workers and they invited the foreign medical graduates to participate. In addition to hospital support, housestaff were able to attract a variety of "outside" anti-Democratic groups which were willing to challenge Mayor Daley on the issue of control of the hospital. The key to the success of the housestaff association was its internal unity and outside support. The outcome was a new governing board to replace the old county board.

The actual results of replacing the board were mixed. Although the coalition succeeded in its demands, the new board remained conservative and politically responsive.[154] The governing commission that took over the hospital appointed a new hospital administrator whose mandate was to end the insurrection and rationalize the Chicago hospital along the lines of the New York model, the Health and Hospitals Corporation. This meant replacing the overt political control that was the target of demands from community groups with the more indirect control represented by the semi-corporate structure.[155] The highly politicized climate at the hospital itself proved a liability; in the early 1970s, left-sectarian groups brought divisiveness and turmoil to the formerly strong organization which fell apart between 1973 and 1975.[156] Although the housestaff regrouped and were successful in a later strike for specific patient care items, the housestaff association ran up against the same patterns noted earlier: nonimplementation of contract gains and economic retrenchment. Furthermore, the continuing political reorganization of the hospital led to the county's refusal to honor the housestaff contract and housestaff had to fight an additional battle to get their contract back.

NATIONAL ORGANIZING: PHYSICIANS NATIONAL HOUSESTAFF ASSOCIATION

During the same period that local housestaff were organizing, a national organization came into being. The idea of a national organization for housestaff had been discussed as early as 1968 by Student American Medical Association (SAMA) leaders and former SHO activists who noted that compared to medical students, housestaff were a "forgotten" and unrepresented group.[157] The impetus to organizing however, was the competitive interest in housestaff shown by other professional organizations such as the AMA and the National Association of Interns and Residents (NARI).[158] Rather than have "outsiders" organize us, many argued that we should "do it ourselves first."

The Physicians National Housestaff Association (PNHA) was established in October 1972, as a loose confederation of local associations of interns, residents, and fellows.[159] Its objectives included ending discrimination in training and hiring, medical care as a human right, adequate educational, working, and living conditions for members and social, educational, and political action toward these ends.[160]

Between 1972 and its demise in 1981, PNHA struggled with issues of identity and strategy: its relation to professional organizations such as the AMA on the one hand, and organized labor on the other, the relation between the national and the local associations, and between different political and ideological factions of housestaff. Prior to 1975, PNHA put much energy into AMA's newly formed Interns and Residents Business Session, pursuing first a reformist and then a takeover strategy. Working within the large and powerful AMA, however, required large inputs of time, energy and money and proved to be cooptive for young housestaff; in its bid for housestaff membership, the AMA also took over PNHA positions, including endorsing collective bargaining.[161]

Beginning in 1974, PNHA moved into closer alignment with organized labor and began to articulate a position as an independent labor organization along the lines of the American Nurses Association. In 1974, PNHA was instrumental in amending the NLRA to extend collective bargaining rights to employees of voluntary non-profit hospitals. Foreseeing an expanded role for itself, and again, pushed into action by the competitive interest in housestaff shown by established unions as well as the AMA, PHNA hired an executive director with a labor organizing background, delegated a committee to examine the pros and cons of unionization and moved its headquarters to Washington, D. C., where it accepted office space and financial support from the American Federation of State, County and Municipal Employees Union (AFSCME).[162] In 1975, PNHA voted to become an official labor organization and to affiliate with the Coalition of American Public Employees (CAPE) and AFSCME.

Although PNHA's official position was to build a dues supported membership base and to consolidate its identity as a labor organization, after the 1976 NLRB "student" ruling, PNHA became increasingly involved in an expensive legal battle to overturn the decision. This created considerable tension within PNHA. One faction, represented by CIR, criticized PNHA for becoming a "top-down" and a "paper" organization. The more radical program, according to CIR, was to organize among city, county, and state hospitals. An opposing position, held by Cook County, was that PNHA should be a mass organization with a primarily symbolic role. Representing one-half of PNHA's dues-paying members, CIR was unwilling to keep up its financial and leadership commitment unless PNHA directed itself to base building along trade-union lines. When PNHA voted to continue to work for the reversal of the NLRB student ruling, CIR withdrew and PNHA subsequently folded.[163]

Unionization as a Progressive Strategy: Problems and Contradictions

Over the course of the past several decades, housestaff have become primary physicians for indigent and low-income populations, particularly in urban areas. This reflects economic and organizational trends such as increased specialization, the use of hospitals as primary care institutions, and federal underwriting of intern and resident services through Medicare and Medicaid.[164] It also reflects demographic shifts.[165]

While the emergence of patient care demands expresses a changed consciousness among housestaff who have come to see themselves less as students than as providers of care to minorities and the poor, the case studies show that these changing patterns were not sufficient in or of themselves to revise housestaff agendas. Two additional factors increased the political consciousness and broadened the objectives of housestaff associations: the entry and leadership of a socially concerned and activist generation of medical students, and the impact of fiscal crisis and economic retrenchment in the 1970s on staffing, equipment, and services. Still, the emergence and resolution of the activist agenda for patient care has differed, depending on legal, political, historical, and organizational variations among the housestaff associations.

The attempt to combine traditional objectives of economic security with new housestaff objectives such as control over training and patient care within a collective bargaining frame-work proved to be conflictual and contradictory. The traditional focus of collective bargaining constrained broader housestaff demands for control over training and patient care and reframed these issues to fit a narrower, depoliticized context. This remained true despite the observation that housestaff associations won more of all their demands where there was more rather than less contract, and that the lack of legal status deterred organizing and discouraged public support for job actions or strikes.

If we compare the several housestaff agendas, economic objectives have obviously done best within this framework. Wages and benefits have risen dramatically for housestaff who formed collective bargaining units.[166] Demands for control of education and training showed some gains but met with a counterattack by hospital administrators and medical schools whose economic and political interests were threatened. Demands related to patient care and limited by the traditional scope of collective bargaining, for the most part evolved indirectly and were hurt by long-term economic trends. Housestaff associations have had the greatest success where the collective bargaining tradition has been weak, where legislation has been enabling, and when housestaff have been innovative in testing labor law.[167]

Another issue was backlash. To the extent that the housestaff movement aimed at control of salaries, working conditions, and patient care, it threatened "the most powerful medical lobby in Washington"—the American Association of Medical Colleges (AAMC)—and provoked an attack.[168] According to housestaff, the March 1976 NLRB decision which designated housestaff as students and thus took away the recently won right to strike was "a political decision" and a "social reaction to a revolution."[169] The AAMC and the American Hospital Association (AHA) mounted a massive legal attack and PNHA has argued that the NLRB adopted the AAMC argument "almost verbatim."[170]

Although the student ruling was a setback for the housestaff movement and involved PNHA and its local affiliates in costly and time-consuming legal battles, the attack also became a rallying cry for local and national efforts, and served to raise political conscious-ness.[171] PNHA analyzed the conflict of interest centered on control of postgraduate medical training in a series of articles which argued that over the course of the decade, the AAMC and the academic medical establishment had superseded the AMA as villains.[172] In PNHA's words, the "hidden housestaff agenda" of the super deans of expanding medical centers was to win capitation grants for house-staff similar to those already granted for medical students.[173] Accord-ing to one editorial, the irony of this development is that although "progressive voices in medicine once welcomed greater power for academics in health planning," the AAMC's recent positions on housestaff licensure and foreign medical graduates make it "more regressive than the AMA ever was."[174] With the PNHA aligned with the AMA in asserting that employees are not students, and with both groups opposed to the AAMC and the AHA, it became possible for physicians—as well as critical social scientists—to see the shifting factions within medicine and the emergence and consolidation of corporate rational interests at the expense of the old professional elite.[175]

Implementation was also a problem. Despite the fact that con-tracts and grievances were won, gains were not always implemented because, in the language of the labor organizer, the contract is "just a piece of paper" to be tested and filled in. Even where members were active and informed, housestaff unions found that in the face of fiscal crisis, "the great financial alligator is eating every contract alive."[176] Issues won as working conditions or as patient care become trans-formed from political to technical or economic issues as limitations of time, money, and space foreclosed innovations won in the political arena.

The escalating nature of the threats made action difficult. In the face of a continuing economic crisis and the accompanying threats to the public sector, contracts and other legal means proved increas-ingly ineffective. Housestaff organizations needed to revert to poli-tical mobilization and confrontation, to organizing community groups and recreating alliances with other hospital workers—to the tactics of the 1960s. Thus political threats to the public health sector reduced the significance of doctors as social change agents even while doctors were becoming activated by those threats which affected their jobs as well as the care they gave.

In addition, outright political attack on the public sector based on a rationale of "excess beds," helped transform analysis from a more simplistic conspiratorial notion of expansionist medical empires to a more complex discussion of the relation between public and private sectors in capitalism and the role of the state. This led to a call for research and analysis as a basis for political education and for mobilization of broader constituencies, consumers as well as health workers.

Finally, housestaff objectives also conflicted with patient care and social needs in such areas as manpower redistribution and public hospitals. For example, plans to create service obligations for physicians in exchange for education, and to address the problem of supplying housestaff to urban and rural poverty areas, were attacked by both local and national associations as threatening the freedom, education and working conditions of doctors. Thus, the same association that pioneered the patient care fund stated that "housestaff may become indentured servants if the Board approves the education plan."[177] The general rule of thumb appeared to be that when progressive issues dovetailed with housestaff interests, they were supported.

It is in the public sector in particular that contradictions stand out and hard choices may have to be made. Issues in the public hospitals were not limited to budgetary items on which doctors, staff, and consumers could unite, but extended to more divisive issues such as the needs of housestaff and medical students for patients on whom they could practice. One doctor expressed the dilemma this way, "If everyone had an M.D. who admitted them and they were withdrawn from the fodder mills, this would create a problem of a teaching base."[178] In Los Angeles, when the county tried to pass a law limiting the salaries of physicians at the county hospitals, the housestaff at Harbour General faced a similar issue: They feared the law would ruin their program, one of the most popular in the country. And, as noted above, despite CIR's policy of trying "not to strike the city," housestaff who served in both public and private hospitals tended to strike on the public service where they were less concerned about professional consequences. Although one housestaff officer said, "There are no two sides in the public system,"[179] it may be more accurate to say, in the words of another, that "The issues are getting closer to the grain."[180]

The existence of issues on which community, patient, and doctor self-interest diverge raises questions as to how progressive a force housestaff can be. In the cases examined above, activist agendas converged with structural change. To the extent that housestaff have become principal providers of care for indigent populations in public hospitals, and economic conditions have endangered these services and positions, patient care demands—whether or not they began as overt political challenges—became quickly infused with demands for participation and control in decision making. This lends support to the view that activism is in part a reaction to an increasing rationalization that limits doctors' ability to practice medicine as they wish. If so, housestaff may only be temporarily aligned with activist concerns for redistributing health services to benefit minorities and the poor.

7

Transforming Society: Professionals as a Political Vanguard

From virtually every strategic perspective, the prevailing radical analysis of health appeared insufficient. Either the medical delivery system—used interchangeably with "health"—was viewed statically as an object of retrenchment and we were called upon to 'Fight Cutbacks' or a monolithic 'Health Empire' was conjured up which greedily hoarded money and power like some multimedia Kong. So, we decided that developing theory was the most relevant practice.
Evan Stark, **Review of Radical Political Economy** (Spring 1977)

Unlike the sixties when we deprecated our professional selves, we can now come out and speak as professionals and experts in the planning field. The notion of a planner carries weight that a community activist doesn't.
Tony Schuman, New York Planners Network Conference, 1976

How will radicals distinguish themselves, in ideology and in struggle, from the ever-more-dominant forces of rationalization and reform? How can they use, and not be used by these forces?
Rhonda Kotelchuck, Health/PAC **Bulletin** 75 (March/April 1977)

A second strategy of social transformation emphasized professions as increasingly important agencies of a class state. Planners, for example, participated in the pro-growth programs of the 1950s, the "social justice" operations of the 1960s, and the "planned shrinkage" of the 1970s. Medicine was viewed as the sector that would make or

break capitalism, a key source of contradictions. Having emerged as
a prime growth area with escalating costs, capitalism had to rationalize this sector and bring it under control, lest it topple capitalism.

From this perspective, the strategic role for activists was ideological: to criticize dominant professional paradigms and institutions
and to construct an alternate socialist model. Activist professionals
were to function as a vanguard,[1] analyzing their domains to distinguish between what the influential New Left theorist Andre Gorz
called "reformist" and "non-reformist" reforms.[2]

The attempt to escape the dilemmas of other strategies led
activists toward more overt political and theoretical frameworks as a
basis for action. To explore the impetus toward vanguard roles as
well as the contradictions of this strategy for planners, I return to the
organizational history of Urban Planning Aid (Chapters 4 and 5),
then look at Homefront and the Planners Network. Homefront, a
New York City organization, began in 1974 as an attempt to build a
citywide coalition around housing. When this failed, it turned to a
study group format and produced an analysis of housing abandonment. Homefront later faltered in moving from an analytic to a
political vanguard role.

The Planners Network began in 1975 as a communications
network for radical planners in North America. It spawned several
regional groups, and despite attempts to make it a formal organization of socialist planners, has functioned primarily as a network. In
articulating the concerns of radical planners in the late 1970s, the
Planners Network illustrates the tensions of the vanguard strategy—
divisions between academic and practicing planners, between radical
planners and community groups; also the changing political significance of political organization by professionals.

URBAN PLANNING AID:
POLITICAL EDUCATION AND ACTION

In its last stage, UPA became more clearly politicized, subordinating
organizing and technical assistance to the development of a "multi-
working class movement . . . a long-term development of left-turning
consciousness."[3] The consensus at UPA was that the housing and
transportation problems of minorities and the poor were the systematic results of a capitalist system in which basic needs had
become profit-making industries. The conclusion: that "socialism in
some form is preferable to capitalism and is a necessary prerequisite
to full solutions to the problems we deal with."[4] UPA's strategy
became political education and action—to locate people's local strug-

gles within broader political perspectives and to encourage political organizing for systemwide change.

Of the factors involved in this shift, two stand out: UPA's disillusionment with community based strategies and the impact of UPA's funding crisis on its staff. *The Empty Promise*, a study of Community Housing Development Corporations by the Housing and Community Research groups of UPA, exemplified the cumulative effect of analysis and action. When UPA started working with community housing development groups in 1969 and 1970, they "believed the political assumptions behind the 'movement were correct."[5] Community development could work. By acquiring ownership of their buildings, poor people could solve their housing problems which included urban renewal threats, changing neighborhoods, high rents, and the abandonment and deterioration of buildings.

UPA noted that it was the professionals who "claimed it was all possible" and who played key roles.

> Housing development requires a great deal of professional input.... Since these people are not residents of any average working class community, it is obvious that no working class community could develop a business of this type without outside assistance.... In many cases this outside assistance is not sought, but comes into the community under its own steam. Professionals such as advocate planners tend to create roles for themselves in order to do their work. A planner who is not satisfied working for an institution where planners have no control over policy, will, often unconsciously, assume a policy making role when there is an opportunity to do so. Because community people have to rely to a large extent on technical assistance in order to produce housing, the professionals most often define the nature and scope of decisions that have to be made.

The pamphlet used case studies to document how "experience convinced us that we were wrong." Community development groups ran into problems with poor quality housing, lack of amenities, high rents, and lack of economic returns. As the new landlord, these conflicts put them at odds with their communities. UPA drew some conclusions:

> Community housing development is a serious attempt to improve housing conditions and community groups are attracted to it because it promises to meet their housing needs. But the promise is an empty one. Community housing development doesn't work because it doesn't confront the basic cause of our housing problems: even though housing

is a basic need, it is only produced when it is profitable to do so. At present, when private producers find producing housing for the wealthier classes to be most profitable, the government has attempted to subsidize low and moderate income housing—making it also profit-able—but has not changed the basic profit oriented structure of the housing industry.

The pamphlet outlined alternative approaches such as rent control and collective bargaining. These approaches "avoid the trap" of "government programs which make the development process seem possible and attractive to community groups and end up reinforcing the communities lack of real power to get what it needs." UPA's preferred solution was a tenants' union. Here, "the govern-ment [cannot] switch the blame for poor and inadequate housing from itself and the housing industry to the community sponsors and the people who live in these projects."

The funding crisis of 1970 brought the question of UPA's political commitment to the fore. Internal memos noted: "we've let the issues slide . . . a hired/salary relation has stood in the way of a stronger political unity and support community." Debates during 1971 reflect-ed a growing uneasiness about government support. "Do they know something about us that we don't know about ourselves?" "Are we contributing to the loyal opposition" or are we "committed to a movement for basic change?" In 1973, a funding crisis made the issue particularly clear. As one staff member put it, "if we are to continue to work without pay and without security, we need a clear political rationale."

New leadership, the firming up of a radical political identity, and a retreat from decentralization meant a return to form and structure. Again, the positioning of research and media relative to organizing reflected shifting organizational goals and identity. Functional issue groups replaced the dispersed regional groups; issue organizing replaced area organizing; and media and research became inde-pendent units, no longer just "respond[ing]" to the short-term needs of substantive areas or organizations."

Research assumed renewed importance during this period. A 1970 memo on public housing organizing illustrated how UPA was "led into research" by tactical needs. Although UPA's stated objec-tive was to "build strong local tenants' organizations which are capable of both winning short-term benefits for their members and relating to the broader movement for basic change," all the tactics listed—code enforcement, modernization, the provision of additional services, and bankruptcy—required research or technical backup. As the organization became openly political, research provided ammunition for organizers and their communities as well as for the publication of increasingly more analytic documents. The growing size and autonomy of the controversial media group symbolized the greater importance given to political education and outreach.[6] Although UPA still described itself as a "conduit" for the resources of the member organizations, UPA attempted to take the lead and to choose issues and constituencies according to its political objectives.

While UPA changed its orientation to planning and planners, the other side of the coin was the difficulty that planners (and other professionals) had remaining in UPA.[7] A conflict between personal and movement needs surfaced in 1974 in a debate about giving individual book credits on a reprint that had collective authorship in its first edition. The precariousness of funding for radical positions and the failing strength of the larger political movement made it hard to sustain a radical career and revived traditional professional concerns.

Although UPA survived many defunding crises, the policies and cutbacks of the Reagan administration cost UPA its large annual operating budget and finally led to UPA's demise in 1983.

HOMEFRONT: PROBLEMS OF A VANGUARD ROLE

UPA managed to keep its feet in the community while moving toward a vanguard role, but without a similar starting point or history, not many groups could combine these roles. The history of Homefront in New York City addresses this issue.

Homefront originated in 1974 out of the "failed attempt" to build a citywide coalition to stop the dislocations caused by urban renewal, institutional expansion, and "redevelopment land grabs."[8] Many of the people involved in the new organization subtitled Citywide Action Group Against Neighborhood Destruction and for Low-Rent Housing, had participated in local struggles. They were frustrated with issue organizing because "when we left, it all just stopped."[9]

Homefront felt the coalition failed because of the impact of the recession and the lack of a sharp analysis that could bring activist efforts and the recession together. Without redevelopment as the major force destroying neighborhoods, activists felt stranded. Homefront saw the need for a mid-level organization which reassessed the situation and addressed itself "to organizers, not a mass base."[10] While Homefront did not feel it should necessarily be "the initiator of actions on local issues," neither did it see itself limited to the issues at hand or to requests from local groups. The feeling was that "when Homefront decides it can have a positive role to play, it will actively seek to participate."[11]

After much debate, Homefront adopted an explicit socialist identity and formed study groups to place "short-range stuff"—local events and struggles—into a long-range perspective. One result was a leaflet on the Morningside squatters. The squatters were examined in terms of the destruction of Manhattan's West Side, the role of their liberal sponsors, the Episcopal Church, and the worldwide displacement of people due to policies of redevelopment.[12]

To construct a strategy for recession, Homefront began a two-year study of the causes and effects of landlord abandonment. The report, *Housing Abandonment in New York City*, was released in November 1977.[13] Contrary to explanations which blamed abandonment on building deterioration, tenants, rent control, greed, crime or welfare, the study of abandonment led them to political economy: "We need to understand the macro level before the building level . . . how investment patterns create the pre-conditions for abandonment." The report argued that abandonment was a "result of the way capitalists create and distribute wealth"; that the major causes of abandonment were "the disinvestment of banks in residential real estate," "the movement of capital—from the city to the suburbs, and to other regions of the country and world where it yields higher profits," and "the pressures of the urban land market, which make centrally located working-class neighborhoods ripe for redevelopment." If the problem was capitalism, then a housing movement could play an important role by creating a demand for a housing system based on peoples' needs.

Homefront criticized city and federal response, particularly the community management and sweat equity programs, on a number of grounds:

> These city programs, and the many privately-funded self-help projects, sap the energies of tenants and housing activists, often diverting them from political organizing which can have a much wider impact than small-scale local self-help programs. *The most serious problem with these programs, however, is that they place most of the responsibility for housing improvement on individuals and local communities, which have the least resources, and get the government (which has the resources) off the hook.*[14]

Rather than self-help, Homefront called for "public ownership with tenant control."

Having established an analytic framework and a strategy—that city owned housing should be an additional source of public housing, the next step was to move beyond the study group and use analysis to inform practice. Beginning in mid-1978, Homefront helped organize a series of actions mobilizing community activists against the auctioning of city-owned property. This led to a citywide moratorium on auctions.

In the case of city-owned property, Homefront's objectives meshed with strong grass roots sentiment against the auctions. But the substance of Homefront's analysis and its vanguard claims—particularly with regard to self-help housing—made action difficult. Having concluded that the popular self-help housing efforts were tokenism at best, Homefront put itself at odds with many grass roots groups and struggles. These groups wanted technical or research assistance, not political leadership.[15]

Although the abandonment report had significant political payoff, Homefront as a group was not able to transform itself from study to action—to develop, in the words of its recruitment brochure, a mass movement dedicated to "decent housing at affordable rents as a right" and based on the assumption that "housing is a class question" and that "the people must hold the government accountable."[16] Following the publication of the abandonment report, several members organized the In Rem Tenants Coalition for tenants in city-owned property. While they saw this as Homefront's praxis, others disagreed about the strategic significance of grass roots organizing, and still others were already committed to local turf struggles and "had only twenty-four hours in the day."[17] After 1980, Homefront did not meet again as a group.

THE PLANNERS NETWORK
AND PLANNERS IN THE 1970s

Chester Hartman, a well-known advocate planner of the 1960s, began the Planners Network to put "the few hundred North American radical planners" in touch through a newsletter. The impetus to networking was to allay the "political and professional" isolation that many politically oriented planners felt in the 1970s and to discuss the impact of retrenchment policies on job opportunities for community-oriented planners.[18] Soliciting personal statements from the several hundred names on the Network mailing list, the newsletter provided a forum for debates and recorded the concerns of radical planners at the time.[19]

The first mailing (August 1975) outlined what were to be the key issues for both the national newsletter and the regional organizations which formed in response to the newsletter: Who is a planner?

What do we mean by radical? Who is our constituency and what are our activities?

Because planners had such diverse credentials and entry routes, the debate about who was a planner centered on planners themselves, not on paraprofessionals, as with law, or on other supporting professionals, as with medicine. Respondents wrote:

> I never liked the term *city planner* because I could never recognize any special discipline, anything like an architectural or a medical discipline. I prefer urbanist (which the French use) meaning someone who studies cities intensely and applies the knowledge won in the process to the solution of urban problems.[20]

> I would favor *planners* (over *urbanists*) by which I mean people who are concerned with rationality in the choice of means and with the consequence of such means as long as they don't have to have professional degrees.[21]

> One important issue is whether the network ought to expand to include organizers working in housing and development.[22]

> A radical planner to some extent is an organizer. Probably organizers who consider themselves also planners are so whether they are so educated and labeled or not.[23]

> I am terribly uncomfortable with the word *planner*. We are virtually never in the position to plan, and we should not be represented in the public's mind as generators of the mess.[24]

The introduction of social action roles in the 1960s and the widening of knowledge and disciplinary bases as federal legislation required comprehensive social plans from planners in one generation and environmental impact statements in another, fueled the old debates about the continuing boundary openness of planning.

The political identity of a radical was also at issue. One of the strongest impulses behind coalescing in the 1970s came from planners who felt that it was time to come out of the closet about socialism. In comparison to the 1960s, when *radical* referred to those who wanted to "help underdogs," the term *radical* had a more ideological reference point in the 1970s.[25] This led to debates: should the Network limit itself to socialists or include the whole liberal establishment? If socialist, should it have an explicit political identity? Some, including the founder, "would like to see our Network be somewhat more to the Left than the amorphous 'liberal' and 'progressive types' that PEO tended to attract."[26] Supporters of a socialist identity argued for the need to move beyond liberal critiques and for the usefulness of "the socialist perspective . . . as a critical tool." They wanted to address the "fundamental questions— private property, racism, monopolies" and to "disabuse the public of the notion that it is planners or urbanists who actually *do* the planning in this country." Others felt that an explicit socialist identity would exclude too many planners, particularly those involved in government work. In the attempt to find a name "we can all live with," the association remained the Planners Network.

The debate over who we are and what we should do took several directions: one group wanted the Network to "crystallize North American planners into a coherent body, capable of taking unified political action and assisting the political and organizational efforts of others." This was a vision of an alternative professional association of radicals on the Left, replete with a journal, and stimulated by "the need to understand our profession first . . . the forces which create our work."[27] Another group feared that such a Network would create a new elite of radical planners. "I believe the Network must be populist in nature, geared to demystifying expertise and knocking down the false god of credentials."[28] Whatever else it did, many wanted the Network to provide an institutional affiliation for unemployed members and to function as a clearinghouse for jobs.[29]

While technical assistance and organizing remained the everyday activities of many of the planners in the Network, they reported that those efforts were frustrating because local experience "gets lost" and is too easily coopted. They wanted an analytic framework to assess the proliferating alternatives at local and federal levels.

> The Network can be a resource bank for those organizing around planning related issues, many of which lack the understanding of basic social forces involved and some of the technicalities that come up.[30]

Compared to the 1960s, there had been a redefinition of what radical planners could offer. In addition to technical aid or organizing, they could contribute theory and analysis as a prerequisite and guide to action.

Several regional organizations formed in response to the national newsletter, but they were, for the most part, short lived. By June 1978, the Planners Network reported: "Reports from the local groups are not encouraging. The Mid-west group may be in trouble and both Boston and New York seem to have lost their initial steam."[31] Beyond their common concerns, the regional organizations differed in leadership and direction.

In San Francisco, an offshoot of the North California group established a "radical counterpart" to the local citizens housing and planning association. Its aim was to provide "technical assistance to progressive community organizations," to "watch-dog public agencies to spot issues on which a radical planning voice and presence are needed," and to "initiate studies and organizing efforts on issues around which no one now is in motion."[32] The group became involved in a number of projects, both funded and unfunded. Hartman's presence and a strong local issue (the International Hotel) fostered an advocacy orientation reminiscent of the 1960s.[33] But unlike the 1960s, the projects gave greater importance to the planners' independent initiative, emphasized technical skills, research, and testimony over organizing, and placed overall importance on job creation and institutional affiliation. Dependent on high levels of voluntary staff energy, the group petered out by 1980.

The Boston Network moved in a different direction, away from advocacy.[34] After a year of meetings which mixed social and educational concerns, the members voted to adopt a radical identity and form a socialist study group to address "the relation between the urban crisis and the crisis of Capitalism."[35] An equally important concern in Boston was jobs for planners because one-half of the members were underemployed or unemployed. This led to suggestions for a job and skills bank, a professional guild or union for those working on a consulting basis, and a learning co-op to "retrain" planners in social policy.[36] Although meetings were well-attended, most people were overcommitted in "narrower areas" and the organizational work fell upon a few. The Boston Network became dormant in 1978.

The New York Network attempted to establish an alternate planning organization from the start. Despite general initial interest in jobs and community, the steering committee focused on political analysis and called one general meeting during the first year, a conference in June 1976 to address the group's organizational structure and the substantive issue of building abandonment. In a lively discussion sparked by the Homefront report on abandonment, criticism of local self-help struggles was met, in turn, by criticism of vanguard groups such as the Network, for being white, professional, and "intellectual."[37]

During 1976 and 1977, the steering committee worked on a proposal for an "organization that was to be a radical alternative to the mainstream." The agenda for the second conference (April 1977) was to adopt this proposal and move into work groups to link the planning profession to New York's fiscal crisis. The tenor of the second conference was captured by the new sense that "The notion of a planner carries weight that community activist doesn't"; that "Unlike the sixties when we deprecated our professional selves, we can now come out and speak as professionals and experts in the planning field."[38] The community groups present at the conference responded by debating "whether we need another group with its own political agenda." Their consensus was that communities only wanted planners to carry out needed research and to testify for them when they needed support.

There were also divisions within the New York Network as to the work to be done. Some felt that the Network's primary effort should be directed toward building an alternative institution or think tank; others argued that the Network should be working within existent bureaucracies relating the fiscal crisis to community groups.

At the second conference, attendance was down from the more than 100 participants to 20. The working groups which were to be the structure of the new organization faltered and the organization became dormant during 1977 and 1978. In the spring of 1979, the New York group combined forces with the Architects Forum to conduct a well-attended Network/Forum discussion series on "problems, policies, and planning in New York which continued to at least 1989.[39]

At the national level, there have been several attempts to transform the Network into a formal national membership organization capable of political action—a progressive alternative to the American Planning Association: The Blacksburg Conference (May 1978), the Cornell Conference (April 1979), and the Washington Conference (December 1981). At the Blacksburg Conference, "The Structural Crisis of the 1970s and Beyond: The Need for a New Planning Theory," an "exclusively academic" audience of 60 participants discussed the need to "unify theory and practice" and to broaden the participation by including "practicing planners."[40] Along these lines, the Cornell Conference, "Planning Theory and Practice: Economic Context, Emerging Coalitions and Progressive Planning Roles," had 250 participants including practicing planners. It was still predominately academic (two-thirds of the group including students), and was characterized by tensions between community oriented planners and academics.[41]

The mandate for the Washington Conference was explicitly organizational. Spearheaded by two New York Network planners, the Network moved to semiformal status, adopted a statement of purpose, elected a steering committee, instituted voluntary dues, and established a series of functional work groups (along the lines of the earlier New York model). While the work group on housing produced a successful reader, and the network as a whole gained "with the greater political self-definition and broader leadership structure the conference led to," the net assessment of the attempt to transform the Network into a vanguard organization was "something of a disappointment."[42] Retrospectively, several felt the project was too ambitious.

The limits of a vanguard strategy for planners are reflected in the difficulties of the New York group and the similar inability to make the national network an activist professional association. Although regional members expressed the need for political community and radical analysis, efforts to formalize a professional organization along more sectarian lines contributed to a high drop out rate except among academics. Given the diverse training, jobs, and interests of the planners, many felt that it made more sense for a person who wanted to "do something" to join a functional issue group than a professional association—a group which focused on housing or energy—issues that cut across disciplines as well as the producer/consumer divide and that had a better chance of creating a national movement for change.[43]

This raises the issue of the self-serving function of the vanguard strategy and whether it was in part an attempt to establish radicals within the profession. Recurrent references in the national newsletter and the regional meetings to the Union for Radical Political Economics (URPE) as a model are illuminating in that URPE established a niche for itself in the academic world by elaborating a Marxist paradigm and then turned to action.[44] But network planners and planners in general are less academically based or identified and more diverse in training and interest. The vanguard movement within the Planners Network came up against what Hartman referred to as the "unresolvable tension between the 'theory-oriented' people and the 'practice-oriented' people."[45] To have become an "umbrella organization" as some wished rather than remain a network, the Planners Network would have had to function as a combination trade union and professional association.[46]

Research and analysis as a primary thrust for health activists emerged in the late 1960s in health as in other areas. Along with the attempt to restructure institutions came the need to understand them. Chapter 4 discussed the beginnings of research in SHO and in early MCHR activities where it grew out of the failures of liberal reform and the requirements of political action. Some of this research was federally initiated and supported; some originated with activists and was supported by their own efforts.

The following case studies are of two primarily research organizations whose analytic perspectives shaped the thinking of the health movement as a whole. I want to understand the impetus to research, how and why ideas changed over time, as well as the strengths and limitations of research as a primary activist strategy in health. The Health Policy Advisory Center (Health/PAC) was the organization responsible for providing political analysis and leadership for the health movement for over a decade. Health/PAC pioneered and popularized the "medical empires" analysis of the health care system and published the *Bulletin,* the "longest continuously publishing insurgent health publication in the United States."[47]

The emergence of the East Coast Health Discussion Group (ECHDG) marked the beginnings of a new analysis. Compared to Health/PAC's concrete mid-level focus on political actors and interests, the ECHDG emphasized theory building and the explicit use of Marxist analysis. Compared to Health/PAC's power structure research, it identified ideology and culture as important "political battlegrounds."[48] Compared to the 1960s, when health was often a means to an end, health was now viewed as constitutive of the social order. The emerging consensus was to build a health Left based on a more powerful paradigm.

HEALTH/PAC: HEALTH POLICY
AND HEALTH POLITICS

Health/PAC grew out of an assessment of health policy in New York City, funded by the Samuel Rubin Foundation and conducted by Robb Burlage under the auspices of the Institute of Policy Studies.[49] The "Burlage Report" documented how the medical empires of the private sector benefited from policies supposedly geared toward upgrading the public sector. It underlined the need for ongoing monitoring of health policy in New York and for a publication which provided concrete analysis of political actors and interests in the health arena.

Organized and directed by Robb Burlage and supported by the Rubin Foundation, Health/PAC began in June 1968 with the publication of its first issue of the *Bulletin.* Within a year, the staff tripled in size to include two physicians, a medical student, an urban planner, and an urban health economist. Between 1969 and 1977, Health/PAC averaged between six and 12 staff members in addition to associate members and interns. There have been as many as three physicians on its staff concurrently.[50]

A West Coast office opened in 1972 to follow important health innovations in that region. This office was "functionally tied to the New York office but 'financially independent'" and produced issues of the *Bulletin* as well as separate reports.[51] In 1976, there was a sharp internal split among staff members in the West Coast office and the West Coast office closed.

If the widespread dissemination of Health/PAC's views is one measure of Health/PAC's success, then Health/PAC succeeded with several significant audiences—the liberal establishment, the general public, and the health Left. Health/PAC had an important and formative influence on the health movement in the late 1960s and early 1970s. In the heyday of health activism, Health/PAC staff were called upon to speak before activist groups all over the country. They organized workshops and seminars for health science students and participated in a Health Free University in New York City.[52] Discussing Health/PAC's influence on the SHO, one leader said:

> Health/PAC was where people went to look for the sources of their dissatisfaction. They [Health/PAC] supplied a new paradigm, a new map of the terrain.[53]

Bulletin subscribers and readers also included "health professionals, academics, civic leaders, and interested public officials." Describing the number of readers at state and federal levels as a large fraction of the mid-level health policy adiministration, one staff member stated: "We are a respected left flank with a constituency in the real world."[54]

Health/PAC's views were also widely popularized through a number of special reports, pamphlets, and two well-known books: *The American Health Empire*, a summary of Health/PAC's analysis of the health system published in 1971, and *Prognosis Negative*, its sequel, in 1976.[55] Both books have been required reading in many college courses.

Over time, Health/PAC lost intellectual and political leadership as well as financial support. By 1977, there was a sense that a decade had ended. Health/PAC's view of federal policy was that it would "fail again" because it did not take into account "new contradictions" in health care such as the high cost clinical model.[56] The Rubin Foundation withdrew its support because it felt that Health/ PAC had already received generous amounts of seed money and must now stand on its own. From the Left, the response to the *Bulletin* was that Health/PAC was delivering "the same old message."

Within Health/PAC there was a sense that the medical empires model had "run out." On the pages of the *Bulletin,* new voices outlined new dilemmas.[57] Internal debates concerned Health/PAC's constituency, the relative importance of institutional versus cultural elements in analysis, and the need to develop theory. The national economic and political climate had changed from the "economic expansion of the sixties, to the economic contraction and crisis of the seventies" and the "federal turnabout has created confusion, anger, and despair among many concerned about the inadequacies of the present health system."[58] Moreover, there was no longer a health Left movement. "Whom do we speak for and to? With no political clout in the real world, we just offer ideas when we speak."[59]

Along with the loss of foundation support, research contracts (another source of organizational income) also became difficult to obtain. Health/PAC was the first critical health policy research organization, but as health policy research boomed and universities established their own research institutes, they assembled resources with which Health/PAC could not compete. In the early 1970s, for example, Health/PAC had a contract with the National Institutes of Mental Health (NIMH) for a major study of community mental health centers; by 1978, the staff were hard pressed to find funding for their projects. Funding priorities also shifted along with politics and in the late 1970s, self-help and consumer action groups were "getting the grants."

After foundation funding ended in 1977, Health/PAC entered a period of uncertain survival. The *Bulletin* was sporadically published in 1978, and two staff members who were the backbone of the *Bulletin* for many years left New York City. In 1979, publication was resumed on a new footing. Health/PAC kept editorial control vested in a volunteer editorial board, published the *Bulletin* through Human Sciences Press, and began to fundraise to cover office expenses. While the relationship with Human Sciences Press ended within a few years, the editorial board expanded and became more politically diverse and the magazine continues publication to this day.

The Medical Empires Model and the Health Movement

Much of what came to be Health/PAC's analysis of the health system was contained in the groundbreaking Burlage Report. This analysis of the 1961 affiliation agreements between private and municipal hospitals in New York City concluded that the public sector—municipal or county hospitals and health centers, and the private sector—voluntary nonprofit hospitals and university medical schools and teaching hospitals, were opposing and unequal forces; that the impact of successive public policies ostensibly directed at improving services in the public sector was

> to bring under private institutional control the potentially competitive resources of municipal hospital financing, facilities, professional staffs and unionized hospital employees.[60]

This meant that:

> hospitals of last resort and the family physician for many of New York's medically needy—are becoming private utilities, reflecting the private research and financial priorities of private and academic institutions.[61]

In conceptualizing American medicine as increasingly dominated by "medical empires" which were part of a "medical-industrial complex," Health/PAC's analysis broke with the older image of the physician dominated system represented organizationally by the AMA. In line with the "Old Left," the study found that the leadership of the city's health establishment overlapped with the private sector; that the role of city government was at best weak and ineffective, merely a rubber stamp. But the analysis went beyond the "simplistic left economism" of earlier institutional critics to introduce "ideological and political elements" in the spirit of the New Left.[62]

Along with identifying the emergent corporate shape of American medicine, Health/PAC also identified agents of change:

> There is a new creative energy emerging from new forces; neighborhood organizations demanding decent health services and a say in that service; health worker organizations demanding not only better wages and better hospital and health center working conditions for the benefit of the patient, but a totally new career opportunity and training system, especially in the largest employer of low-income and minority group people in the city, the municipal hospitals; and health science students seeking alliance with community people to change the system.[63]

Given the nature of the problem—a private takeover of public funds and facilities, a weak and ineffective government, and the growing movement for change—Health/PAC called for decentralized, community controlled planning and facilities. It saw itself as an "independent nongovernmental center" to monitor and analyze health policy, to give technical assistance to "citizen and professional groups, and to serve as a communication center both for interested professionals and concerned citizens."

Central to all these roles was the research function:

> to gather relevant information about health standards, problems, institutions, powers, forces and political and institutional alternatives as seen particularly in the diverse New York City context, but with awareness of developments elsewhere in the nation and the world.[64]

One 1971 issue of the *Bulletin,* entitled "Health Research Guide," contained a summary statement of what research was, how to do it, and its relation to organizing around the health system.[65] The rationale for research was that it led to a "real source of understanding of how and why an institution works, how decisions are made, and in whose interests." The objective of power structure research was not theory building but action: to map the contours of the health delivery system, to locate the pressure points for change, and to use them. In fact, theory was not considered to be particularly useful. "No guide like this one can actually tell you how to find out the most important issues or the most important power relationships in a particular setting." The document said that "understanding an institution is like the work of a spy." Such work must be empirical and approached as an artform.

Research was also "a powerful organizing tool." The doing of research by a collective could "help identify points of leverage and points of weakness in an institution"; Interviews could "[help] people understand their own grievances and their own situation with respect to an institution." Even the demand for information "may become an organizing and agitating goal, one easily coupled to a more strategic demand for an on-going release of information to the people affected by it and for an on-going role of those people in making decisions based on that information."[66] Although one of the long-time staff members at Health/PAC adamantly insisted that "we've been absolutely constant. We were never organizers," the divide between research and organizing was not so clear-cut. In Health/PAC's early period, research as a consciousness raising and organizing tool underscored its student internship program, the action-research groups associated with the Health/PAC sponsored Health Free University, and projects such as the monitoring of New York City's various medical empires.

Doctors had an important role in Health/PAC's power structure research. Not only were they part of the new "creative energy," they were also medical insiders. One doctor on the Health/PAC staff, assigned to "monitor" Bellevue, said that he had the kind of access to hospital decision making that it would be difficult and probably impossible for anyone other than a physician to gain. Doctors were also particularly important to Health/PAC in its early period, when the emphasis was on community controlled facilities and when medical credentials gave legitimacy to the study of community health efforts.[67]

Developing Analysis and Strategy

Over the course of the decade in which it provided running coverage of the health system and the health movement, Health/PAC came to reassess both its analysis and strategy. Neither proved impervious to historical change.

Beginning in the 1960s, the health movement had brought together three streams of activists: community groups concerned with health services, nonprofessional health workers, and progressive health science students and professionals. Health/PAC initially emphasized community or grass roots action as the key part of the equation. At the time, community groups in New York City were challenging medical empires at a variety of locations,[68] and beyond New York in Chicago and San Francisco. It looked to Health/PAC as if "the shots ringing out in the struggle over a South Bronx Community Mental Health Center are being heard around the medical world."[69]

In the course of monitoring community struggles in New York and elsewhere, Health/PAC was forced to reexamine the role of community as agency. By 1972, Health/PAC published a strong indictment, not only of community as a force for change in the health system, but of community control as a solution to medical empires and as a strategy for general social change.[70] One staff member pinpointed Health/PAC's own bias stating, "we built community up. We gave short reports of romanticized struggles."[71] By 1972, however, the community romance was over:

> Time and practice have shown . . . that the workers at the hospital are
> in fact pivotal. Their actions have made the greatest inroads and have
> had the most continuity. This arises in part out of the differences in the
> relation of workers and community residents to a hospital.[72]

Professional workers and unions were viewed skeptically from the start as agents of change for minorities and the poor. Health/PAC judged New York City's CIR as elitist for refusing to join with nonprofessionals or nurses, as primarily self-serving, and even reactionary. CIR received little and mostly nonsympathetic coverage.[73] The experience of the Lincoln Collective, a "critical mass" of radically oriented health professionals and a key experiment in institutional organizing, crystallized many of the doubts on the health Left about doctors as agents of social change. Health/PAC felt that deeply ingrained professionalism was responsible for "the incapacity of doctors at Lincoln to work with the community and with worker organizations."[74] Reports from elsewhere confirmed the tendency of professionals to remain aloof from workers and the community and to be easily intimidated by their hospital administration.[75] The other side of the coin was that activist doctors were distrusted by workers and community groups and that interns and residents were a particularly poor bet due to the fact that they were only passing through the institutions employing them.[76]

During the early 1970s, Health/PAC identified nurses as pivotal health professionals. Strategically located between doctors and nonprofessional workers, nurses were believed to be more class conscious for having been "consistently denied positions of administrative or professional authority"; less inhibited from acting by a "barrier of professionalism"; and already politicized by the women's movement. It seemed likely that they would unite with activist groups inside and outside of the hospital because "the institutional and attitudinal sources of oppression are the same for both women workers and consumers."[77]

But nurses and nonprofessional hospital workers were increasingly unionized and many of their unions channelled health activism into narrow wage and benefit demands. In the struggles of hospital workers at Gouverneur and Lincoln Hospital Mental Health Services, Health/PAC criticized the union for

> [its] tendency to isolate dissenters and prevent the development of local initiative, the inability to deal with issues related to health care save in bread and butter terms, the identification of the union's interests with the hospital industry's interests.[78]

Nurse militancy looked promising but it too was contradictory in action. Examining a 1974 Bay Area strike by the California Nurses Association for control of working conditions and improved patient care, Health/PAC wrote that the strike highlighted "race, class, and sex antagonisms." Noting that the association represented the elite strata of registered nurses, they asked:

> Given the existing hierarchical division of labor within the hospital, will bargaining along narrow skill lines by a relatively privileged group of professional nurses serve to create even more tension and divisions?

And concluded:

> RN's alone cannot shut hospitals down and bring significant change to their workplaces. In the long run, demands for professional upgrading by RN's are made at the expense not only of other workers but of the RN's themselves.[79]

By 1974, the opinion at Health/PAC was that institutional organizing had also failed. Events in New York City and elsewhere in the country suggested that health workers, like the community, did not represent a homogeneous group and that health institutions proved to be a limited site for action. At this point, one staff member said, "there was a push toward more theoretical work. We formed a study group and read some of the neo-Marxist literature, the Frankfurt school. . . ."[80]

As early as 1970 the Health/PAC *Bulletin* began to describe the health system as "more than a matter of producing and distributing adequate medical care."[81] In a series of pioneering articles on a diverse range of topics such as medicine and the military, prison medicine, the medical treatment of drug addicts, and women and the health system, Health/ PAC—albeit in a nonsystematic fashion— moved beyond distributive problems and private and public sector conflicts to explore the broader question of medicine's relation to dominant structures and values.[82]

Both the women's movement and the occupational health and safety movement were particularly important in refocusing health research. The analysis of women as health consumers suggested that medicine had played and continued to play an important part in creating and reproducing traditional sex roles.[83] Studies of sterilization abuse and abortion explored how the health system reproduced class structure and values as well as sex roles.[84] Occupational health and safety provided similar intellectual stimulus. As a low prestige specialty neglected in medical school and in practice, occupational health was the sort of anomaly which called for historical and comparative explanation. Research on occupational health initially focused on the role of industrial elites versus rank-and-file organizations; later articles, such as a case study of asbestos, shifted from power structure research to a more fine-grained examination of how dominant interests came to be reflected within medical science.[85]

Large-scale economic developments had also become more important at Health/PAC throughout the decade. As early as 1970, Health/ PAC staff were aware of the need to provide more of a "citywide or national framework for local struggles."[86] *The American Health Empire* (1971) moved in this direction—from "isolated hospitals to hospitals as part of a system"—by locating health priorities within capitalism and describing the emergence of monopoly capitalism in the health sector. Critics on the Left still faulted the analysis for its "historical specificity"; its "static" and undialectical quality; and its failure to deal with science, technology, and the role of the state.[87]

1975 marked the beginning of a period of intellectual ferment. The health movement was in disarray as was the Left. New developments in the health sector made it necessary to revise the theoretical map "to get at the heart of what clinical medicine does. Not systems analysis or political analysis, but to focus on the health outcome."[88] "We got the notion that what had been lacking was the content of medicine. We talked about power structures, about everything but that."[89] Study groups formed at Health/PAC and Health/PAC staff participated in a conference on health sponsored by URPE and in the newly formed East Coast Health Discussion Group. The readings of these groups included new Marxist writings on the social relations of productions, on ideology, and on the role of the state.

A 1976 editorial entitled "Economic Crisis" outlined a more economistic model for health.[90] Scientific medicine was identified as medicine's "Trojan horse." Having provided the formula for medicine's early professional success, science and technology had led to the logic of corporate medicine, heavily dependent upon government funding. This, in turn, brought government regulation and control. Compared to the earlier Health/PAC image of conflicting sectors, this model suggested dialectical motion: scientific medicine gave rise to a cost crisis that, in turn, could be solved by "voluntarizing" the public sector. The problem was not the mode of delivery but the model of care.

This model also gave greater analytic importance to the role of government.

> When we started, we had a slightly non-economistic analysis which argued that the powers in health were monopolies. Government was viewed as a rubber stamp. Now we have a tripartite analysis—labor, government and capital, with an independent role for government.[91]

The logic of development suggested that health empires might themselves be superseded by government control. Just as the organizers of care had replaced the deliverers in the 1930s, the hospital model of technological medicine would be replaced in the 1980s because it had come to stand in the way of the rationalization of the health sector.[92] The strategy that emerged from this analysis was to "return to the public health perspective" and to elaborate a preventative, out-patient model of care.[93]

Although Health/PAC had begun to identify new arenas of conflict and struggle, in the words of one staff member, "We couldn't develop them. We had less staff and money. The timing was wrong."[94] Caught in a series of binds as the economic and political environment changed, as the health movement faltered, and as its analysis "ran out," several issues emerged.

Health/PAC faced a continuing organizational problem: its targeted agency of change and its reader and sustainer base, did not, for the most part, overlap.[95] The readers and sustainers were middle-class professionals whose interests Health/PAC served by providing health policy analysis when no one else was doing it and by acting as a link between the liberal health establishment and the health movement. With the subsequent growth of a large health policy industry, the failure of the health movement, and the change in federal directions, Health/PAC lost political clout in the real world and with it, financial support.

Health/PAC members identified several other factors that made it difficult to create a wider readership: a difficult style, a substantive focus on issues more relevant to the poor, and an unwillingness to use the sort of "non-radical organizational bases that exist in many communities such as unions and church groups" or to engage in legislative and legal arenas.[96] For example, despite growing union activism during the period, Health/PAC's own work with unions on health and safety issues, and the increasingly strategic importance of unions in the area of occupational health and safety as well as in the fight for the public hospitals, Health/PAC did not reassess the role of unions in the *Bulletin*.

The question of constituency was raised as early as 1970.

Who we are is white, middle class, college trained. We can't organize blacks, the poor, blue collar workers. Anyhow these groups have their own organizations. We can do some things well, like research, talk, write. . . .We should aim at white, mid-America.[97]

Discussing Health/PAC's precarious financial situation in the mid-

1970s, one staff member spoke at length about Health/PAC (and the Left's) neglect of the middle class.

> Many on the health Left, like the women's movement, are not in-
> terested in us. We didn't appeal to people on the fringes of the Left,
> into nutrition or vitamins, although something was griping them. Or
> those into the free clinics. This was a very important movement. Many
> were involved, but we said little. My critique [of the free clinics] was
> fine as far as it went, but what it left out was the whole question of
> what it was subjectively that got people involved in free clinics. We
> made only a structural critique. This didn't and wouldn't make people
> involved in free clinics leave or deal with why people were there in the
> first place.[98]

Staff turnover was an on-going organizational problem, but it was as much a product of Health/PAC's career making function as it was a consequence of political struggle or economic need. When collectivity was at its height during 1971 and 1972, Health/PAC discussed and rejected the suggestion of collective signatures on books and articles. According to one staff member:

> Our prime reason for rejecting collective signature was our concern
> with accountability. Individuals should be held responsible for the
> research they had done. The converse was less discussed, that indi-
> viduals should get credit for their work. Although we did have a stong
> ideological sense that the collectivity had value for what it can do for
> its individuals.[99]

Drafts were collectively criticized until the politics became clear, but authorship remained individual. This enabled several members to establish reputations through their work at Health/PAC.[100]

Several staff members accused Health/PAC of political oppor-
tunism and a lack of critical focus: "We chose the community because that's where people were in motion. We were afraid to drop the community focus earlier for fear of losing funding."[101] The same criticism was also expressed about Health/PAC's approach to workers. Workers became objects of attention because they too were in motion, and they were closely scrutinized and treated initially, like the community, "as tools or agents of change for the Left."

Similar criticisms were voiced about Health/PAC's coverage of community and worker struggles. About Lincoln:

> I remember reading what they said about us and feeling it's not us.
> What I said was translated into non-ambivalent statements. Ultimately

this was very destructive. People read Health/PAC and came to Lincoln thinking the revolution was occurring.[102]

From the Lower East Side,

With Gouveneur all was seen as positive. We weren't critical enough. City hospitals were viewed as colonized territory by academic empires and patient/community activity against the empire was always reported optatively, never critically.[103]

One former staff member gave an example of Health/PAC's eulogistic appraisal of the United Harlem Drug Fighters: "Read what we wrote about them and compare it to the revelations about them later in the *New York Times*. Now we knew they were really evil, but we didn't care who they were."[104] While there was internal debate about the need for a more critical analysis, the criticism that did emerge tended to be criticism after the fact.[105] When Health/PAC's two agendas—the critical and the political—came into conflict, political needs won out.

Although Health/PAC was involved in many intellectual crosscurrents, it remained committed to mid-level critical analysis and unwilling to become either overly theoretical or practice oriented. Two internal struggles reflected this position. At Health/PAC's New York office, a losing battle was waged by a member who wanted to adopt a "more cultural analysis." The second conflict was between the New York office and a faction in the West Coast office. The West Coast office criticized Health/PAC's "heavy analytical style" oriented to middle-class professional readers. They became active as organizers, writing a Spanish-English newspaper for hospital workers and community groups. Health/PAC East accused the West Coast of having been taken over by a Marxist sect which wanted to serve minority and poverty groups as opposed to doing serious research.

The theory/practice issue took the form of a continuing debate: whether Health/PAC should move beyond a critical function of "opposing and exposing" to propose some sort of political program as a Left alternative.[106] Although individual members took such stances in support of the National Health Service/Dellums Bill or the public hospital system, the organization as a whole deferred from politics as well as organizing. One staff member said, "All around us there are the corpses of those who left us to organize and failed. They never came to grips with the intellectual and empirical questions."[107]

By sticking to "political analysis of concrete situations" however, Health/PAC did not escape the dilemmas of the organizers. One manifestation was the convergence of the federal government on Health/PAC's health empires analysis. A 1977 editorial noted that "public officials have for all appearances accepted Health/PAC's 'profits, prestige and politics' analysis of the private sector," and succinctly stated the problem for Left political analysts: "How will radicals distinguish themselves, in ideology and in struggle, from the ever-more-dominant forces of rationalization and reform? How can they use, and not be used by, these forces?"[108] Without a Left movement, the author argued, Left analysis would probably be absorbed into the liberal corporate social agenda.

THE EAST COAST HEALTH DISCUSSION GROUP: TOWARD A SOCIALIST MEDICINE

The emergence of the East Coast Health Discussion Group (ECHDG) and the publication of the Health Movement Organization packets were concrete expressions of the dissatisfaction and intellectual ferment that characterized the health Left in the mid-1970s.

The ECHDG had its origins in a conference on health called by the Union of Radical Political Economists (URPE) in New Haven in spring 1975. Stimulated by URPE's focus on health as an important and inadequately explored sector of American capitalist development, the response of the health Left was to seek a format to continue the discussion. In fall 1975, a group of about 30—of whom almost one-third were doctors—including members of Health/PAC, the Institute for Policy Studies, the American Public Health Association (APHA) Socialist Caucus, and URPE, began to meet every six weeks in various eastern cities.

The group's objective was "to publish, to popularize, to be a propaganda group—not just another organization group."[109] The ECHDG saw itself as the nucleus of a Health Movement Organization (HMO), an organization which would serve as a "network for Marxist analysis in health" and as an "interchange" for study groups across the country, issuing "periodic mailings of theoretical papers, reports on organizing projects and commentary on praxis."[110] The first packet, mailed to 400 in the spring of 1976, proposed the HMO framework, presented an explicit socialist perspective and called for intellectual work to inform politics.

In contrast to Health/PAC's mid-range political analysis of concrete organizations and events, HMO, had an explicitly theoretical orientation. Members were determined to go beyond the guilt-ridden anti-intellectualism of the 1960s and "do our thing." "We

came in and said, god-damn it, we'll be a group of theoreticians."[111]
The reasons were clear:

> From virtually every strategic perspective, the prevailing radical analy-
> sis of health appeared insufficient. Either the medical delivery system—
> used interchangeably with 'health'—was viewed statically as an object
> of retrenchment and we were called to 'Fight Cutbacks!' or a monolithic
> 'Health Empire' was conjured up which greedily hoarded money and
> power like some multimedia Kong. So, we decided that developing
> theory was the most relevant practice.[112]

In contrast to Health/PAC's avoidance of Marxist terminology, the
ECHDG would explicitly make use of Marxist analysis:

> Not all of us are Marxists; nor are these packets directed to Marxists.
> But most of us are self-consciously trying to employ Marxist methods
> to move beyond liberal and radical analyses of health.[113]

In contrast to the closed nature of the Health/PAC editorial collective, HMO would be an "open forum for ideas," a publication of
"works-in-progress." The ECHDG reprinted its own reading list in
the first packet and called for local study groups to form, enter into
dialogue, and publish their own works-in-progress. There were over
100 responses to the first mailing, and by the second packet, feedback from newly formed or existing groups.

The history of the ECHDG falls into two parts: a period of
"creative discussion" and production. Then, beginning in 1977 and
1978, a period characterized by membership turnover, organizational
change and a sense of drift. Between 1975 and 1979, the group put
out four packets: the first packet was a collection of "introductory
papers" which outlined basic areas of critical inquiry;[114] the second
and third packets presented a theory and methodology of health
and illness called historical materialist epidemiology; and the fourth
packet explored ideology in medicine.[115]

Toward a Socialist Model

Taken together, the ideas put forward in the packets constituted a
new paradigm for the health Left. Critical of Health/PAC's tendency
to focus on mid-level empirical analysis and remain rather vague
about the larger context of health politics, the ECHDG located the
problem squarely at the level of the political economy and called for
a "socialist" not a "socialized" medicine.[116] The cover letter to the
first packet proclaimed:

> We see the existing health system as ultimately based in, or an extension of, the pervading capitalist structure, and we think it is counter-productive to try to understand and contemplate strategies for change in the health system, without wider social change.

Distinguishing itself from Health/PAC, the ECHDG called attention to the more complex role of the state and to the subtleties of ideological hegemony in advanced capitalist society. Influential neo-Marxist writers listed in the ECHDG bibliography, (*HMO Packet* #1) included O'Connor, Poulantzas, and Gough on the role of the state and Althusser, Habermas, Gramsci, and Williams on culture and ideology.[117]

If American capitalism set the "boundary conditions for health and disease," then one must look for causation in the social relations of production.[118] The theory of historical materialist epidemiology (HME) put forward in *HMO Packet* #1, located disease within the social organization of a given society:

> HME maintains that the history of human disease is a single, non-repetitive process, which obeys discoverable laws and results from discoverable relationships. These relationships are essentially social in nature. It is the same social environment which forms the context within which we live that also forms the context within which disease arises.[119]

And within a given historical period, "the physics and chemistry of disease may recur again and again. But the causes of those phenomena and the reason for their spread are socially rooted and historical in nature."[120]

Proponents of this theory rooted it historically in the work of Engels and Virchow and distinguished it from biological explanations and liberal "social epidemiology."

> Epidemiology is the study of the distributions and determinants of states of health in human populations. What differentiates materialist epidemiology from bourgeois social epidemiology is the attempt to relate the patterns of disease and illness in a society to the economic and social relations which are the determinants of the functioning of that society.[121]

Devoid of its radical roots in a critique of society, they argued that social epidemiology lent itself to individual units of analysis such as lifestyles, and had been used by liberals and progressives in the 1960s to "buttress the war on poverty programs."[122] Applying HME to the examination of coronary heart disease, Peter Schnall argued that HME began where social epidemiology left off; that while social epidemiological models elaborated a series of risk factors such as cigarette smoking and personality type and marked an advance over biological models,

> the task for HME is to explore the basis for each of the identified risk factors for coronary heart disease. Each of these risk factors have specific historical and socioeconomic determinants which are rooted in the mode of production and social relations generated thereby, and are unique to modern capitalism in America and a greater or lesser extent to Western Europe.[123]

Central to HME was the concept of stress:

> Stress arises when the human system is called upon to behave in a way such that the person either is unable to behave in that way or is uncertain of the behavior. The body experiences changes in the distribution of the blood and other physiological occurrences. Gradually the body returns to its pre-stress condition. Over time, chronic stressful conditions can cause permanent pathological conditions—hypertension, chronic heart disease, etc. This is the chemistry of stress and is experienced similarly by most. However the cause of stress and the type of stress vary depending on the social organizations within the society.[124]

Social stress was put forward as "the most common alternative understanding of disease causation in recent social science and medical literature," and was identified as a "major problem today."[125] Working conditions, unemployment, family disorganization, were all mediated by the body through stress.

HME was seen as a critical tool by the health Left, a theoretical construct which countered the tendency to depoliticize health-related phenomena.[126] Applied to the field of occupational health, a field developed by health activists, HME led to a critique of then current forms of activism for having "narrowed" the definition of work and occupational health to immediately dangerous work conditions amenable to worker control or medical benefits. A critical perspective suggested that work be broadened to include all productive activity and that the fight for occupational health "must be determined in myriad struggles in and out of the workplace, which have nothing to do with medicine or safety, but challenge the relations of production," because "heart disease, stroke, alcoholism and cancer" were "occupational diseases of post-World War II social capital in the same way that black and brown lung are the diseases of competitive capital."[127]

HME's proponents claimed that in addition to underlining the failures and limitations of scientific or "bourgeois" medicine, HME had explanatory power in its own right.[128] According to one sociologist of science, it was in epidemiology and occupational health that it was becoming obvious that there were "at least two sciences." Epidemiology—coming under attack from inside and outside medicine, and occupational health—generally devalued within scientific medicine, were central to a new "socialist medicine" that starts "not with tissues in a laboratory but with the social relations of production."[129]

While HMO packets contained political and economic as well as cultural analyses, reflecting different and conflicting perspectives within the ECHDG, HMO's particular contribution was its exploration of ideological aspects of medicine and health.[130] Having expanded the domain of ideology to the very core of scientific medicine, modes of diagnosis and even the model of the human body, were seen to harbor assumptions that obscured social responsibility and attributed individual blame.[131] Scientific medicine was described as a historical product rather than a true reading of nature. This meant that rather than a science, "medicine is a social science subject to all the weaknesses and biases that the other social sciences have."[132]

The turn to ideology as a cutting edge also reflected an attempt to come to grips with the experience of socialist countries.

> We must begin to critique the myth that medicine is 'objective science' because changing the delivery or financing of medical care will not change the nature of medicine. The experience of the socialist countries, with the possible exception of China, clearly bears this out.[133]

One of several articles that examined the Chinese experience confirmed the critical role of ideology and ideological struggle. Despite the revolution, the Chinese health system did not change until a massive ideological campaign disseminated a new definition of health along with an army of health workers.[134] Similar conclusions were drawn from the American experience. Assessing liberal and Left health programs, Sander Kelman concluded:

> The most important struggles currently going on in health are ideological; this includes not only the struggle for 'correct' ideas, but also the struggle for the definition and selection of legitimate 'consumers' for placement on and control of HSAs [Health Systems Agencies].[135]

Workshop to Network?

By spring 1978, ECHDG was adrift. HMO publication was suspended because it had become too labor intensive[136] and the group recruited new members and experimented with a new format. As one member noted, in making the commitment to "being a group of theoreticians," ECHDG did not escape the syndrome of "Left guilt over praxis." This took two forms—commitment to movement building and questions of identity or "where to?"

One of ECHDG's objectives had been to organize the health Left into a federation of study groups dialoguing through an exchange of packets of work-in-progress. Several reasons were given for why this did not happen. Some felt that HMO papers had become "pre-papers" for journals in the field.[137] Others noted the use of Marxist and academic jargon. The enthusiastic response to the first packet was mixed with criticisms as well as questions about how to translate the theoretical work into political strategy for those committed to local action.

Even though the HMOs were successfully being used by groups to organize, there was no commitment to sustained collective practice. One factor was HMO's political diversity.[138] About one-third of the group played an active role in writing the Dellums Bill for a National Health Service; one-third were the nucleus for the APHA Socialist Caucus—a growing arena for health activists with a much broader outreach; and others were involved in struggles around municipal cutbacks and occupational health. The conclusion was that

> while we continue to share and debate our activities, we still feel too tentative individually and professionaly or too committed to local groups and struggles to formalize a collective politics we can organize others around.[139]

ECHDG's relation to existing health movements was also made difficult by its criticism of them. *HMO Packet* #3 published an analysis of occupational health projects based on "the empirical and historical discussions taking place within historical materialist epidemiology." The article concluded:

> Occupational Health Project strategists rarely treat health as an important theoretical issue—consensus is assumed on the meaning of health —let alone debate how rank and file struggles on issues other than health can generate the preconditions for eliminating illness. Instead, persons who are extremely radical on a range of other issues carry the

most banal conceptions of illness, medicine and health to the work-place.[140]

Similar issues were raised with the growing holistic health movement. While holistic health had the potential to be a popular base for a "people's health strategy," in its current form it was criticized for being "individualistic" and "apolitical"; for lending itself to governmental victim-blaming strategies; and for creating new professionals, esoteric knowledge, and further medicalizing life.[141] Although the group as a whole agreed about the importance of critical analysis and debate, in the case of occupational health and holistic health, there were differing opinions as to whether the movements could be redirected and given progressive political content. Those who argued they could, felt the HMO analysis was hard on current efforts and unrealistic in its suggestions.

Identity and commitment also became issues. During its early period, ECHDG was formally a workshop for ideas and informally a social and professional network. As publication made individual members professionally visible and as the ECHDG went into a less creative and more routine phase, other activities displaced ECHDG for its members. In spring 1978, the ECHDG reorganized itself into workgroups, each responsible for an HMO packet, but the workgroups did not work: "Six weeks was not enough time to produce a joint theoretical work." Another person commented, "We couldn't find anything we wanted to do together." Requiring output put off newcomers as well as old members for whom "it wouldn't come together." Having become oriented to producing the HMO packets, there was a feeling that without it, the group might not be legitimate.[142]

ECHDG's difficulties must also be given historical context. The Health Services and Policy workgroup fell apart during 1978 and 1979 when its members could not decide on a project. All agreed that part of the problem was the "lack of national level movement."[143] At the same time, the Sex, Culture and Everyday Life workgroup became a sort of catchall, reflecting, some felt, the depoliticization and drift within the radical community itself. As one person succinctly put it, "We tend to blame dropping out on the group, but times have changed."[144]

Apart from organizational and contextual issues, the emerging model of a socialist medicine itself raised questions within the group. By helping to delegitimize scientific medicine, activists expressed concern that they had opened the way to a series of new threats: a resurgence of right wing reactionary movements around self-help and folk health; the imposition of federal programs that would substitute less costly, nonmedical models particularly for minority and poor clients; and new structures of specialization based on the self-help, environmental, and holistic health movements.

A multifactoral model with complex social causation implied different research methods, actors, and outputs. A socialist medicine which started with the analysis of the social relations of reproduction, not "tissues in a lab," might not require doctors or scientists.[145] For example, an occupational health researcher studying cancer in a steel mill, might begin with a collective discussion rather than individual questionnaires or physical examinations, assuming that one can not easily separate objective from subjective information or emphasize the scientific importance of one set of data at the expense of the other.[146] A new understanding of the relation between stress and heart disease led to a suggestion that hypertension not be medically treated, particularly among minorities and the poor, because medical treatment further obscured its social, economic, and political causation. A broad preventative approach to health made traditional medical practice neither desirable nor a cutting edge of change. In contrast to liberal strategies which called for an expanded medical sector, these examples suggested a more limited and ambiguous role for traditional health workers and for the traditional health sector.

Finally, health problems redefined in terms of social structural arrangements required large-scale social change—adequate jobs, housing, and food in addition to a clean environment and a reorganized production line. This meant that they ran the danger of remaining a Utopian vision, leaving health activists to decide how to relate to those fighting for relief from inequities of access, quality, and delivery of care within the current health system.

Taken as a whole, activist strategy became more, not less, problematic with the advent of a new paradigm. With the scientific model, conflicting interests seldom surfaced. It was assumed that all wanted better health and that scientific and technological developments produced better health. This meant that the costs of renal dialysis were not weighed against increased welfare benefits. But as activists moved toward a socialist model, conflicting interests became more explicit. This meant that issues such as controlling hazardous wastes or limiting the growth of the nuclear industry could pit the working class against the middle class on the issue of jobs versus health.[147]

Part III

The Politics of
Professional Knowledge

8

The Political Significance
of Activism

Advocacy and reform efforts became politicized and changed over time. Although there were considerable differences between medicine and planning, these differences did not substantially affect activists' political strategies. But they did affect outcomes. This chapter examines the impact of organizational differences (particularly the organization of knowledge) on outcomes. Chapter 9 looks at the common trajectory of activists' political strategies.

The same strategies were not equally effective in planning and medicine and the overall significance of activism also differed. Planners and doctors mobilized at both workplace and community sites but planners had relatively more success in the community while doctors were more successful in the workplace. This can be better understood by examining the nature of health care and plans as goods and the comparative institutional strength of doctors and planners.

Health care and plans as goods. Low-income and minority communities were more concerned about housing than health care and more interested in defending what they had, than in making new demands. The explanation seemed to be that communities more typically viewed neighborhoods and housing as *collective goods* much as Mancur Olson has used the term. *Collective goods* are defined in relation to specific groups and in regard to the feasibility of excluding potential consumers.[1] Moreover, urban renewal posed a direct threat to preexisting homes and neighborhoods. Whether it was communities which organized first to protest renewal plans, or planners and others who took the initiative and organized and mobilized communities, the issue—defense of the collective home or neighborhood—was a direct and immediate concern to the communities involved.

In contrast, health care was typically viewed by low-income and minority communities as individual or noncollective and most health care actions involved the creation of new as opposed to the defense of existing health care facilities.[2] These distinctions shed light on the community's support for health care facilities as "job centers." When viewed as jobs, health care became a more collectively defined good which carried individual incentives as well as collective benefits.[3]

Health care had other disadvantages as a mobilizing issue for activists. Health was typically viewed as the secondary consequence of more immediate and collective needs for housing and jobs. Moreover, people tended to be concerned about health care only when they were sick, and when they were sick, they could not mobilize. This meant that whereas part of the impetus for planning advocacy came from low-income and minority clients, in medicine, the clients tended to be apathetic and the impetus most often came from medical activists.

Because low-income communities viewed health care in terms of jobs, health care engendered more conflict than did planning. Not only did health activists find that the community was "conservative," they also concluded that health was a "poor cover" for social change. But as planning issues shifted from defense to offense—from urban renewal threats to community development strategies—planners began to experience many of the same patterns of conflicting interests as did health activists. Conversely, when health care issues became more collective and defensive as in battles for participation and control of ongoing neighborhood health centers staffed with community workers, or during New York City's fiscal crisis in the mid-1970s, when the public hospital system came under attack, there was more community mobilization and support.

Social analysts from such differing political perspectives as Daniel Bell and Manuel Castells have argued that social and political conflict in contemporary society will shift from struggles over production to struggles over patterns of allocation or consumption.[4] The consumer campaigns associated with Naderism as well as urban political movements around housing and schools have been cited as examples of this trend. Although the case studies in this book show that many of the activist organizations began as struggles over allocation—over the distribution of outcomes—their developmental histories suggest a countertrend. Low-income and minority clients often pushed activists beyond giving services (redistribution of consumer goods) to challenge the relations of production and political dominance. Thus, what began as struggles over distribution often became struggles over control (jobs, career tracks) and then over production systems (who makes the decisions).

Upon inspection, many of the consumption and distribution issues that mobilized communities turned out to be either production or production/distribution issues. In the area of health services, activists had trouble getting community and clients involved in health care unless jobs were involved. In planning, community groups were similarly interested in gaining decision making power. In neither sector were consumption issues alone central to conflict. This suggests that theoretical attempts to distinguish struggles over consumption and distribution from production are somewhat artificial as well as politically problematic.

Both Bell and Castells view government intervention into service delivery as central to subsequent social and political conflict. This is certainly true in terms of the overall context of professional activism. It is also true that government sponsored projects made for widespread and sustained disenchantment both due to their size and scope and to the increased opportunity to experience daily the workings of the system. But when the range of activist efforts is examined, it is evident that conflict has been associated with all types of service delivery, not just governmental programs. Furthermore, the same kinds of problems arose in independent as well as in sponsored efforts and in politically radical as well as liberal projects.

Theorists also argue that the emergence of struggles over the distribution of services allows classes to unite in political action.[5] This case material suggests that issues retain their class character in the service sector and that political mobilization and action have been problematic at best. Different groups had differing views and objectives with regard to services and putting forth a unified perspective was difficult. Mobilization was hampered by multiple divisions along both status and class lines. Finally, although mobilization around consumption issues was in the direction of a multiclass and multidisciplinary constituency, it was the work of activists and involved their sustained criticism of professional knowledge and social function. It has not followed the populist or class formations predicted by either Bell or Castells. Furthermore, it has been accompanied by its own contradictions for both analysis and action.

Knowledge, expertise, and institutional strength. Another factor influencing outcomes was the relative strength of doctors, compared to planners, in the workplace. This is related to their control of knowledge (standardized models and methods, credentialing, etc.) independent of the bureaucratic context. Doctors also dominate the division of labor in health care. This makes their activities highly salient to their employers and central to the ongoing economy of their employing organizations.[6] The resulting organizational strength has meant that doctors will fight at the workplace on the basis of claims to knowledge when their political control is threatened.[7] This has also meant that activist doctors could draw upon the institutional strength of their own occupation even as they challenged its basis.

Along these lines, the case studies show that activist doctors functioned more successfully than planners in workplace collectives and in unions. The collective I studied won control of its department. The housestaff unions in which activists mobilized increased membership, political commitment, and shifted from a primarily economic agenda to a broader and more political set of demands including training, work control, and patient care.

Planners, in comparison, do not control their knowledge independently of their organizational context. Their career aspirations as well as actual careers often fall within line as opposed to staff positions. Their product is politically defined, subject to political interpretation, and requires political implementation. As Glazer has noted, planners represent a "minor" or subordinate profession.[8] Weak in the organizational environment, planners have had less workplace success and have needed the support of the community for political clout. The same factors have made bureaucratic reform cooptive for planners. Their collective was effective only when asked by community groups to support its efforts. The planners could not mobilize other planners nor create community support for subsequent political or workplace issues, and unionization has been ineffective.

The limits of difference.   Although these outcomes illustrate the continuing relevance of structural differences between medicine and planning, particularly those differences related to the organization of knowledge, these differences seemed to hold *only up to a point.* Political autonomy was both more fragile than activists initially thought and less decisive in terms of their objectives.

Doctors who won workplace issues in both collectives and unions, found that organizations had the ability to endure and outwait them; to transfer decision making from one level to the next; and to redefine political issues as technical or economic so that demands of time, money, and space often foreclosed innovations they had won on political grounds.

Doctors also learned that their autonomy at the workplace was superseded by political and economic events at higher levels. For example, the New York City fiscal crisis revealed the dependence of doctors' autonomy upon economic and political conditions outside the worksite. Activists saw that winning political control of a department, or winning an effective citywide union contract for housestaff, or even saving a particular public hospital, were, in turn, overridden by threats to the whole public sector generated by economic constraint. At this point, doctors like planners, also needed to mobilize the community for political support.

The viability of political roles. Another factor which contributed to the differing outcomes was that the community was more critical of politicized doctors than planners. This relates to the shared perception of medicine's "scientific" and apolitical nature and to the fact that clients felt that doctors had a clearly revelant technical role to which legitimacy was accorded. Planners, in contrast, were more commonly linked to political processes and both the planners' role and expertise were poorly defined.

This finding suggests a dysfunction of medicine's superior cognitive base. The narrow and clearly defined knowledge base made it easier to challenge activist doctors when they stepped out of line. It was also used against them by clients and sponsors to restrict their attempts to expand scope and role. Jamous and Peloille have described the double-edged function of a narrow technical knowledge in a similar manner. They found that technicality helps a profession gain autonomy but at the cost of representing a condition for outside intervention.[9] These case studies suggest another duality: that while technicality furthers the cause of professional autonomy, it makes certain kinds of internal change—such as broadening or politicizing professional knowledge and role—difficult and even impossible.

Planners, in contrast, had less trouble becoming and remaining political. Although their political activity was circumscribed, they institutionalized a community organizing role. An additional factor of significant comparative advantage for planners in the community was that federal legislation from the late 1950s on made planning a legislatively defined channel for federal funds. This gave planners important positions in the community in comparison to their weak positions in work organizations.

The other side of the coin was that activist doctors and health science students did not deprofessionalize to the extent that planners did. Few left medicine entirely. Dropping out in medicine tended to mean dropping down—finding low-status areas within health as opposed to nonhealth-related employment. This was not only a response to differences in length of training, prestige, salary, and work satisfaction. The adoption of critical research as a primary activist role posed an ideological conflict for medical activists alienated by the ascendancy of scientific research and academic goals in medical school. Many sought a return to service. This meant that working in the community was politically legitimate, while research —political as well as scientific—was viewed as a "cop-out." In contrast to doctors, planners had less of an investment in training and less clearly defined career lines. Typically moving from job to job, planners did not experience the gap between alternate and main line careers which was so marked in medicine.

ACTIVIST PROFESSIONAL MOVEMENTS
IN CONTEXT

When activist professional movements are placed in their historical and developmental context, not only do outcomes differ, but so does the overall political significance of activism for planning and medicine.

In planning, activism in the 1960s appeared in response to the impact of federal programs such as urban renewal on minorities and the poor. Federal legislation, which directed planners to redevelop slums and blighted areas and to relocate the poor, led to the subsequent displacement of poor people from their homes to the advantage of commercial interests. This gave rise to a *crisis of legitimacy* for planning—a confrontation between professed ideals and real social out-comes.[10]

In Chapter 2, planning was described as a "new" profession, a product of increasing state intervention over the past 50 years. This close identification with government has been contradictory for planning; it has been both a source of growth as well as criticism. It has meant that planning has been invidiously linked with both socialism at the national level (the New Deal) and with the politics of zoning at the local level. While the post-World War II period marked the beginning of what was to be a "golden age" for planning, a period of growth and expansion related, in part, to legislatively defined opportunities, the widespread criticism of urban renewal posed a check to postwar expectations for continued growth and expansion.

What ensued was an internal crisis as well as a public outcry. The failure to ask whether a slum was a home set off a round of self-criticism among planners. If the mainstream of physically oriented planners had failed to perceive the difference, then it was necessary to broaden the planning model to include social, psychological, and economic aspects—to create a social as opposed to a physical or land use planning. Within planning, an academically based, social science oriented segment of the profession had been proposing just such a broadened model. Activists who questioned the traditional claim to serve a unified public interest turned to strategies which served targeted groups of clients. Whether there was a unified public interest, it had become clear that certain groups had no one planning in their interest.

Activists' initial attempts at social reform and advocacy, were also attempts to remove barriers to expanding opportunities by creating new models, new practice options, and new sources of community support for planners—an identity and a degree of autonomy apart from government bureaucracies. From a developmental perspective, liberal and reform-minded planners pursued a strategy of professionalization.

Medical activism in the 1960s appeared as a response to the gap between science and service—also a crisis of legitimacy. Federal funding had enabled postwar medicine to become technologically sophisticated and scientifically oriented, yet, at the same time, each large medical center was surrounded by community populations which did not see a doctor during an average year. Medical students felt alienated from patient care. Broader social issues pertaining to the delivery and financing of health care or whether the boundaries of health care included abortions and drug use were not openly discussed in the medical school curriculum, nor was the discomforting fact that the organization and practice of American medicine was racially segregated for many clients and practitioners.

American medicine had been dominated by a conservative, entrepreneurial elite represented, organizationally, by the AMA. Until the 1960s, the AMA was able to forestall federal underwriting of services and to limit government intervention to funding research and hospital construction. Medical care was organized as a two-track system, with fee-for-service care in the private sector for those who could pay and charity care in the public sector for those who could not. It claimed to give equal care to all who needed care.

In the postwar period, a growing civil rights and student movement and urban unrest, along with the increased introduction of federal funds into the privately controlled system, generated internal criticism directed at unequal outcomes, the scientific priorities of American medicine, and the conservative policies of the AMA. The proponents of change were a socially minded group of physicians, mostly academically based, and a new generation of medical students. Like their counterparts among the planners, they also sought a broadened social medicine which gave attention to service as a priority. In the face of adamant AMA opposition to health care insurance, the activist strategy was to link up with a progressive federal government to expand services and to encourage other innovations in the organization and delivery of care. It was a strategy of bureaucratization.

Alford's analytic description of underlying structural interests— social, economic, and political forces that are dominant, challenging, and repressed—helps clarify the particular alignments within each profession and the resulting difference in strategies of change.[11] In medicine, the dominant interests were "professional monopolists" represented by the AMA, and the challenging groups aligned themselves with "corporate rationalizers" represented by the government, the American Association of Medical Colleges (AAMC), and the American Hospital Association (AHA). In planning, the dominant interests can be described as corporate rationalizers aligned with the state and the challenging forces as aspiring professionals.

Although the AMA's hold was broken, academic and corporate medical interests (represented by the AHA and the AAMC) rose in their place along with increased governmental regulation and control. This was due, in part, to the fact that medicine in the postwar period has been a key sector for economic growth. This has led to government and corporate intervention to rationalize and control costs as well as to break the power of the professional monopolists represented by the AMA. Planning, which has been under greater governmental control, has not been as contradictory or as consequential (until recently).[12] Consequently, government intervention has attempted to reform planning but never to attack it in the same way that medicine has been attacked.

Medical activists initially felt threatened by professional monopolists and aligned themselves with the government in the attempt to initiate change. Over time, the threat became government and corporate rationalization and an increasing impetus to action has been the loss of autonomy in the workplace. In planning, activism has been more concerned with ideological struggles for legitimation that serve the cause of profession building.

Although the alignment of underlying structural interests differed, both cases illustrate the tenuous location of professions between the state and major class interests. Both cases show how liberal and reform elements in medicine and planning attempted to renegotiate these linkages by redesigning service delivery and knowledge, how they attempted to position themselves within their respective professions so as to gain degrees of freedom of action. We cannot understand the changing fortunes of these professions over the past few decades without looking at the role of internal movements in generating and shaping change.

In summary, the structural and historical differences between medicine and planning did affect outcomes. Planners were more successful in the community and doctors in the workplace. The analysis of these findings suggests that although medicine's superior knowledge base and control of its knowledge independent of organizational context gave activist doctors strength in their institutional environment, it proved to be a liability for them as political actors. Clients and sponsors were better able to restrict them to their clearly defined and "relevant" technical roles.

However, these differences seemed to hold only up to a point. Activist doctors discovered that their work autonomy was neither as secure as they had believed nor as decisive regarding outcomes. When issues escalated from the level of a department or a hospital to the public hospital system as a whole, victories were converted to paper wins, and doctors, like planners, found that in the face of large-scale economic and political forces they needed to mobilize the community for political support.

A similar point can be made in comparing health care and plans. Although a plan seems to be as far from health care as one can go and still deliver services and although the community response to these services differed, when health care was provided collectively and came to mean jobs, status, and control, as well as services, and when planners produced plans with, and for, specific community groups, these very different products became more structurally alike and thus subject to similar forces and struggles.

Finally, activism in planning took the form of professionalization, and in medicine, bureaucratization, because the underlying constellation and linkage of structural interests differed. This suggests that the similarities of activists' political strategies resulted from conflict; that they represent dialectical and not convergent patterns. To the extent that both medicine and planning became involved in delivering services to minorities and the poor, they were both caught up in similar struggles relating to knowledge, service, and autonomy.

9

The Problem of
Professional Knowledge

Despite the structural and historical differences between medicine and planning, activists faced similar problems and adopted similar strategies. Although their overt aim was to weaken or radically transform professionalism—defined as claims to knowledge, value neutrality and autonomy—they ended up supporting it in unexpected ways.

The changing ideologies and strategies of these activist organizations reflect the basic character of professionalism; in particular, the constraints of occupations whose prerogatives are based on claims to knowledge. The central dilemma for activists was their dependence on claims to privileged knowledge. Whether these claims were challenged by community clients or discredited by radical ideology, the loss of these claims meant an unexpected loss of legitimacy as actors. What was at stake was the ability to work, not only status and prestige.

New clients—low-income and minorities—are important to this tale for their role in redefining and challenging professional knowledge, and more generally, for questioning the rationality of activists' political assumptions. While these particular interactions have given activist politics a certain direction and flavor, the focus of this concluding chapter is on what activism in turn reveals about the nature of the professions. This chapter describes the challenges posed by new clients, examines the emergence of a radical critique of professional knowledge among activists, and explains their shifting political strategies by the constraints posed by attempts to combine political and professional roles.

NEW CLIENTS AND MODELS OF THE COMMUNITY

Most analyses of the professions have focused on the problem of controlling the producers and creating a market monopoly.[1] In locating conditions under which institutional control of the professions is challenged or breaks down, most studies have ignored how changes in the social composition of clients become a source of internal criticism and change.[2]

Beginning in the late 1950s, low-income and minority groups became categorically defined clients for doctors and city planners. Federal legislation targeted them as the subjects and objects of services through such programs as urban renewal, the Hill-Burton Act and the War on Poverty legislation, and created new channels of service delivery such as Neighborhood Health Centers, Medicaid, and OEO-funded advocacy planning. Activists also selected these clients on the basis of need. These clients, however, proved to be a continuing source of conflict and criticism. At the same time, the interaction was a collective experience for a generation of professionals and raised their political consciousness regarding their role and function.

Activists started with two political assumptions: that low-income and minority communities were "rational" but unserved and that activists' professional and political interests were not necessarily at odds. But as activists worked with minorities and the poor, these unexamined assumptions were challenged and proved inadequate or wrong.

First, activists found that medical and planning services had unexpectedly *low salience* for low-income and minority communities as measured by support for issues related to these services. The exceptions were cases in which urban renewal threats to destroy homes had led to community mobilization before advocates took on these causes.[3] But more often than not, the community was found to be relatively indifferent to activist efforts on their behalf. This was true not only for planning, but for health care, which had been thought to be of such universal importance. Activists typically found health a matter of concern "only when people are sick," and when, paradoxically, they were unable to organize around medical issues.

Activists also discovered that health care and planning meant different things to low-income and minority communities. They felt that services were commonly viewed "instrumentally"—in terms of stratification and social mobility. Planners learned that community groups were as interested in gaining power as in specific outcomes. In several cases, doctors who met with community groups to initiate health centers found, "to their surprise," that the groups were not interested in health care for its "intrinsic value," but that the health center had appeal as a "job center."

Finally, as low-income and minority communities organized,

which was, in part, a response to activist efforts, they began to criticize the advocates as well as the professional establishment. Finding themselves left out of technical discussions and procedures, they pointed to racial, class, and cultural biases in the definition of the ends and means of technical aid.[4] One advocacy organization which prepared alternate plans and statistical presentations as a defense against official relocation plans was criticized by its client groups because of their "hard to read" technicality and "nonfeeling" way of dealing with the issues. This led to a revised strategy in which the community directly pressured the relevant public agency to represent their interests and advocate planners were relegated to a back-seat role.

Instead of technical aid, some community groups demanded the transfer of technical knowledge along with participation and control. Community helpers on a hypertension screening program were hired to introduce the health workers to the community. First, they demanded equal pay and supervisory control because "we are teaching you health workers about our community." Later they demanded the skills to do the screening themselves. Community groups also began to demand that federal funds be channelled directly to them and not through a layer of service providers.

The disparity between professional expectations and community views made for a much more complex reality. It exposed the lack of consensus about supposedly universally held values and raised the possibility that many of these assumptions were class based and occupationally self-serving.[5] Middle-class activists, many of whom were professional idealists, were forced to recognize that their credentials represented a basis for exploitation. The professions possessed scarce and valued resources: both services (which along with income and property were a primary mode of social stratification) and positions (entry into which was controlled and which provided good livings, carried social prestige and promised career mobility). Finally, the diagnoses of experts were the labels that controlled wide areas of social life and carried enormous symbolic power.

Given their initial expectations, categorically defined clients, and new work situations, it is not surprising that many professionals became increasingly self-critical. C. Wright Mills has noted that professional groups are typically locked into individualistic methods and concepts both by training and practice. Their experience presents them with a "scatter of individual situations" and denies them the chance to see the social structure as a whole.[6] These experiences changed as they began working with clients defined collectively by economic criteria, in federal programs such as poverty or urban renewal or in independent advocacy organizations and free clinics. All of these programs either failed to achieve their objectives, or in part, benefited the very groups they set out to reform. The consequence was that these professionals adopted a progressively more structural perspective. They dropped their initial notion of institutional malfunctioning and began to view professional services and roles more systematically, in terms of social, political, and ideological functions.

THE EMERGENCE OF A RADICAL CRITIQUE
OF PROFESSIONAL KNOWLEDGE

At the heart of the relationship between activists and their clients were issues related to knowledge. Even critics of the professions such as Freidson and Larson have assumed the stability of professional knowledge and its resistance to encroachments of bureaucratic authority. For both Freidson and Larson, the strength of a given knowledge base rests on a combination of inherent (abstract versus commonsense knowledge) as well as political factors. Freidson stated that managerial control of knowledge based labor was limited "by the very nature of the skill and knowledge it possesses and by its tendency to organize itself into stable occupations."[7] Larson found that the cognitive base of a given profession was the key intervening variable in determining the nature of its market control over labor and services.[8] Concerned with the organization of professions and the use of knowledge to obtain sheltered positions in the labor market, both ignored the possible development of critical knowledge which could attack a dominant paradigm's claims to scientific and objective status as "interested," not just inaccurate. Along the same lines neither of them foresaw political radicalization coming from within the professions.[9]

While Starr argued that medicine has undergone a significant erosion of professional authority including claims to knowledge, he emphasized the failure to satisfy claims in undermining public confidence, not knowledge per se. Furthermore, the sources of declining confidence are for the most part external—consumers, government, and corporate interests. Medicine's contribution has been its self-aggrandizing behavior. In his scenario, activists play a minor and somewhat programmatic role in a process whose motive force is cost containment. This accords with his prediction of a serious threat, if not the literal end, to professional dominance with the "coming of the corporation."[10]

These case studies of activist organizations over an 18-year period show a different picture: the destabilization of the central core of professional knowledge and the role of activist professionals in initiating and facilitating this process. As we have seen, delivery strategies did not set out to challenge claims to professional knowledge or to hand over control to client communities. Activists sought to broaden this strategy by introducing economic, social, and psychological aspects of medicine and planning. These "social reform" models emphasized the linkage between new knowledge and social change and criticized establishment professionals for their ivory tower isolation, for their focus on science not service, and for assuming that interests were equitably served. But the new clients were political realists who viewed skills as commodities and power. Working for poor and minority communities, often in federally funded programs, set the stage for the contradictions that emerged from advocate efforts. Along with their clients, activists began to view their technical aid as a form of control and began to question the efficacy of technical expertise in solving the problems before them.

Some of the most incisive criticism of both advocacy planning and patient advocacy came from first generation advocates. Planners, for example, found that advocacy was not the solution to the problems of planning but raised many of the same issues in microcosm—at the level of the community. Who are the clients? What are the issues? Whose definition of the problem should be used?[11] If advocates working in communities with broader professional models did not solve these problems, then perhaps the problems were related to factors other than the narrow scope of knowledge or the limitations of service delivery?

It became a commonplace among health advocates that their services were neither community priorities nor necessarily the most efficacious means to a given end. "Jobs, housing and the elimination of police brutality" were more essential to improving daily life than health. Futhermore, if lead poisoning was related to poor housing and poor housing was related to lack of jobs and income, then efficacy dictated political mobilization, not one-to-one treatment. One doctor put it this way: "After working as a patient advocate for four of the families in the building, I decided that an effort should be made to confront the landlord and make him pay for his negligence."

Even where specific health problems were a priority, one-to-one strategies such as patient advocacy and technical aid were criticized for being slow and ineffective means to a given end. Advocacy was also criticized for engendering dependence. While advocacy might pay off in outcomes during the time that projects were funded and in place, activists felt that in the long run, communities were left more dependent upon outside professional help. Like planners, doctors came to believe that their analysis and strategy were wrong. In the words of one doctor at the conclusion of his project, "We are treating a symptom, rather than the cause."

In the context of ongoing experience, many activists reconceptualized their function. If medicine and planning were less important priorities to communities than to professionals, then why were they being funded? For what purpose? They began to revise their view of what was wrong with medicine and planning. Rather than poorly functioning systems, they began to speak of systematic structural biases. Rather than blaming conservative professional elites, critical attention turned to a combination of elite and state domination.

Activists started with a model of the community as rational but unserved. Rejecting the traditional professional model in which claims to legitimacy rest upon expertise, needed services, and autonomy (from elites, the state, and major class interests), many activists adopted a critical model in which medicine and planning played a mediating role vis-à-vis the federal government and the poor. This meant that providing services cooled out the dissent that might be used to change the system. Critical of their own reform efforts—whether federally sponsored or independent—for patching a system in need of more basic change, activists rejected technical service as a political strategy and turned to community organizing and empowerment.

Deprofessionalized strategies.   Community mobilization and empowerment did not prove more stable than delivery strategies for activists. Clients were neither a consistent source of support nor an effective agency of social change. Attempts to mobilize communities to demand their rights; to collapse distinctions between professionals, paraprofessionals, and clients; to transfer expertise; and to create community control through participatory democracy and decentralization were satisfactory neither to the activists, the community, nor the sponsors of reforms.

In abandoning claims to knowledge and adopting political roles, activist professionals found themselves without viable client or organizational bases. Mobilized communities rejected professionals in overt political roles as did their sponsors. Communities claimed that the adoption of political roles deprived them of power. Militant groups viewed these roles as expansionist and "neo-Colonial." These views were shared by less militant organizations. The director of a child care agency criticized the two doctors placed in her service. "We want them," she said, "as patient advocates—not as imitations of Cesar Chavez." A planning group was told: "The community has its own political leaders," and to "come back when you have something to offer us."

Activists discovered that they had romanticized the community, not only its unity and desire for service, but its degree of support for political action. Activists learned that when community members stepped into provider roles on health center boards, community housing corporations, or even as paraprofessionals, more often than not, they adopted the identity and interests of providers. One of the most innovative projects of a doctors' collective was to train "barefoot" doctors to work out of community storefronts. According to the director, the biggest issue for the project was its internal contradictions. The community workers did not want to remain outside the hospital. They wanted status inside the system. They also wanted their jobs to have career potential. A recurrent refrain among activist professionals was that the community was "conservative."

From the community's perspective, professionals who were politically radical were often found to be professionally conservative both with regard to defining the contents of services and in sharing expertise and control. The community organizer of one health clinic accused its radical medical staff of undermining the clinic's medical innovations which included independence from larger medical institutions. She felt that, medically, the staff wanted the more prestigious affiliation and tended to negate the importance of patient care reforms. She concluded, "Their support for radical community groups distracted them from the real health work." On the other hand, when community groups were politically radical, they posed other problems for activist professionals. Seeking to use activists and their services to gain power for their own ends, they were quite willing to make use of middle-class guilt.

Sponsors of activist efforts also reacted negatively. The federal government and medical and planning schools threatened to discontinue funding to many of the organizations which turned to political action. This further raised activists' political consciousness. They learned that sponsors were willing to support activities that quieted, not further inflamed, the ghettos. Activists turned toward professional constituencies and institutional sites both as federal funding for community efforts began to disappear and as it was rejected by activists.

Client based legitimacy proved organizationally as well as politically problematic. National organizations such as PEO and MCHR, which based their authority on service to low-income and minority clients, were adversely affected when repudiated by these clients. Unwilling to give leadership "to the people" and lacking an analysis which enabled them to act on their own behalf, they ran into difficulties. They felt coopted by their attempts to reform professional organizations and found themselves at the mercy of other equally volatile movements to which they had switched their allegiance. The problems of "serving" social and political movements reinforced the need for independent analysis, the search for other sources of legitimacy, and the turn from community to professional constituencies.

Finally, activists were themselves dissatisfied with community mobilization and empowerment. Within their own ranks, the rejection of technical expertise alienated many for whom legitimacy was based on putting the ideals of professional service into practice. Changes in the opportunity structure for activism—a more conservative political climate, declining federal funding, and increasingly fragmented social and political movements—coincided with the movement of a generation of activists through the life cycle. Having overestimated the community, participatory democracy, and decentralization, many found that they had underestimated their own needs for meaning, status, leadership, and making a living.

The adoption of overtly political and nontechnical roles led to an impasse. Activists discovered that their legitimacy before their clients was based on their narrow and "relevant" technical knowledge; before their sponsors, on their "apolitical" role and general social acceptance. This meant that in rejecting technical aid and adopting nontechnical roles on political grounds, activists undermined their legitimacy and thus their ability to act.

Reprofessionalization.   Viewed ideologically, strategies of social transformation presented a radical critique of traditional professional knowledge and methods; viewed structurally, however, they represented a return to more traditional client-professional relations characterized by renewed claims to knowledge, increased social distance from clients, and professionally defined service objectives.

To understand the reasons for this shift we need to see how activist professionals grounded their political action. Rein has proposed a typology of bases of legitimacy for change which provides a useful framework for this discussion. These are expertise, bureaucratic position, consumer (client) preference, and professional values.[12] Rein states that the typology is historically based but does not make explicit developmental claims. Expertise and bureaucratic position are respectively, pre- and post-World War II rationales for change;

consumer preference and professional values are associated with the late 1950s, 1960s, and the 1970s.

The case studies show that "who we serve" became a problem for activist professional movements and that certain sequences were likely to develop. Let us take delivery strategies. Assuming that the community was rational and that professionals could and should redistribute services, activists initially grounded political action by reference to the unmet needs of minorities and the poor. But advocacy proved unstable. These assumptions almost invariably proved inadequate or wrong, and activists shifted their claims to client preference (Figure 1, Type 1).

Client preference did not prove a tenable base for activist professionals for the reasons described above. If activists accepted the community's views as rational and decided not to serve, they faced a crisis of legitimacy (Type 2). Their analysis dictated political —not technical roles—but their acceptance in the community was based on their technical knowledge, apolitical role, and general social approval. From their own perspective, activists often found communities conservative and self-serving.

If they decided that the community was irrational—that one could not ground political action on what people say they want—and if they still chose to serve, activists faced the realization that technical aid shored up a system in need of major change (Type 3).

If they decided that the community was irrational and not to serve, the question then became how to transform society? How to ground political action if not by direct reference to the wants of client communities? Many concluded that it was necessary to act by reference to other values or reference groups. This led to a shift from client preference to a political ideology of social transformation as a basis for action (Type 4).

As a source of legitimacy, a vision of social transformation resolved some of the dilemmas of prior claims. Compared to expertise and bureaucratic position, it allowed the professional a critical and nontraditional role. Compared to client preference or professional values, it provided a knowledge based claim. Compared to client preference, it allowed the professional to "speak for" clients thus defusing clients as a source of conflict and criticism.

Although ideologically radical, strategies of social transformation reestablished claims to expertise and knowledge. This was due to their underlying socialist models and to the identification of political analysis and theory building as key tasks. Theory became a requisite for political analysis, and political analysis a requisite for action. This led to the popularity of study groups and reading lists among

Model of Community	Traditional Service Orientation	
	Accepted	*Rejected*
Rational	Advocacy (Traditional Activism) (Type 1)	Crisis of Professional Legitimacy (Type 2)
Irrational	Technical Aid Helps the System (Cooptation) (Type 3)	Social Transformation (Utopian Ideology) (Type 4)

Fig. 1 Consequences for Activist Strategies of Differing Models of Community and Differing Service Orientations

members of activist organizations, and to the resurgence of professional identities and intellectual projects. The self-selected task of vanguard groups was to critically examine professional knowledge and social function, and to construct socialist paradigms to replace "scientific models" of medicine and planning. Political analysis was also important to unions and workplace collectives which sought to put their struggles into a broader perspective for the purpose of political education and organizing.

By emphasizing political analysis and theory building, strategies of social transformation extended as well as reestablished leadership roles. Unlike empowerment and to some extent delivery, socialist strategies allowed activists to speak for these groups. By introducing political theory as an explanatory framework, they added a claim to political as well as technical expertise.

Finally, although the socialist model was used to demystify "scientific" models of medicine and planning and to expose their social and political functions, radical political discourse also represented a new source of indeterminacy and mystique in the sense that Jamous and Peloille have used the phrase—as a barrier to outside intervention.[13] This came at a time when scientific models provided the basis for an increasing rationalization and control of professional work.

The political implications of a radical critique.   The emergence of a radical critique of professional knowledge became another source of contradiction for both activists and their low-income and minority clients. As a return to knowledge based expertise, these strategies posed problems of praxis. This was related to the tendency to criticize grass roots efforts, to the nature of Marxism as an esoteric political discourse, and to the unwillingness of community groups to take political leadership from outsiders.

Radicalization was also associated with the displacement of initial service objectives as the goal of substantive benefits for minorities and the poor gave way to a commitment to long-term political agendas. Although there were some attempts to formulate "nonreformist" reforms,[14] nontechnical solutions often failed to produce any short-term gains. In the pursuit of systemwide political change, activists often placed themselves at odds with the very grass roots groups they sought to serve. This suggests a tendency for things to have come full circle. First, activists dropped technical roles to better serve political ends; then, activists defined clients and substantive gains in terms of desired long-term change.

Strategies directed at institution building as opposed to service can also be self-serving.[15] Attempts to institutionalize change based on new paradigms followed the unsuccessful attempts of the 1960s to base change on client service. Compared to values, cognitive claims were less institutionally threatening and Marxism itself enjoyed a recent popularity within academia.

Although part of the impetus to theory building was the failure of unguided action, activists found that critical analyses were not more immune to processes of cooptation than were organizing roles. Their critiques and paradigms were adopted, but in support of entirely different priorities and interests. In helping to delegitimate professional knowledge, they had opened the way to new dangers ranging from right wing attacks to increased corporate rationalization based upon cost control.

Finally, the trajectory of radical analysis was itself at odds with roles for professionals as actors. As socialist models of medicine and planning relocated problems and solutions within broader multi-disciplinary contexts, traditional professionals and professional organizations were no longer relevant or effective agents of change. While some theorists have been critical of professional knowledge, they have also viewed knowledge based skills as stable and contributing to the resistance of professionals to managerial control. By tying knowledge to work autonomy, there has been a tendency to ignore other sources of instability and change, in particular the substantive content of a given body of knowledge.

AUTONOMY AS AN ACTIVIST ISSUE

How did activist strategies affect professional autonomy? In the sociological literature, autonomy has been variously described as deriving from the inherent characteristics of certain occupations,[16] from the political activities of occupations,[17] or from class conflict.[18] But central to all these discussions are claims to knowledge.

The case studies suggest that autonomy must be examined in terms of clients, work organizations, and the federal government and at both the political and the ideological level. *Political autonomy* refers to control over the immediate work environment, occupational self-regulation, and market control.[19] *Ideological autonomy* refers to the relation between professional knowledge and practice and dominant belief and authority systems.[20] Although professional norms have traditionally assumed the value of political autonomy, these case studies suggest that we look more closely to see whose interests autonomy serves at a given time. This includes the various internal groupings within a given profession which are jockeying for position and power.

Initially, political autonomy was not a concern for medical activists. Autonomy was the norm in medicine and its defense was associated with the conservative professional establishment (the AMA) and the opposition to federally financed health care and group practice. Given this context, liberal and reform-minded activists sought to move into closer alliance with their clients and with a progressive federal administration to innovate and change. From the activist perspective, autonomy was a rationale for conservative interests or a rhetorical device at best. Certainly at the start, its benefits were either taken for granted or dismissed.

In planning, autonomy was relatively nonexistent given the realities of centralized political decision making and the typically bureaucratized work situation. Political autonomy was also contradictory as a goal, for without political implementation, plans remain Utopian blueprints. Planning's involvement in the much criticized urban redevelopment programs of the 1950s and 1960s led activists to seek pluralism, not autonomy, as a strategy for change and to use clients to balance political and bureaucratic pressures.

The case studies of medicine and planning show that in the course of activism, challenges to knowledge and service claims undermined activists' real political autonomy. While the turn to professional constituencies and work sites was partly a response to community-activist conflict, activists found that the workplace held similar challenges. As they attempted to gain political control of the workplace in order to change both delivery and process, they found their control challenged and variously circumscribed by other workers (paraprofessional, semiprofessional, and professional), by the administration, and ultimately by the escalation of fiscal and political threats.

In addition to undermining political autonomy, activists' experience with low-income and minority communities more crucially undermined their belief in their own ideological autonomy. Activists who worked in federally funded service programs became critical of and were criticized for their involvement in these programs. Specific programs such as Neighborhood Health Centers and community housing development corporations came to be reevaluated as "traps." Activists found that community people were coopted to serve on conflict ridden boards where they could do little better than the local government in operating facilities, and where they were made scapegoats in times of fiscal constraint. Alternate service institutions, both independent as well as government sponsored, were relabeled *counterinsurgent* for cooling out the activists as well as for "patching" the system. Whereas activists had initially seen the state as weak and a potential partner in reform, the problem was redefined as elite domination by professions allied with the state. A new realm of discourse centered upon the social control functions of the professions.

In strategies of social transformation, autonomy displaced service delivery as a key issue for activists, both at the political and ideological levels. With state rationalization and service cutbacks, activists gave more attention to issues relating to workplace control. As noted in the discussion of unions and work based collectives, these concerns did not necessarily converge with client service issues. Ideologically, because professions are viewed as agencies of the state which reproduce the dominant belief and authority systems, many saw their strategic role as intellectual—to demystify current "bourgeois" models and to create socialist models of medicine and planning. To the extent that service issues were redefined in terms of autonomy, this represented, in part, a turning to professional constituencies and away from low-income and minority clients.

The conclusion that activists undermined and then rebuilt the structure (if not the ideology) of professionalism, suggests that perhaps critics of the professions have gone too far both in dismissing attributes such as knowledge and in asserting that professionalism is "ideological." While professionalism has overly packaged claims to knowledge, expertise, service, and autonomy, there may not be other alternatives. As activists moved away from the traditional poles along each of these dimensions, the whole package began to pull apart and their positions polarized.

Several conclusions emerge. First, knowledge is not bedrock to be relied upon. Although professional status is based on knowledge, the substantive content can be radical and destabilizing. Because knowledge is power, the intellectual project is not complete and comes alive as an arena of social conflict.

Second, claims to knowledge are indeed central to professionalism. As nonpropertied middle-class experts, the structural position of planners and doctors is defined by their claims to privileged knowledge. These claims created the opportunities for action, shaped the forms action took and ultimately decided their fate. Radical changes in practice proved to be self-limiting because of their tendency to undermine claims to knowledge, the basis of the legitimate authority of experts.

Third, the search for a viable political strategy floundered on the double and contradictory role of knowledge. Activists in professions needed knowledge as professionals, but as political actors, knowledge was viewed as elitist and self-serving. While the shift from a redistributive to a transformative politics took place within a given historical period that in the long run may begin to look fairly unique, the issues raised are more enduring. They reflect a more permanent contradiction and suggest, in answer to the question of the 1960s, that it is difficult to be both professional and political at the same time and in the same place. Combining them may be possible under certain conditions but will not be stable.

If this is so, then on structural as well as historical grounds, there are good political reasons to keep alternate visions of society alive. Regardless of the seemingly pessimistic outcome of this analysis—no political strategies seemed to have worked—we have learned that social change cannot rely upon professionals as a vanguard and that social theory can play a role in teaching us both the power and the limits of theory itself as a source of change.

Notes

Chapter 1

1. M. Carr-Saunders and P. A. Wilson, *The Professions* (London: Oxford University Press, 1933) 284-318; Ernest Greenwood, "Attributes of a Profession," *Social Work* 2 (July 1957):44-55; William J. Goode, "Community within a Community: The Professions," *ASR* 22 (April 1957):194-200; "Encroachment, Charlatanism and the Emerging Profession: Psychology, Sociology, and Medicine," *ASR* 25 (December 1960):902-14; "The Librarian: From Occupation to Profession?" *The Library Quarterly* 31 (October 1961):306-20; Robert K. Merton, "Some Preliminaries to a Sociology of Medical Education," in *The Student Physician: Introductory Studies in the Sociology of Medical Education,* ed. Robert K. Merton, et al. (Cambridge, Mass.: The Commonwealth Fund, 1957) 3-79; Joseph Ben-David, "Professionals and Unions in Israel," *Industrial Relations* 5 (1965):48-66; Richard H. Hall, "Professionalization and Bureaucratization," *ASR* 33 (February 1968):93-104; and Morris L. Cogan, "Toward a Definition of Profession," *Harvard Educational Review* 23 (Winter 1953):33-50.

2. William J. Goode, "The Theoretical Limits of Professionalization," in *The Semi-Professions and Their Organization,* ed. Amitai Etzioni (New York: Free Press, 1969); Joseph Ben-David, "Professionals and Unions in Israel"; and Dietrich Rueschemeyer, "Doctors and Lawyers: A Comment on the Theory of the Professions," *The Canadian Review of Sociology and Anthropology* 1 (February 1964):17-30.

3. The emergence of a literature critical of traditional attribute and functional analysis reflects the convergence of several streams of work: the Chicago School (Hughes and Becker); the power elite approach of C. Wright Mills (popularized by the student movement and the New Left); conflict theory in general; the work of revisionist historians on the Progressive period and political sociologists and political scientists on urban service

bureaucracies. Empirically based critiques of medicine, law, planning, and social work also began to appear. Taken together, this work represents an "occupational benefits" approach to the professions.

4. A particular knowledge base can be an important factor in a profession's attaining self-control but does not by itself guarantee such control. Eliot Freidson, in *Profession of Medicine: A Study of the Sociology of Applied Knowledge* (New York: Harper and Row, 1970) and other works emphasizes political process as opposed to inherent qualities. Magali Sarfatti Larson has examined the contribution of a particular cognitive base to the successful professional project in *The Rise of Professionalism* (Berkeley: University of California Press, 1977).

While the occupational benefits perspective has shown that knowledge is used as a weapon, it has also taken knowledge as a given. More recent "cultural" critiques have corrected this bias and focused on the social construction of knowledge and on knowledge as ideology. See, for example, P. Wright and A. Treacher, eds. *The Problem of Medical Knowledge* (Edinburgh: Edinburgh University Press, 1982.)

5. Rue Bucher and Anselm L. Strauss, "Professions in Process," *AJS* 66:4 (January 1961):325-34 is an alternative perspective to Goode's "Community within a Community."

6. See H. Jamous and B. Peloille, "Professions or Self Perpetuating Systems: Changes in the French University Hospital System," in *Professions and Professionalization*, ed. J. A. Jackson (Cambridge: Cambridge University Press, 1970) 111-52. See also, Rueschemeyer, "Doctors and Lawyers," and Friedson, *Profession of Medicine*.

7. Robert H. Wiebe's *The Search for Order, 1877-1920* (New York: Hill and Wang, 1967) reinterprets the period and suggests that professionalism, a structure of loyalties based on occupational identity and cohesion, served as a new basis for stratification and provided the rationale for introducing the expert to the public.

Revisionist analyses of the Flexner Report and the institutionalization of "scientific" medicine include E. Richard Brown's, *Rockefeller Medicine Men: Medicine and Capitalism in America* (Berkeley: University of California Press, 1979); Howard Berliner, "A Larger Perspective on the Flexner Report," *IJHS* 5:4 (1975):573-92; and James G. Burrow, *Organized Medicine in the Progressive Era: The Move Toward Monopoly* (Baltimore, Md.: Johns Hopkins University Press, 1977.)

8. James O'Connor, *The Fiscal Crisis of the State* (New York: St. Martin's Press, 1973), for the most part, writes at the level of state or capitalist class. However, he has a suggestive last chapter in which he describes the impact of fiscal crisis on class relations in the service sector. Medicine and planning become sites for conflict due to the economic development activities of the state in the 1950s. See also Claus Offe, "Advanced Capitalism and the Welfare State," *Politics and Society* 2:4 (Summer 1972):479-88.

9. On the class position of educated workers: for new working class theory, see Serge Mallet, *Essays on the New Working Class,* ed. and trans. by Dick Howard and Dean Savage (St. Louis: Telos Press, 1975); Alain Touraine, *The Post-Industrial Society,* (New York: Random House, 1971); André Gorz, *A Strategy for Labor* (Boston: Beacon Press, 1967); and André Gorz, ed., *The Division of Labour* (Sussex: The Harvester Press, 1976); and Martin Oppenheimer, "The Proletarianization of the Professional," *Sociological Review Monograph* 20 (1973):213-28. For educated workers as a "third" class, see Barbara Ehrenreich and John Ehrenreich, "The Professional-Managerial Class," in *Between Labor and Capital,* ed. Pat Walker (Boston: South End Press, 1979) 5-45. As a contradictory class, see Erik Olin Wright, "Intellectuals and the Class Structure of Capitalist Society," in *Between Labor and Capital,* ed. Pat Walker 191-211, and *Class Structure and Income Determination* (New York: Academic Press, 1979).

10. *The Coming of Post-Industrial Society* (New York: Basic Books, 1973). Other contemporary theorists who have described a post-industrial model include Raymond Aron, Zbigniew Brzezinski, and Jean Meynaud. See Krishan Kumar, *Prophecy and Progress* (London: Penguin Books, 1978) for a discussion and critique of the post-industrial model.

11. On professional decline, see Eliot Freidson, *Professional Powers: A Study of the Institutionalization of Formal Knowledge* (Chicago: University of Chicago Press, 1986). Focusing on professions within the political economy, Freidson sees change but not decline. On medicine, see Freidson's "The Reorganization of the Medical Profession," *Medical Care Review* 42:1 (Spring 1985):11-35; and Paul Starr, *The Social Transformation of American Medicine* (New York: Basic Books, 1982).

On deprofessionalization, see Marie R. Haugh, "Deprofessionalization: An Alternative Hypothesis for the Future," *Sociological Review Monograph* 20 (1973):195-211; "The Deprofessionalization of Everyone?" *Sociological Focus* 3 (1975):197-213; and "Computer Technology and the Obsolescence of the Concept of Profession," in *Work and Technology,* eds. M. R. Haugh and J. Dofny, (Beverly Hills, Calif.: Sage Publications, 1977) 215-28; Nina Toren, "Deprofessionalization and Its Sources," *Sociology of Work and Occupations* 2 (November 1975):323-37; R. A. Rothman, "Deprofessionalization: The Case of Law in America," *Work and Occupations* 11 (May 1984):183-206.

On proletarianization, see Oppenheimer, "The Proletarianization of the Professional"; Stanley Aronowitz, *False Promises: The Shaping of American Working Class Consciousness* (New York: McGraw-Hill, 1973); Larson, *The Rise of Professionalism,* 232-37, and "Proletarianization and Educated Labor," *Theory and Society* 9 (January 1980):131-75; C. Derber, "The Proletarianization of the Professional: A Review Essay," in *Professionals as Workers: Mental Labor in Advanced Capitalism,* ed. C. Derber (Boston: G. K. Hall, 1982) 13-33; J. B. McKinley, "Toward the Proletarianization of Physicians," in *Professionals as Workers,* ed. C. Derber 37-62.

12. Daniel P. Moynihan, who coined the phrase "the professionalization

of reform," voiced this view most explicitly. *Maximum Feasible Misunderstanding: Community Action in the War on Poverty* (New York: Free Press, 1969). See also, Frances Fox Piven, "Professionalism as a Political Skill," in *Personnel in Anti-Poverty Programs: Implications for Social Work Education* (New York: Council on Social Work Education, 1966); and Martin Rein, *Social Policy* (New York: Random House, 1970) chap. 15. For a debate, see B. Bruce-Briggs, ed., *The New Class?* (New Brunswick, N. J.: Transaction Books, 1979).

The New Right picked up and extended this critique in the 1980s. See Charles Murray, *Losing Ground: American Social Policy, 1950-1980* (New York: Basic Books, 1984). For a discussion that attempts to distinguish New Left from neoconservative and New Right criticism of the role of the intellectual elite in expanding social welfare, see Barbara Ehrenreich, "The New Right Attack on Social Welfare," *The Mean Season: The Attack on the Welfare State,* ed. Fred Block, et al. (New York: Pantheon, 1987) 161-95.

13. Richard Cloward and Frances Fox Piven suggest that professionals in insurgent roles serve the same functions vis-à-vis the poor as traditional professionals—social control and political socialization. Services represent the new political goods—the "grist of urban politics." Despite their focus on minorities and the poor, their empirical analysis of who got what and why in the 1960s and the evidence that insurgents caused as much disruption as they headed off, suggests we look at provider groups as well as at the poor. *The Politics of Turmoil* (New York: Vintage, 1975) 274, and *Regulating the Poor: The Functions of Public Welfare* (New York: Vintage, 1971.)

14. Ehrenreich and Ehrenreich "The Professional-Managerial Class."

15. See note 9 above.

16. See, for example, Sheryl Burt Ruzek, *The Women's Health Movement: Feminist Alternatives to Medical Control* (New York: Praeger, 1978). Ruzek, who examines feminist attempts to reshape the health care system, describes the impact of feminists on the Free Clinic Movement, Medical Committee for Human Rights and Health/PAC.

17. Talcott Parsons, "Professions," ed. David L. Sills, *International Encyclopedia of the Social Sciences* (New York: Free Press, 1968)12:536-47; "The Professions and Social Structure," in Talcott Parsons, *Essays in Sociological Theory* 2nd ed., (New York: Free Press, 1954) 34-39; and Bernard Barber, "Some Problems in the Sociology of the Professions," *Daedalus* 92 (Fall 1963):669-88. Much of this analysis is modeled on the physician/patient relation as analyzed by Parsons in "Illness and the Role of the Physician: A Sociological Perspective," *American Journal of Orthopsychiatry* 21 (July 1951):452-60. This model is criticized by Dietrich Rueschemeyer in "Doctors and Lawyers."

18. See, for example, Larson, *The Rise of Professionalism* 236-38.

19. Critics such as Freidson and Larson tend to view knowledge as relatively stable and resistant to change. But cognitive rationality has its critics. Jamous and Peloille in "Professions or Self-Perpetuating Systems,"

warn that cognitive rationality must be viewed as a "duality." Wilensky states that the optimal knowledge base must be neither too vague nor too narrow, "The Professionalization of Everyone?" *AJS* 70 (September 1964):137-58; Ben-David, "Professionals and Unions in Israel," and Goode, "The Theoretical Limits of Professionalization," interpose the nature of the task as an important intervening variable. Finally, cognitive rationality itself invites rationalization according to Jamous and Peloille. The rationalization of the underlying knowledge base of the professions may make for a "fit" between knowledge base and bureaucratic organizations. See Wolf V. Heydebrand and James J. Noell, "Task Structure and Innovation in Organizations," *Comparative Organizations*, ed. Wolf V. Heydebrand (Englewood Cliffs, N. J.: Prentice-Hall, 1973) 294-322.

Chapter 2

1. Amitai Etzioni, ed. *The Semi-Professions and Their Organization* (New York: Free Press, 1969).

2. Nathan Glazer, "The Schools of the Minor Professions," *Minerva* 12:3 (July 1974):346-63.

3. Goode, "The Theoretical Limits of Professionalization."

4. See, among others, Mel Scott, *American City Planning* (Berkeley: University of California Press, 1971); Roy Lubove, *The Urban Community: Housing and Planning in the Progressive Era* (Englewood Cliffs, N. J.: Prentice-Hall, 1967); and John L. Hancock, "Planners in the Changing City: 1900-1940," *JAIP* 33:5 (1967):290-304.

5. Scott, *American City Planning* 163.

6. At that time, many of these planners moved to Washington and tackled national issues. Scott, *American City Planning* chap. 5.

7. The index of the *JAIP* reveals the popularity of this continuing debate.

8. See Melvin M. Webber's classic statement, "Comprehensive Planning and Social Responsibility: Toward an AIP Consensus on the Profession's Roles and Purposes," *JAIP* 29:4 (1963). Gans, "City Planning in America: A Sociological Analysis," in *People and Plans* (New York: Basic, 1968); also Ernest Erber, "Urban Planning in Transition," in *Urban Planning in Transition,* ed. Ernest Erber (New York: Grossman Press, 1970). Planners tended to describe themselves as generalists in the late 1950s and 1960s, and as specialists in the late 1970s.

9. There have been ongoing campaigns to accredit planning programs and to certify planners. Both the former and current professional organizations of the American Planners Association, are membership organizations which give exams. Current requirements for certification include a mix of

schooling and experience. The certificate is not mandatory for employment except when stated.

10. Erber, "Urban Planning in Transition," xvii.

11. Henry Cohen, "The Changing Role of the Planner in the Decision-Making Process," in *Urban Planning in Transition*, ed. Erber 174.

12. William Alonso, "Cities and City Planners," in *The Professions in America*, ed. K. Lynn (Boston: Beacon Press, 1963) 170-85.

13. For a historical and comparative discussion of professional development, see Corrine Lathrop Gilb, *Hidden Hierarchies: The Professions and the Government* (New York: Harper and Row, 1966). For the development of the medical profession, see James G. Burrow, *Organized Medicine;* Rosemary Stevens, *American Medicine and the Public Interest* (New Haven, Conn.: Yale University Press, 1971); E. Richard Brown, *Rockefeller Medicine Men;* and Eliot Freidson, *Profession of Medicine.*

14. For descriptions of medicine in nineteenth-century America, see Burrow, *Organized Medicine;* Gilb, *Hidden Hierarchies* chap. 2; Brown, *Rockefeller Medicine Men;* William G. Rothstein, *American Physicians in the Nineteenth Century,* (Baltimore, Md.: Johns Hopkins University Press, 1972); Barbara Ehrenreich and Deidre English, *Witches, Midwives and Nurses: A History of Women Healers* (Old Westbury, N. Y.: Feminist Press, 1973): and Stevens, *American Medicine,* Part 2.

15. Gilb, *Hidden Hierarchies* 11-14; Stevens, *American Medicine,* Part 1; Joseph Kett, *The Formation of the American Medical Profession: The Role of Institutions, 1780-1860* (New Haven, Conn.: Yale University Press, 1968); and Richard H. Shyrock, *Medical Licensing in America, 1650-1965* (Baltimore, Md.: Johns Hopkins University Press, 1967).

16. George Rosen, "What is Social Medicine? A Genetic Analysis of the Concept," in *From Medical Police to Social Medicine: Essays on the History of Health Care,* ed. George Rosen (New York: Science History Publication, 1974) 60-119; Erwin H. Ackerknecht, *A Short History of Medicine* (New York: Ronald Press, 1968); Brown, *Rockefeller Medicine Men* 74-80; and Howard S. Berliner and J. Warren Salmon, "Toward an Understanding of Holistic Medicine," *HMO Packet* #4 (n.d.).

17. Abraham Flexner, *Medical Education in the United States and Canada,* Bulletin 4 (New York: Carnegie Foundation for the Advancement of Teaching, 1910). For a revisionist analysis of the report and the subsequent reforms see Howard Berliner, "A Larger Perspective on the Flexner Report"; Brown, *Rockefeller Medicine Men;* and Burrow, *Organized Medicine.*

18. Stevens, *American Medicine,* Part 1; Brown, *Rockefeller Medicine Men* chap. 4; and Burrow, *Organized Medicine* chaps. 2-3. For the impact of the Flexner Report on women healers, see Ehrenreich and English, *Complaints*

and Disorders; for the impact on blacks and on the class composition of the profession, see Brown, *Rockefeller Medicine Men* 146-56.

19. Burrow, *Organized Medicine;* Stevens, *American Medicine;* and Gilb, *Hidden Hierarchies.*

20. Brown, *Rockefeller Medicine Men;* Berliner, "A Larger Perspective on the Flexner Report."

21. Rosen, "What is Social Medicine?"; Howard Berliner, "Ideology in Medicine," *HMO Packet* #1 (1976):5-7; Berliner and Salmon, "Toward an Understanding of Holistic Medicine"; and Howard Waitzkin, "A Marxist View of Medical Care," *Annals of Internal Medicine* 89 (1978):264-78.

22. Rosen, "What is Social Medicine?"

23. Rosen, "What is Social Medicine?" 107-16.

24. George Rosen, *A History of Public Health* (New York: M. D. Publications, 1958); Rosen, "What is Social Medicine?"; Burrow, *Organized Medicine* chap. 6; Barbara G. Rosenkrantz, *Public Health and the State: Changing Views in Massachusetts, 1842-1936* (Cambridge, Mass.: Harvard University Press, 1972); and Kurt W. Bach, et al., "Public Health as a Career in Medicine: Secondary Choice within a Profession," *ASR* 23 (October 1958):533-41.

25. Richard H. Shyrock, *Medicine in America; Historical Essays* (Baltimore, Md.: Johns Hopkins University Press, 1966); George Rosen, "The Evolution of Social Medicine," in *Handbook of Medical Sociology,* eds. Howard E. Freeman, et al. (Englewood Cliffs, N. J.: Prentice-Hall, 1963); George Rosen, "The Hospital: Historical Sociology of a Community Institution," in *The Hospital in Modern Society,* ed. Eliot Freidson (New York: Free Press, 1963).

26. Rosen's "What is Social Medicine?" For Virchow's political demands, see Waitzkin, "Marxist View."

27. Rosen, "The First Neighborhood Health Center Movement," in *Medical Police to Social Medicine* ed. Rosen 304. Burrow, *Organized Medicine,* discusses public health practice, contract medicine, and social insurance movements.

28. See Rosen, "What is Social Medicine?" for a discussion of this professional segment and its association with industrial society and social welfare.

29. On this contradiction, see Sander Kelman, "Toward the Political Economy of Medical Care," *Inquiry* 8 (September 1971):30-37; Stevens, *American Medicine;* Brown, *Rockefeller Medicine Men* chap. 3; and "Economic Crisis," *Health/Pac Bulletin* 69 (March/April 1978):175.

30. See, among others, Rick J. Carlson, *The End of Medicine* (New York: Wiley-Interscience, 1975); John Knowles, *Doing Better and Feeling Worse: Health*

in the United States (New York: W. W. Norton, 1977); and Paul Starr, "Medicine and the Waning of Professional Sovereignity," *Daedalus* 107:1 (Winter 1978): 175-93.

31. Rhonda Kotelchuck, "The Depression and the AMA," Health/PAC *Bulletin* 69 (March/April 1976):13, and Stevens *American Medicine* chap. 7.

32. Rueschemeyer, in "Doctors and Lawyers," raises the importance of the competence gap.

33. Larson, *The Rise of Professionalism* chap. 3.

34. Freidson, *Professional Dominance* and *Profession of Medicine.*

35. See predeeding note 9.

36. Glazer, "The Schools of the Minor Professions."

37. Gilb, *Hidden Hierarchies.*

38. Moore, in *The Professions,* 17, does not believe that individual clients are necessary to professional status; clients may be corporate or communal and service need not be face-to-face. For a contrasting view, see Wilensky, "The Professionalization of Everyone?" See also Larson's discussion of the public service professions of which city planning is a good example. *The Rise of Professionalism* chap. 11.

39. Peter Marcuse discusses this and the more general case of the planner's complex and expanding role set in terms of conflicting interests and ethical obligations, in "The Ethics of the Planning Profession," Working Paper DP 43 (Los Angeles: University of California, School of Architecture and Urban Planning, 1974).

40. Harder to regulate from without, it requires greater elements of interpersonal trust. See Goode, "Theoretical Limits." Freidson qualifies the equation of solo practice with profesional autonomy by noting the possibility of patient tyranny and, in hospital or group settings, collegial tyranny. *Profession of Medicine* chaps. 2-5.

41. Among others, Glazer, "The Schools of the Minor Professions"; Gilb, *Hidden Hierarchies;* Goode, "Theoretical Limits"; Moore, *The Professions;* Larson, *The Rise of Professionalism;* and Wilensky, "The Professionalization of Everyone?"

42. The first formal gathering and articulation of MDS views was a conference, "Radicals in the Professions," in Ann Arbor, Michigan, July 1967. The thematic paper by Alan and Barbara Haber, "Getting by with a Little Help from Our Friends," introduced what were to be the main concerns of MDS. See Bob Gottlieb and Marge Piercy, "Beginning to Begin to Begin," in *Selected Papers from Radicals in Professions Conference,* published by Radical Education Project of SDS, October 1967.

43. Martin L. Needleman and Carolyn Emerson Needleman make this distinction in *Guerrillas in the Bureaucracy* (New York: John Wiley and Sons, 1974).

44. Contrary to popular opinion, there is a long tradition of health activism. Among medical students and housestaff, for example, there was the Association of Interns and Medical Students (AIMS) which took a progressive stance to national health insurance and which fell victim to cold war anticommunism in the 1950s. Prior to MCHR, there were other organizations committed to civil rights objectives. Thomas L. Perry, Jr., and De Forest Ely, "AIMS, Past, Present and Future," *The Interne* (March 1947).

45. For a discussion of public hospitals in New York City, see Samuel Wolfe and Hila Richardson Sherer, *Public General Hospitals in Crisis* (Washington, D. C.: Coalition of American Public Employees, 1977). For policy analysis, Robb Burlage, *New York City's Municipal Hospitals: A Policy Review* (Washington, D. C.: Institute for Policy Studies, 1967).

46. Barney G. Glaser and Anselm L. Strauss, *The Discovery of Grounded Theory: Strategies for Qualitative Research* (New York: Aldine, 1967).

Chapter 3

1. John Mollenkopf uses the phrase to refer to postwar federal urban policy, which involved a coalition of business, politicians, and federal government in rebuilding central city business districts. This underwriting of infrastructure—new facilities, improved physical plants, technology build-up—pertained to schools and hospitals as well as to urban cores. "The Post-War Politics of Urban Development," *Politics and Society* 5:3(1975):247-95.

2. The Association of Interns and Medical Students (AIMS) in medicine, and in planning the Federation of Architects, Engineers, Chemists and Technicians (FAECT). Perry and Ely, "AIMS, Past, Present and Future" 125-78, and Morris Zeitlin on FAECT in *Planners Network* #5 (June 18, 1976):4.

3. Gouldner, *The Dialectic of Ideology and Technology* (New York: Seabury Press, 1976) chaps. 11-12, 269-73. See also Martin Rein, "Social Planning: The Search for Legitimacy," *JAIP* 35:5 (1969):233-45.

4. Webber, "Comprehensive Planning and Social Responsibility"; Scott, *American City Planning* 464; Edward C. Banfield and James Q. Wilson, *City Politics* (Cambridge, Mass.: Harvard University Press, 1963); and Newton Quigg, "Planning Comes of Age," *JAIP* 23 (1957):185-91.

5. Scott, *American City Planning* chap. 4, and Gans, "City Planning in America," in *People and Plans*. Although many see World War II as the great divide, they differ as to why. Banfield and Wilson emphasize federal aid policies; others cite local conditions and special interests in local politics. See

Alan A. Altschuler's discussion in *The City Planning Process: A Political Analysis* (Ithaca, N. Y.: Cornell University Press, 1965) 417-19.

6. Altschuler, in *The City Planning Process* 417; Scott, *American City Planning;* and Mark I. Gelfand, *A Nation of Cities* (New York: Oxford University Press, 1975).

7. In *A Nation of Cities* (chaps. 4-5) Gelfand describes the three major blocks of interest in the Housing Act: the housers, real estate and business, and the planners.

8. For example, Section 701 of the 1954 Housing Act. In 1961 and 1962, comprehensive area plans became prerequisites for the highway program. Altschuler, *The City Planning Process* 425.

9. Scott, *American City Planning* 542.

10. On the growth of the academic establishment see Scott, *American City Planning* chap. 6, and Jerome L. Kaufman, "Contemporary Planning Practice: State of the Art," *Learning from Turbulence*, ed. David R. Godschalk (Washington, D. C.: American Institute of Planners, 1974).

11. David R. Godschalk, "Introduction: Learning from Turbulence," in *Learning from Turbulence*, ed. Godschalk; Francine Rabinowitz, "Introduction," *City Politics and Planning* (New York: Atherton Press, 1969); Scott, *American City Planning* 543; Quigg, "Planning Comes of Age"; and Kaufman, "Contemporary Planning Practice."

12. See articles by Gans, Glazer, Seeley, and Rein in the *JAIP* during 1959. Also, Scott, *American City Planning* 474, 547.

13. John W. Dyckman, "What Makes Planners Plan," *JAIP* 27:2 (1961).

14. Alonso, "Cities and City Planners" 172. See also Kaufman, "Contemporary Planning Practice"; Rabinowitz, *City Politics and Planning;* Andreas Faludi's introductory discussion of "Expansion of Planning as a Bureaucratic Function of Urban Government," in *A Reader in Planning Theory*, ed. Andreas Faludi (Oxford: Pergamon Press, 1973) 232; and Webber, "Comprehensive Planning and Social Responsibility." Lawrence E. Susskind describes how federal programs led to new roles and skills in "The Future of the Planning Profession," *Learning from Turbulence* ed. Godschalk. Harvey Perloff, in "Education of City Planners: Past, Present and Future," describes a dual line of development: on the one hand, a more traditional orientation to the physical environment and clients and, on the other, as advisory staff. *JAIP* 22:4 (1956).

15. Norton Long, "Planning and Politics in Urban Development," *JAIP* 25:4 (1959):167.

16. Thad L. Beyle and George T. Lathrop, "Introduction," *Planning and Politics: Uneasy Partnership*, eds. Beyle and Lathrop (New York: Odyssey Press).

17. The federal requirement regarding participation shifts from the 1954 amendment to the Housing Act of 1949 which called for a "workable" program, to the "maximum participation" of OEO, to the modified "widespread citizen participation" of Model Cities. See Scott, *American City Planning,* and Gelfand, *A Nation of Cities.*

18. Gelfand, *A Nation of Cities* chaps. 4-5.

19. Long, "Planning and Politics in Urban Development."

20. Jewel Bellush and Murray Hausknecht, "Entrepreneurs and Urban Renewal," *JAIP* 32:5 (1966):289-97.

21. Charles A. Beard, "Some Aspects of Regional Planning," *APSR* 22 (May 1926):276. See also statements by other members of the Regional Planning Association and the Chicago School.

22. Martin Anderson focuses on implementation in *The Federal Bulldozer* (Cambridge, Mass: MIT Press, 1964). In *A Nation of Cities,* Gelfand discusses the legislative process. For criticism of physical planning see the work of Herbert Gans. Also, John Seeley, "The Slum: Its Nature, Use, and Users," *JAIP* 25:1 (1959); and Nathan Glazer "The School as an Instrument in Planning," *JAIP* 25:4 (1959).

23. The volume edited by James Q. Wilson, *Urban Renewal* (Cambridge, Mass: MIT Press, 1966) is full of expletives.

24. Jacobs identified city planners as the culprits and put planning on the defensive. *The Death and Life of Great American Cities* (New York: Randon House, 1961).

25. Herbert J. Gans, "The Human Implications of Current Redevelopment and Relocation Planning," *JAIP* 25:1 (February 1959):15-25.

26. Peter Marris, "The Social Implications of Urban Redevelopment," *JAIP* 28:3 (1962); and Walter Thabit, "Renewal—A Planning Challenge," *JAIP* 26:2 (1959). Among the early critics was Robert C. Weaver. See "Social Issues: The Disadvantaged and the Amenity Seekers," in *The Metropolitan Future: California and the Challenge of Growth* (Berkeley: University of California Prss, 1965) 114. Also, Scott, *American City Planning* chaps. 6, 8; and discussion with Herbert Gans.

27. The progressive wing included the Chicago School and the School of Planning at the University of Pennsylvania. Meyerson and Gans went from Chicago to Pennsylvania. At Pennsylvania, Meyerson influenced Gans, Davidoff, and Reiner, among others. Involved in reconceptualizing planning around rational mid-range approaches, they wanted plans to be more useful to policymakers and more geared toward social action. Scott, *American City Planning* 528-31; Martin Meyerson, "Building the Middle-Range Bridge for Comprehensive Planning," *JAIP* 22:2 (1956); and discussion with Herbert Gans.

Prior to the 1960s, the "actionists" of the Regional Planning Association proposed seven major projects of basic research on the urban environment to the Ford Foundation (1950). Scott, *American City Planning* 474.

28. Peter Marris, "A Report on Urban Renewal in the United States," in *The Urban Condition*, ed. Leonard J. Duhl (New York: Basic Books, 1963); Gans, "The Human Implications of Current Redevelopment."

29. Bernard J. Frieden, "The Changing Prospects for Social Planning" *JAIP* 33:5 (1967):311.

30. Paul Davidoff, "Advocacy and Pluralism in Planning," *JAIP* 31:4 (1965):334.

31. *People and Plans*, Part IV—"Planning against Urban Poverty and Segregation."

32. Stevens, *American Medicine* chap. 13; Stephen P. Strickland, *Politics, Science and Dread Disease: A Short History of United States Medical Research Policy* (Cambridge, Mass.: Harvard University Press, 1972); John T. Grupenhoff and Stephen P. Strickland, "Introduction," *Federal Laws: Health Environment, Manpower*, eds. John T. Grupenhoff and Stephen P. Strickland (Washington, D. C.: Science and Health Communications Group, 1972); and Eli Ginzberg, *The Limits of Health Reform* (New York: Basic Books, 1977) chap. 3.

33. Grupenhoff and Strickland, *Federal Laws* 2.

34. Strickland, *Politics, Science and Dread Disease* 79.

35. Ginzberg, *Limits* chap. 3.

36. For a 1944 survey of physicians and their favorable response to group practice, see Perry and Ely, "AIMS, Past, Present and Future." On group practice, see Edwin P. Jordan, "Group Practice," *NEJM* 250:13 (April 1, 1954):558.

37. Ginzberg, *Limits* chap. 3; Stevens, in *American Medicine* chap. 13, discusses the G. I. Bill and government subsidy of medical education and research.

38. Basil E. Barton, "The Appreciation of Medical Politicians," in *NEJM* 250:20 (May 20. 1954):852-56, and Ginzberg, *Limits* chap. 7.

39. Grupenhoff and Strickland, *Federal Laws*; Strickland, *Politics, Science and Dread Disease*; and Elton Rayack, *Professional Power and American Medicine: The Economics of the American Medical Association* (Cleveland, Ohio: World Publishing, 1967).

40. Grupenhoff and Strickland, *Federal Laws*.

41. Editorial, "The Health Needs of the Nation," *NEJM* 248:2 (1953):77. This editorial discusses the Magnuson Commission report.

42. Strickland, *Politics, Science and Dread Disease;* and Grupenhoff and Strickland, *Federal Laws.*

43. On research, Strickland, *Politics, Science and Dread Disease;* on hospital construction, see Stevens, *American Medicine* 194; and on federal aid to the public and the voluntary hospital system in the 1930s, see Rhonda Kotelchuck, "The Depression and the AMA."

44. Strickland, *Politics, Science and Dread Disease* 56.

45. Federal programs include: Community Mental Health Centers, 1963; the OEO funded Neighborhood Health Centers, 1964; the Health Professions Educational Assistance Act of 1963; Medicare and Medicaid, 1965; and the Health Manpower Act of 1968. See Strickland, *Politics, Science and Dread Disease,* for the discussion of the National Science Foundation and the National Institutes of Health. See also Ginzberg, *Limits.*

46. Stevens, *American Medicine* chap. 7; and Barbara Ehrenreich and John Ehrenreich, *The American Health Empire: Power, Profits and Politics* (New York: Vintage, 1970) chap. 2.

47. Ehrenreich and Ehrenreich, *The American Health Empire* 29-32.

48. Ehrenreich and Ehrenreich, *The American Health Empire* 32.

49. Ehrenreich and Ehrenreich, *The American Health Empire,* chap. 2; Richard Harris, *A Sacred Trust* (Baltimore, Md.: Penguin Books, 1969) 75; Stevens, *American Medicine* Part Four; and Ginzberg, *Limits* 166, 200.

50. Harris, *Sacred Trust;* and Stevens, *American Medicine.*

51. See Harris, *Sacred Trust,* on the interests of the American Hospital Association.

52. Anne R. Somers and Herman M. Somers, *Medicare and the Hospitals: Issues and Prospects* (Washington, D. C.: The Brookings Institutions, 1967) 108-113.

53. Somers and Somers, *Medicare* chap. 6; Stevens, *American Medicine* 15 and Ginzberg, *Limits* 160-69.

54. See, for example, "The Health Needs of the Nation," *NEJM* 248:2 (1953):77. This editorial criticizes the domination of medical training by highly scientific and technical orientations.

55. See Eli Ginzberg and Alice M. Yohalem, eds., *The University Medical Center and the Metropolis* (New York: Macy, 1974), and Health/PAC *Bulletin's* ongoing examination of "medical empires."

56. For a critical examination of the National Health Planning and Resources Development Act of 1974 see Louise Lander, "HSAs," Health/PAC *Bulletin* 70 (May/June 1976).

57. Strickland, *Politics, Science and Dread Disease* 210.

58. Ginzberg, *Limits* 95-96; Louise Lander, "PSROs," in Health/PAC *Bulletin* 59 (July/August 1974).

59. Robert Stevens and Rosemary Stevens, *Welfare Medicine in America: A Case Study of Medicaid* (New York: Free Press, 1974), and Wolfe and Sherer, *Public General Hospitals in Crisis.* More recently see, Harry Schwartz, "A Medicare Standoff with Doctors Looms," *Wall Street Journal,* November 3, 1983; and Ronald Sullivan, "Priorities Revised in City's Hospitals," *New York Times,* August 20, 1983.

60. Elliott A. Krause, *Power and Illness* (New York: Elsevier) 241-43.

61. For an example of one such attempt and the struggle that ensued, see Howard Waitzkin, "Expansion of Medical Institutions into Urban Residential Areas," *NEJM* 282:18 (April 1970):1003-07.

62. Robb Burlage, *New York City's Municipal Hospitals.*

63. Stevens, *American Medicine* 383. See also, Robert J. Weiss, et al., "Foreign Medical Graduates and the Medical Underground," *NEJM* 290:25 (June 20, 1974):1408-13; and Robert J. Weiss et al., "The Effect of Importing Physicians—Return to a pre-Flexnerian Standard," *NEJM* 290:26 (June 27, 1974):1453-58.

64. Stevens and Stevens, *Welfare Medicine in America;* and Wolfe and Sherer, *Public General Hospitals in Crisis.* Schwartz, "A Medicare Standoff with Doctors Looms"; and Sullivan, "Priorities Revised in City's Hospitals."

65. For a sense of the ferment within left/liberal medical circles, beginning in the late 1950s, see Paul Lowinger, "The Doctor as a Political Activist? Progress Report," *American Journal of Psychotherapy* 22:4 (October 1968):616-25.

Chapter 4

1. Gordon Fellman and Barbara Brandt, *The Deceived Majority: Politics and Protest in Middle America* (New Brunswick, N. J.: Transaction Books, 1973) 68. Fellman and Brandt describe the origins and early stages of UPA. My account also draws on the UPA files and interviews with several UPA members, active at different periods in the organization's history.

2. Fellman and Brandt 67. UPA put advocacy planning as proposed by Paul Davidoff and others into practice.

3. Fellman and Brandt 126.

4. Fellman and Brandt 129. This description of UPA's early period draws heavily on Fellman and Brandt chap. 5.

5. Fellman and Brandt 130.

6. "Advocacy Planning: What it is, How it Works," *Progressive Architecture* (September 1968):114-15.

7. Fellman and Brandt chap. 5; "Advocacy Planning: What it is, How it Works; and Robert Goodman, *After the Planners* (New York: Simon and Schuster, 1971).

8. Lisa Peattie, "Advocacy Planning in the United States," July 1968 (Mimeographed) 5.

9. Peattie 6.

10. Fellman and Brandt 126.

11. Fellman and Brandt 126.

12. "Whom does the Advocate Planner Serve?" *Social Policy* (May/June 1970):47. See also, Chester V. Hartman, "The Advocate Planner: From 'Hired Gun' to Political Partisan" in Cloward and Piven, *The Politics of Turmoil* 59-65. Hartman's is a more optimistic account of noncooptive reform.

13. Fellman and Brandt 129-30.

14. Fellman and Brandt 129.

15. See Goodman chap. 7, on the importance of cultural change.

16. Peattie 8.

17. Peattie 9.

18. Goodman 172.

19. Chester V. Hartman, "The Urban Field Service," *The Architectural Forum* 135:2 (September 1971):50-53, and "The Harvard Urban Field Service: A Retrospective View," *11 Views: Collaborative Design in Community Development*, ed. D. Batchelor (Durham, N. C.: North Carolina State University School of Design, 1971) 119-30; Jon Pynoos, "Urban Field Service," *Planning Comment* 5:2 (1969):56-70; Jon Pynoos, Interview, July 1976; and Chester Hartman, Interview, November 1977.

20. Pynoos 56.

21. Hartman, "The Urban Field Service" 53. The following description draws upon this account.

22. Hartman, "The Urban Field Service," and Interview.

23. Hartman, "The Urban Field Service" 51.

24. Hartman, "The Urban Field Service" 52.

25. Hartman, "The Urban Field Service" 50.

26. On planning education, see Harvey S. Perloff and Frank Klett, "The Evolution of Planning Education"; and Barry C. Nocks, "Case Studies: A Decade of Planning Education," in *Learning from Turbulence*, ed. David R. Godschalk.

27. The National Committee on Full Employment channelled funds to SDS. NCUP grew out of a 1964 SDS summer project to organize the unemployed around community improvement. For general information on NCUP and Economic Research and Action Project (ERAP) see Kirkpatrick Sale, *SDS* (New York: Vintage Books, 1974) chaps. 6-9; Richard Rothstein, "Evolution of the ERAP Organizers," in *The New Left*, ed. Priscilla Long (New York: F. Porter Sargent, 1969) 272-88; Wini Breines, *The Great Refusal: Community and Organization in the New Left: 1962-1968* (New York: Praeger, 1982) chap. 7.

28. Robert Heifitz, "Project Report on Work of the National Committee for Full Employment with the Newark Community Union Project," Newark, N. J. November 1965 (Mimeographed); Rothstein, "Evolution of ERAP Organizers"; and Sale, *SDS*. For movement ideology, see Staughton Lynd, "The New Radicals and Participatory Democracy," *Dissent* 12:3 (1965):324-33.

29. Tom Hayden, quoted by Hamish Sinclair in "Field Interviews with Student and Community Associates of NCUP Evaluating NCUP-NSFE Accomplishments," Newark, N. J., Summer 1965 (Mimeographed).

30. Heifitz, "Project Report."

31. Tom Hayden, "Open Letter to ERAP," quoted in Heifitz, "Project Report."

32. Sale, *SDS* chap. 9 146-47; and Rothstein, "Evolution of the ERAP Organizers." On the problems of community organizing at NCUP, Breines, *The Great Refusal* 139-49.

33. Heifitz, "Project Report"; and Sinclair, "Field Interviews."

34. Jacqueline Leavitt, "Report on Four Months as Resident Planner," Newark, N. J., 1965 (Mimeographed); "Diary of Activities at Newark, New Jersey, June through September," Newark, N. J., 1965 (Mimeographed); and Interview, May 1976.

35. For the historical origins of SHO see William Bronston and Michael McGarvey, "A Treatise on Reformation: The Student Health Movement," paper presented at Conference on Radicals in the Professions, Ann Arbor, Michigan, July 14-16, 1967 (Mimeographed); Michael R. McGarvey, Fitzhugh Mullan and Steven S. Sharfstein, "A Study in Medical Action—The Student Health Organizations," *NEJM* (July 11, 1968):74-80; Fitzhugh Mullan, "A New Mood in Medical Students," *Medical Opinion and Review* 4:3 (March 1968); SHO *Bulletin*, ed. Lee Hyde (Spring 1966); and Fitzhugh Mullan and Robert G. Page, "History and Hope," *Chicago SHP, Summer 1967*, ed. Lois Gordon (Chicago: 1968) 1-17.

36. On the context of student health activism see Michael McGarvey, "The Creation of the SHO," Opening Address, *Second National Assembly of the SHO,* Bronx, New York, February 1967; Mullan, "A New Mood in Medical Students"; McGarvey and Bronston, "A Treatise"; and SHO *Bulletin* (Spring 1966):12. For the relation of SHO to the student movement, see "The Context," *1967 Califronia SHP: A Critical Report,* ed. Thomas Brod (California: 1967):2-5.

37. McGarvey and Bronston, "A Treatise" 2.

38. McGarvey, Mullan and Sharfstein, "A Study in Medical Action"; Bronston and McGarvey, "A Treatise"; and SHO *Bulletin* (Spring 1966).

39. Ehrenreich and Ehrenreich, *The American Health Empire* 244-45.

40. Larry Brillant, interviewed in "Inside the SHO," *AMA News* (March 11, 1968). Figures for national membership and local chapters of this loose-knit organization are approximate as is the proportion of medical to health science students. The latter is based on my survey of the distribution of students in summer projects, by discipline, and is taken from Final Reports.

41. Bronston and McGarvey, "A Treatise" 2. Mullan, "A New Mood," discusses the two objectives. On health advocacy see SHO *Bulletin* (Spring 1966) and McGarvey, "The Creation of the SHO."

42. Lee Hyde, "Bandaid Banners," SHO *Bulletin* (Spring 1966):12-13.

43. Bronstein and McGarvey, "A Treatise."

44. SHO press release, "Statement for the AMA," 1967 (Mimeographed).

45. Peter Schnall, "Medical Education Re-evaluated," in *1966 California SHP: A Critical Report* 65-88; Bronston and McGarvey, "A Treatise" 4; and SHO *Bulletin* (Spring 1966):14-15.

46. Bronston and McGarvey, "A Treatise" 1.

47. See, among others, "Student Resolution on Education," *The SHP: A Demonstration of Health Science Student Participation in Community Health Services to the Poor* (California: 1966):51-55; Schnall, "Medical Education"; Bronston and McGarvey, "A Treatise"; Ben Siegel, "Thoughts on the Curriculum" in SHO *Bulletin* (Spring 1966):14-15; and Julie Ingelfinger, Herbert Schreier and Steven Sharfstein, "SHO and Curriculum Change," *Encounter* 3:1 (Spring 1968):7-10.

48. Bronston and McGarvey, "A Treatise" 5.

49. Ben Siegel, "Thoughts on the Curriculum," 14; Bronston and McGarvey, "A Treatise" 5; and "Social Responsibility of the Health Professional," Working Papers of the Asilomar Conference, in *1967 California SHP* 73-75.

50. Schnall, "Medical Education."

51. Bronston and McGarvey, "Social Responsibility of the Health Professional."

52. Bronston and McGarvey, "A Treatise." Also, McGarvey, "The Creation of the SHO" 2.

53. SHO *Bulletin* (Spring 1966):6; and Bronston and McGarvey, "A Treatise" 5. Between 60 and 65 percent of SHO participants were medical students; 20 to 25 percent were nurses, and the rest were divided between students of the social sciences, dentistry, etc. Compared to earlier organizations such as AIMS, this interdisciplinary thrust was unique.

54. See Ingelfinger, Schreier and Sharfstein, "SHO and Curriculum Change" 12-13.

55. One of the many such analyses is Lee Hyde's, "Bandaid Banners" 12-13.

56. Bronston and McGarvey, "A Treatise" 4.

57. *1966 California SHP* 3. Also, Working Papers of the Asilomar Conference, in *1967 California SHP* 71-75.

58. Bronston and McGarvey, "A Treatise" 4.

59. Bronston and McGarvey, "A Treatise" 3; McGarvey, Mullan, and Sharfstein, "A Study in Medical Action" 75.

60. Henry S. Kahn, "Report from Boston Student Medical Conference," SHO *Bulletin* (Spring 1966):3-4; Bronston and McGarvey, "A Treatise" 4; Ben Siegel, "Report from Chicago," SHO *Bulletin* (Spring 1966):7-8; and Mullan, "A New Mood in Medical Students."

61. Bronston and McGarvey "A Treatise" 5.

62. Bronston and McGarvey, "A Treatise"; McGarvey, Mullan, and Sharfstein, "A Study in Medical Action"; McGarvey, "The Creation of the SHO"; SHO *Bulletin* (Spring 1966); and in the *1966 California SHP*, statements by Paul F. Wehrle, M.D., Michael R. McGarvey, and Philip R. Lee, M.D., among others.

63. Supporting organizations included Physicians Forum, the National Medical Association and the American Public Health Association. McGarvey, Mullan, and Sharfstein identify Drs. Martin Cherkasky and Donald Madison of Einstein College of Medicine, New York, Drs. Leon Jacobson and Robert G. Page of University of California, and Drs. Roger Egeberg and Paul Wehrele of University of Southern California, as "providing top level faculty backing for the programs," "A Study in Medical Action" 75. See also Philip R. Lee, "Creative Federalism and Health Programs for the Poor," *1966*

California SHP. For a description of the Washington response see Bronston and McGarvey, "A Treatise" 7.

64. For Dr. H. Jack Geiger on the linkage between progressive members of the medical profession and the New Frontier administration, see the discussion of Neighborhood Health Centers in chap. 5. See also, Robb Burlage, "Toward a New Politics and Economics of Health," paper presented at *3rd National Conference of SHO*, Detroit, Mich., 1968 (Mimeographed).

65. Mullan's account of SHO as spontaneous idealist activism *White Coat, Clenched Fist* (New York: Macmillan, 1976) misses the role of the university and the federal government in the ghettoes and ignores politics within the health sector as well as the changing alignment of the government and health sector.

66. McGarvey, "The Creation of SHO"; SHO *Bulletin* (Spring 1966):5-6; and "Student Health Project, University of Southern California," *Encounter* 1:1 (Summer 1966).

67. The 1966 California *SHP Report* illustrates the OEO impact and makes the case for student health projects in terms of a War on Poverty philosophy.

68. Community feedback comes indirectly through comments of students, preceptors and community agencies with which SHO students worked as well as Neighborhood Youth Corps workers.

69. *1966 California SHP*. Also, Bronston and McGarvey, "A Treatise" 5-7; McGarvey, Mullan, and Sharfstein, "A Study in Medical Action" 75-76; and the description in the *1967 California SHP: A Critical Report*, by Martin Stein 12.

70. *Encounter* 1:1 (Summer 1966).

71. Carl M. Shafer, "The Project Evaluated: A Descriptive Commentary on the Student Health Project" in *1966 California SHP* 3.

72. Michael R. McGarvey, Peter Schnall, and Martin Stein, "Barriers to Comprehensive Health Care," in *1966 California SHP*.

73. Mullan, "A New Mood in Medical Students."

74. Tom Brod, "Thoughts on the NYC Program," *1967 California SHP* 52-54.

75. Brod, "Thoughts" 53.

76. Brod, "Thoughts" 53.

77. Brod, "Thoughts." See Lambert King's similar discussion of the use of high school student interns in Chicago, *1967 SHP* 53.

78. Brod, "The Project in Perspective," *1967 California SHP* 45-46.

226   THE POLITICS OF KNOWLEDGE

79. Comments by Ted Minor, preceptor, *1967 California SHP* 48.

80. S. Douglas Frasier, M.D., "Goals and Directions," *1968 California SHP*, Appendix G, 72-73. The issue was raised for discussion in a position paper by Oliver Fein presented at the *4th National Assembly of the SHO*, Philadelphia, Penn. November 1968. The paper, entitled "SHO, SHP and the Community," summarized SHO/SHP problems with the poor communities within which they worked and proposed a less "exploitative relationship."

81. *1967 California SHP*, comments and conclusions.

82. The *3rd National Assembly of SHO* is covered in *Encounter* 3:1 (Spring 1968).

83. Mike Silverstein, "Letter to SHO from the Stanford SHO," April 15, 1968 (Mimeographed).

84. Ehrenreich and Ehrenreich, *The American Health Empire* 246-47.

85. Lambert King, "The Health Science Student Experience in the 1968 Chicago Student Health Project," *1968 Chicago SHP* 1-4, and *1968 California SHP*, written by Tess Weiner. See Introduction and Appendix materials.

86. *1968 California SHP* 30-57.

87. *Greater New York SHP, Summer 1969* 11-44. *1966 California SHP* 58; *Greater New York SHP, Summer 1968* 56-60. See also Health/PAC *Bulletin* 4 (September 1968).

88. See *Greater New York SHP, Summer 1968* 107; and Lambert King, "The Health Science Student Experience in the 1968 Chicago SHP," *1968 Chicago SHP*.

89. Mullan, "A New Mood in Medical Students."

90. Health/PAC *Bulletin* 4 (September 1968).

91. PEO, "What is Planners for Equal Opportunity?"; and PEO, "Policy Statement," adopted 1968, New York, N. Y.
PEO was conceived as a national organization, meeting annually along with AIP and ASPO. It remained New York based and staffed by its founder and chair, Walter Thabit. At its height (1967-1968) membership numbered 400, attracted by counter conferences held alongside AIP meetings. The Bulletin *Equalop* stopped publication in 1971 and the organization dwindled on until February 1976.
Material on PEO includes *Equalop*, PEO's quarterly bulletin, published from Spring 1965 to Winter 1971; reports on PEO's National Conferences, 1966-1974; and various Memos, Agendas, and Proposals from PEO's organizational files, courtesy of Walter Thabit.

92. Walter Thabit, "Chairman's Corner," *Equalop* 1:1 (Spring 1965); and PEO, "Policy Statement."

93. *Equalop* 1:2 (Summer 1965).

94. On the right to speak out, see *Equalop* 1:1 (Spring 1965) and 2:1 (Spring 1968). The theme was central to PEO's Fifth National Conference, "Planner as Watch-Dog" (1971).

95. AIP was professionally oriented and required qualifications; ASPO was service oriented, with a broader membership than certified planners or planners in general. In 1978, AIP and ASPO joined to create the American Planning Association. This umbrella organization includes the American Institute of Certified Planners with the old AIP members. Membership in the AICP remains qualified.

96. PEO Policy Committee, Minutes of the October 2, 1965 meeting, New York, N. Y. See also, Walter Thabit, "Report to the Policy Committee," July 8, 1966, New York, N. Y.

97. PEO, *Conference Proceedings* for the Second Annual PEO Conference entitled "Urban Crisis=Planning Opportunity" (March 1968).

98. "Urban Crisis=Planning Opportunity," 64.

99. *Equalop* 2:2 (Fall 1968).

100. *Equalop* 2:2 (Fall 1968).

101. *Equalop* 3:3 (Winter 1970). See PEO's Fourth Annual Conference, "New Cities for Black and White" (1970).

102. *Equalop* 3:1 (Summer 1969).

103. Walter Thabit, "The President has the Floor," *Equalop* 2:4 (Winter 1968).

104. *Equalop* 2:1 (September 1968).

105. *Equalop* 2:2 (Fall 1968).

106. *Equalop* 4:2 (1971); 4:3 (1971); and 4:4 (1971).

107. Murray Edelman, *The Symbolic Uses of Politics* (Urbana: University of Illinois Press, 1964).

108. *Equalop* 4:2 (1971) and 3:4 (1970).

109. *Equalop* 3:4 (Spring 1970).

110. Yale Rabin, *Equalop* 2:4 (Spring 1969).

111. Paul Lowinger, M.D., "MCHR in the Health Movement: From the Early '60's to 1968," MCHR monograph, n.d.; Paul Lowinger, M.D., "The Doctor as Political Activist? Progress Report," *American Journal of Psychoanalytic Theory* 22:4 (October 1968): 616-25; and Leslie Falk, M.D., "MCHR Mississippi Project," Report of the Field Medical Administrator, July 12, 1964 (Mimeographed).

112. Dr. Desmond Callan, Interview, Spring 1978. See also, Rhonda Kotelcheck and Howard Levy, "MCHR" Health/PAC *Bulletin* 63 (March/April 1975):4-5.

113. Falk, "MCHR, Mississippi Project"; and Des Callan, M.D., "A Mississippi Health Program: A Modest Proposal," Memo to MCHR program and executive committees, January 15, 1965 (Mimeographed). Dr. John Holloman, Jr., Speech at the MCHR annual dinner, October 15, 1965 (Mimeographed).

114. Minutes of Executive Committee, September 12, 1964, New York, N. Y.

115. MCHR Press Release, June 11, 1966, Statement by John S. Holloman, Jr., M.D. in Washington, D. C., December 1965; and MCHR "Priority Tasks" n.d. (Mimeographed).

116. For a description of the clinic, Falk, "MCHR, Mississippi Project"; M. Cunningham, H. Sanders, and P. Weatherly, "We Went to Mississippi," *American Journal of Nursing* 67 (1967):801; Callan, "A Modest Proposal"; Lowinger, "MCHR in the Health Movement"; and H. Jack Geiger, M.D., Statement in Panel Discussion of Neighborhood Health Centers, Cleveland, Ohio, Summer 1968 (Mimeographed).

117. Kotelchuck and Levy made this point, "MCHR."

118. Dr. H. Jack Geiger felt there was little impact at the level of Holmes County. This led him to speak with OEO and outline a health service to be used for "social change." Interview July 20, 1978, New York, N. Y. Also Geiger, Panel Discussion of NHC, 1968.

119. See the discussion of SHO's experience above and of the OEO funded health centers in chap. 5.

120. Lowinger, "MCHR in the Health Movement"; Dr. H. Jack Geiger, Interview, July 20, 1978; and Geiger, Panel Discussion of NHC, 1968.

121. Lowinger, "MCHR in the Health Movement"; and Robert J. Bazell, "Health Radicals: Crusade to Shift Medical Power to the People," *Science* 173 (August 6, 1971):506-9.

122. Kotelchuck and Levy, "MCHR"; Bazell, "Health Radicals." Dr. Desmond Callan; and Hampton's Family Paper, 1970 (Mimeographed).

123. Bazell, "Health Radicals;" Kotelchuck and Levy, "MCHR." Dr. Desmond Callan.

124. No longer preoccupied with the South, the major thrust was how political priorities shaped health care in the North. Dr. Eli Messinger, Past National Executive Director of MCHR, Interview, February 13, 1979. Also, Lowinger, "The Doctor as Political Activist," 620.

125. "MCHR Challenges AMA in National Statement," *Health Rights News* 1:2, 1967; and Lowinger "The Doctor as Political Activist."

126. MCHR forced the adoption of a "stronger stand against racially discriminatory county societies," Lowinger, "MCHR in the Health Movement."

127. "Bring the War Back Home," Health/PAC *Bulletin* 19 (April 1970). Dr. Howard Levy was courtmartialed in 1967 for his refusal to comply with orders to train green berets with medical skills for Vietnam.

128. Many of the topics were discussed on the pages of the Health/PAC *Bulletin.* There was a close relation between MCHR and Health/PAC, but no real staff involvement until 1971. Dr. Eli Messinger, Interview, February 13, 1970.

129. "Community Clinics and Community Participation in Health Policy Determination," MCHR Proposal for 1971-1972 National Program, submitted by Quentin D. Young, M.D.; *Health Rights News, January 1971; Kotelchuck and Levy, "MCHR" 10-11; and "Free Clinics," Health/PAC Bulletin* 34, October 1971.

130. See, for example, Tom Bodenheimer, "Free Clinics: Strategy for Survival," n.d. (Mimeographed); and Health/PAC *Bulletins* 34 (October 1971) and 26 (February 1972). For a fuller discussion see chap. 5.

131. Bodenheimer, "Free Clinics: Strategy for Survival."

132. MCHR conference at San Diego, California, 1970-1971; Bazell, "Health Radicals"; and Kotelchuck and Levy, "MCHR."

133. Dr. Larry Brillant, *The Body Politic* (July/August 1970):35.

134. Hampton's Family Paper, 1970; and Kotelchuck and Levy, "MCHR" 6.

135. East Coast MCHR Women's Caucus, "A Model Proposal for a Revised National Leadership Structure," February 1971.

136. Hampton's Family Paper, 1970. The National Executive Committee Minutes for June 28, 1970, Eli Messinger presiding, discusses similar issues in regard to challenges to MCHR by North Western University Health Collective and the League of Black Revolutionary Workers. They want MCHR to focus on health workers.

137. Nick Egleson, "Letter to the Movement," *Liberation* (April 1970): 45-50.

138. H. Jack Geiger, M.D., "Hidden Professional Roles: The Physician as Reactionary," *Social Policy* (March/April 1971) 28. See also, the rebuttal by Howard Levy, "Counter Geiger," *Social Policy* (May/June 1971) 57.

139. Bazell, "Health Radicals" 507.

140. MCHR memo, "National MCHR Leadership in Organizational Structure: National MCHR Convention," April 9, 1971; MCHR Proposal for 1971-1972 National Program, submitted by Quentin D. Young, M.D., May 3, 1971; Stephanie Allan and Laura Green, "MCHR: Big Plans, New Style," *Health Rights News* (May/June 1971) 4; and "Health Crusade: Women's Caucuses," "National MCHR," and "Right the War," in *Health Rights News* (May/June 1971) 7.

141. Quentin D. Young, M.D., "Dear MCHR Activist," Letter dated November 1972. This example of MCHR's new public relations effort cites the goal of sending *Health Rights News* to 40,000 people.

142. Tom Bodenheimer, "MCHR Preliminary Position Paper on National Health Care," September 1971 (Mimeographed).

143. Boston MCHR Chapter, "National MCHR—Is It Necessary and Why: A Tentative Answer," n.d. (Mimeographed).

144. "Health Crusade," *Health Rights News* (May/June 1971) 7.

145. Dr. Quention D. Young as quoted by Gregg W. Downey, "Medical Rights Committee Plans Crusade for Medical Justice," *Modern Hospital* (June 1971).

146. Bodenheimer, "Report from the National MCHR Executive Meeting Debate on the National Health Crusade," in *MCHR Western Regional Newsletter* (September 1971).

147. Baltimore Caucus, "Statement to the MCHR," 1971-1972 (Mimeographed).

148. New York MCHR Chapter, "Critique of Current Directions in National MCHR," 1971 (Mimeographed).

149. Bodenheimer, "Report from the National MCHR Executive Meeting Debate on the National Health Crusade."

150. "Health Care is a . . . ?" Report from the Boston Chapter MCHR, 1972-1973 (Mimeographed).

151. "Health Care is a . . . ?"

152. See Cloward and Piven, *Poor People's Movements* chap. 5.

153. For a general discussion, Jim O'Brien, "American Leninism in the 1970s," *Radical America* (November 1977/February 1978):27-62. In terms of MCHR, see Kotelchuck and Levy, "MCHR," 26-27.

Chapter 5

1. Between 1968 and 1969, OEO gave $1,000,000 to advocacy projects in seven cities. UPA remained the only continuing project despite several defunding crises. Earl Blecher, *Advocacy Planning for Urban Development: With Analysis of Six Demonstration Programs* (New York: Praeger, 1971).

2. Urban Planning Aid, "Fund Raising Proposal: Development of Advocacy Planning," Cambridge, Mass., July 30, 1968.

3. Emily Achtenberg, Interview, July 14, 1976.

4. Jeff Tryens, Interview, July 13, 1976.

5. UPA Memo, "Proposal for Evaluation," UPA Files/1970-1971 Demonstration Grant Activity, Boston, Mass.

6. "Notes from the Somerville Group," and Memo from the Ad Hoc Public Housing Group, entitled, "Public Housing Organizing Work," July 28, 1970, Boston, Mass. UPA Files, 1970-1972.

7. OEO requirements for community representation had an impact. See the Memo, "UPA Board Function: Operation and Composition" (n.d.), Boston, Mass. UPA Files, 1970-1972.

8. UPA Files, 1970-1972, Boston, Mass.

9. UPA, "Notes from the Sommerville Group."

10. UPA, "Notes from the Sommerville Group."

11. "Notes on Preparing UPA's 1972-1973 Work Program Submission for OEO," UPA Files, 1970-1972, Boston, Mass. UPA continued to have trouble with OEO and developers related to its tenant organizing. In 1975, Max Kargman filed a conspiracy suit to halt tenant union drives in his projects, charging Tenants' First Coalition and UPA with "conspiracy to redistribute the wealth."

12. *The Student Health Project of Philadelphia, 1968* 42.

13. Greater New York Student Health Project, Summer 1968.

14. *Greater New York SHP, 1968* 12-13.

15. *Greater New York SHP, 1968* 40.

16. *Greater New York SHP, 1968* 77.

17. *Greater New York SHP, 1968* 77.

18. *1968 Chicago Student Health Project* 56; and *Greater New York SHP, 1968,* 77-80.

19. *Greater New York SHP, 1968* 78.

20. *Greater New York SHP, 1968* 76.

21. *Greater New York SHP, 1968* 80.

22. *1968 Chicago SHP* 56-62.

23. *Chicago SHP, 1968* 62.

24. Eleanor Foster, director of a CAP, *1968 Califronia Student Health Project* 65.

25. Richard Unwin, preceptor of a rural Community Action Agency, *1968 California SHP* 67.

26. The Administrator of an OEO funded Neighborhood Health Center, *1968 California SHP* Appendix 66-67.

27. *Greater New York SHP 1968* 90.

28. "Some Questions from the Black Caucus," *1968 California SHP* 69. See also "The Black Students and the SHP—A Position Paper" 70-71.

29. *Greater New York SHP, 1968* 47.

30. Roger O. Egeberg, M.D., "A Letter from the Dean," *1968 California SHP* Appendix 71.

31. *The Student Health Organization of the South Bronx, Summer 1967* 115.

32. *SHO of the South Bronx* 115, 136.

33. *SHO of the South Bronx, 1967* 34. In *The Northern New England SHP, 1968* and *1969*, the projects were referred to as "satellite clinics." See also, *Greater New York SHP, 1968*, and SHO, "An Analysis of the Association of American Medical Colleges," a statement by SHO at the National Co-Ordinating Council Meetings, Fall 1969 (Mimeographed).

34. *Greater New York SHP, 1968* 38.

35. Minutes and Agenda for Chicago meeting between SHP and RMP, July 15, 1968. See also, Ehrenreich and Ehrenreich, *The American Health Empire*, chap. 15.
For post hoc insight into RMP, during the congressional investigation of student demonstrations in Chicago, December 1969, one RMP administrator said of financial support for SHO: "Such information could not be gotten through traditional channels such as formal surveys." Ronald Koziol, *Chicago Tribune*, December 7, 1969.

36. *Greater New York SHP, 1968* 38.

37. "SHO Business: A New Role?" *Medical World News*, May 9, 1969. Parenthetically, the first critique of the OEO funded and university sponsored Neighborhood Health Centers was at a Cleveland SHO meeting in the

summer of 1968. *Proceedings of the Cleveland SHO* (Summer 1968). Also, Dr. Oliver Fein, Interview, July 25, 1978.

38. "SHO Business: A New Role?" *Medical World News* 23.

39. Dr. Oliver Fein; and SHO interorganizational Memos and Notes from the Chicago office. Files of Dr. Ken Rosenberg.

40. See SHP Final Reports for Summer 1968, particularly for New York, Chicago, and California. Most SHOs did not reapply for funding after 1968. Over the winter of 1968-1969, SHO made several inflamatory statements which did not receive media attention until after two summer 1969 contracts had been signed. Thus, there was a mix of student withdrawal and federal unease in response to the 1968 projects, the critical articles, and the investigation of SHO's role in the riots following the Chicago Democratic National Convention.

41. On the origins of the Neighborhood Health Centers, Dr. H. Jack Geiger, Interview, July 20, 1978; Peter Rothstein, "The Community Health Center," Institute for Policy Studies, October 1966 (Mimeographed draft) 6-7. For precursors, George Rosen, "The First Neighborhood Health Center Movement."

42. Dr. Geiger saw health as a major, unused area for community organization, participation, and jobs. He noted: "OEO was restricted regarding voter registration and political activity but there was nothing to stop our community health organization from being coterminous with voter registration." Inteview, July 20, 1978.

43. By 1966, eight centers were funded as demonstration projects. The initial vision was of a nationwide network of health centers which served all area residents not just the poor; which became financially independent through methods such as group practice; and which provided a broad range of preventative and social services. Although the program expanded to 112 centers as of 1978, subsequent legislation and funding cuts circumscribed the early objectives. See Karen Davis and Cathy Schoen, "A New Approach to Health Care Delivery," *Health and the War on Poverty* (Washington, D. C.: The Brookings Institution, 1978).

44. Personal letter, n.d.

45. Dr. Oliver Fein; and *Proceedings of the Cleveland SHO.* See also, Boston MCHR/SHO Chapter, *Catalyst* 2:3 (March 1969) for the symposium on Columbia Point Health Center.

46. NENA Intergroup Health Committee, Gloria Martinez and, David Cook, cochairmen, "A Proposal for a Comprehensive Neighborhood Health Center in the Northeast Section of the Lower East Side," October 1967 (Mimeographed) 13.

47. On NENA's origins, Interview with Ana Dumois, the community organizer who helped the mothers committee formulate the project and obtain funding, June 21, 1978; Dr. Desmond Callan, Interview, January 1978. Dr. Callan was Associate Director and Director at NENA from September 1968 to November 1970 and coauthor of the Health/PAC critique of NENA, Health/PAC *Bulletin* 42 (June 1972).

48. Dr. Desmond Callan; Desmond Callan and Oliver Fein, "NENA: Community Control in a Bind," Health/PAC *Bulletin* 42 (June 1972):3-12.

49. NENA Health Committee, "Proposal."

50. NENA Intergroup Health Committee, Minutes, August 7, 1969.

51. NENA Health Committee, "Proposal" 2.

52. NENA Intergroup Health Committee Minutes, August 7, 1969.

53. *NENA Health Center Staff Report to NENA Board,* February 25, 1970 (Mimeographed).

54. Callan and Fein, "NENA: Community Control in a Bind" 5.

55. Reverend Gerald Vander Hart, Chairman of the Board of Directors, Memo to NENA Health Center Staff, April 20, 1970.

56. Ana Dumois felt the federal requirement was a major disservice. It meant the director and associate director were hired before they were really interviewed and once in place, they limited the community's options. Interview, June 21, 1978.

57. Dr. Desmond Callan; Callan and Fein, "NENA: Community Control in a Bind."

58. Dr. Desmond Callan; Ana Dumois; and Callan and Fein, "NENA: Community Control in a Bind."

59. See Reverend Gerald Vander Hart, Memo to NENA Health Center Staff; Judy Fox, Memo regarding Social Services, March 19, 1970; and Victor Alicea, "Report of findings and conclusions reached on the issue of Social Services," June 3, 1970 (Mimeographed draft).

60. *NENA Annual Report to Public Health Service,* October 1970.

61. Callan and Fein ("NENA: Community Control in a Bind") quote this statement by a NENA physician. For discussion of the issues involved see Memos and Minutes, 1970.

62. Memo regarding Position of Staff Association, from Staff Association to NENA Review Committee, June 1, 1970 (Mimeographed).

63. Memo from Staff Association; Ana Dumois.

64. Callan and Fein, "NENA: Community Control in a Bind" 6.

65. Dr. D. Zimmerman, as reported in Review Committee Meetings Minutes, June 1, 1970.

66. Alex Efthim, "Report on Study of the Social Service Work in the NENA Health Center," June 15, 1970, Detroit (Mimeographed).

67. Ana Dumois. See also "Proposal."

68. Callan and Fein, "NENA: Community Control in a Bind" 3.

69. Dr. Oliver Fein.

70. Geiger posed this dilemma at a panel discussion at the Cleveland SHO meeting in which health centers were attacked by radicals. See also NENA Intergroup Health Committee, Minutes, August 7, 1969.

71. Dumois made this criticism clear in her interview. See a comparable statement about Martin Luther King, Jr. Health Center in Noel M. Tichy, *Organization Design for Primary Health Care: The Case of the Dr. Martin Luther King, Jr. Health Center* (New York: Praeger Publishers, 1977) 135.

72. Dr. Howard Levy, Interview, July 25, 1978. Dr. Levy worked at NENA between 1973 and 1978.

73. "Health Clinic Strikers are Resolute," *New York Times*, April 1978.

74. Dr. Howard Levy.

75. Timothy F. Dugan, "Consumer Control: Real or Imagined?" Paper presented to the Residency in Social Medicine, Montefiore Hospital, August 26, 1977 (Mimeographed). This comparative study of NHC includes both NENA and MLK.

76. Dugan, "Consumer Control" 16; and Gerald Sparer, George B. Dines, and Daniel Smith, "Consumer Participation in OEO-Assisted Neighborhood Health Centers," *American Journal of Public Health* 60:6 (June 1970).

77. Dugan, "Consumer Control" 8-9; and Tichy, *Organization Design*, chaps. 4 and 5.

78. Dugan, "Consumer Control" 8.

79. Dugan, "Consumer Control" 9.

80. On board/staff conflict see Tichy, *Organization Design* 55-56, 72; and Elinor Langer, "Medicine for the Poor: A New Deal in Denver," *Science* 153 (July 29, 1966):511-12.

81. Tichy, *Organization Design* 72.

82. Peter Rothstein, "The Community Health Center," October 1966, draft for the Institute of Policy Studies 10 (Mimeographed).

83. Tichy, *Organization Design* 55; and *The Sixth Report, The Dr. Martin Luther King, Jr. Health Center,* William B. Lloyd, M.D., Project Director, January 1972-July 1973, 12.

84. Rothstein discusses the problem of organizing around health, "The Community Health Center" 18-20; Dr. H. Jack Geiger.

85. Dr. Desmond Callan.

86. Dr. Desmond Callan.

87. Davis and Schoen adopt this explanation for NHC in general.

88. Dr. Peter Schnall, Interview, August 17, 1978.

89. Delores Smith quoted in Dugan, "Consumer Control" 8.

90. Dr. Howard Levy, July 25, 1978.

91. Mike Clark, Interview, May 1978.

92. The first free clinic was established in Haight-Ashbury in 1967. For an outline of the principles of the movement, see "Free Clinics," Health/PAC *Bulletin* 34 (October 1971).

93. "Free Clinics," Health/PAC *Bulletin* 34; See also MCHR Proposal for 1971-1972, submitted by Quention D. Young, M.D., "Community Clinics and Community Participation in Health Policy Determination," May 3, 1971.

94. "The Selling of the Free Clinics," Health/PAC *Bulletin* 38 (February 1972).

95. Tom Bodenheimer, "Free Clinics: Strategy for Survival," n.d. (Mimeographed); and Health/PAC *Bulletin* 34 and 38.

96. Bodenheimer, "Free Clinics: Strategy for Survival"; Dr. Eric Marcus, Interview, January 1978.

97. "Free Clinics," Health/PAC *Bulletin* 34 (October 1971).

98. "Free Clinics," Health/PAC *Bulletin* 34. Also *Bulletin* 38 (February 1972); Raymond M. Glasscote, et al., *The Alternate Services* (Washington, D. C.: American Psychiatric Association, 1975).

Chapter 6

1. For a discussion of theorists of the new working class, see Chapter 1, note 9 above.

2. MDS disseminated the work of the European "new working class" theorists such as André Gorz, *Strategy for Labor;* Serge Mallet, *Essays on the New Working Class;* and Alain Touraine, *The Post-Industrial Society.*

3. Material on the Urban Underground includes interviews with Jacqueline Leavitt, May 1976; Bob Jacobson, September 16, 1977; and Bob Gottlieb, June 6, 1976. Unpublished material includes: "The Urban Underground Resurfaces," Statements of the Urban Underground at Public Hearing of the New York City Planning Commission, February 19, 1969; "Letting the Cat Out of the City Planning Bag," n.d.; "Petition to the New York City Planning Commission *re* R-10 Zoning"; and miscellaneous leaflets for demonstrations and other political events.

4. UU, "Letting the Cat Out of the City Planning Bag."

5. The jobs included positions in the County Planning Commission, the Community Renewal Program, the Department of City Planning, and private consulting firms.

6. Paul Becker, "The Urban Underground Resurfaces" 4.

7. Ruth Glick, "The Urban Underground Resurfaces" 11.

8. Lynne Aston, "The Urban Underground Resurfaces" 5.

9. Glick, "The Urban Underground Resurfaces" 10-11.

10. In its heyday, 70 to 100 planners turned up at meetings.

11. Bob Jacobson, Interview, September 16, 1977.

12. Bob Jacobson.

13. Bob Gottlieb, Telephone interview, June 6, 1976. Gottlieb felt that Sale *(SDS)* was wrong in calling MDS a predominately SDS group. According to some reports only 25 percent were SDS members and the rest were "alienated middle class labor."

14. Bob Jacobson.

15. Barbara and Alan Haber suggest that certain professions will play key roles in revolutionary change due to a combination of their strategic locus and the changing objective conditions of work. "Getting By with a Little Help from Our Friends," in *Selected Papers* 44-62.

16. Alan Leidner, Interview, August 1980.

17. Brad Smith, Interview, March 19, 1988.

18. Brad Smith, Interview, February 1981; Alan Leidner.

19. The Urban Underground faced a similar situation and the existence of special contracts was used to remove some of the activists.

20. Over the years, representation on community boards had been cut back so that the planning staff were no longer involved in advocacy and area planning had stopped being a lively arena for dissent.

21. Subsequently, they successfully defended the politically motivated firing of a planner. The Moberg case is described in Rachel Bernstein, et al., *Building a City/Building a Union* (New York: DC 37 Printing Department, 1987) 26-27.

22. Group discussion. Spring 1980.

23. Leidner.

24. Leidner.

25. Needleman and Needleman, *Guerrillas in the Bureaucracy.*

26. Lawrence Susskind and Anne Aylward, "Comprehensive Planning: A State-of-the-Art Review of Concepts, Methods, and the Problems of Building Local Capacity," prepared for the Advisory Commission on Housing and Urban Growth, American Bar Association, January 29, 1976 (Mimeographed).

27. Susskind and Aylward 57. The question of publics or constituency has been a continuing concern for planning.

28. Susskind and Aylward 76-77.

29. Susskind and Aylward 66-68.

30. Susskind and Aylward 66-67.

31. Norman Krumholz, Janice Cogger, and John Linner, "The Cleveland Policy Planning Report," *JAIP* 41:5 (September 1975):298-304. The quotes appear on pages 298-300.

32. Herbert J. Gans, "Planning and Class Interests"; Norton E. Long, "Another View of Responsible Planning"; and Paul Davidoff, "Working Toward Redistributive Justice," in *JAIP* 41:5 (September 1975):305-18. These articles on the Cleveland Policy Planning Report will be referred to subsequently as "Journal Forum."

33. Gans, "Journal Forum" 305.

34. Davidoff, "Journal Forum" 318.

35. Piven, "Journal Forum" 309. Piven's critical assessment of the Cleveland Report was mixed with praise. Using substantive benefits to minorities and the poor as a yardstick, Piven conceded that the Cleveland planners had been responsible for real benefits to the people.

36. Piven, "Journal Forum" 310.

37. Kasperson and Breitbart, *Participation, Decentralization and Advocacy Planning* 27. The data came from a survey by the Advisory Commission on Intergovernmental Relations, 1972.

38. See Sherry Arnstein, "A Ladder of Citizenship Participation," *JAIP* 35:4 (1969):216-24.

39. Kasperson and Breitbart, *Participation, Decentralization and Advocacy Planning* 28.

40. Needleman and Needleman, *Guerrillas in the Bureaucracy.*

41. Needleman and Needleman, *Guerrillas in the Bureaucracy* 47.

42. See Fitzhugh Mullan's account of his passage from SHO to Lincoln Hospital in *White Coat, Clenched Fist* chap. 4. Interviews with Dr. Charlotte Fein, July 12, 1978; Dr. Ken Rosenberg, April 21, and May 23, 1978; and Dr. Peter Schnall, August 17, 1978. Given the structure and length of the training process for doctors, I believe a cohort analysis of medical activists would show more continuity than for planners.

43. Mullan, *White Coat* 107, 192.

44. Mullan, *White Coat* 98. For a history of Lincoln Hospital see *White Coat,* chap. 5; also, Ron Blum, M.D., "New York: The Lincoln Collective," *The New Physician,* October 1970, 829-31; Cleo Silver for HRUM, "Lincoln Hospital: Three Views," *Health Rights News,* January 1971; and Ehrenreich and Ehrenreich, *The American Health Empire,* chap. 18.

45. Ehrenreich and Ehrenreich, *The American Health Empire* 254.

46. For a discussion of earlier activity at Lincoln Hospital, see Health/ PAC *Bulletins* 23 (September 1970) and 37 (January 1972), and Seymour R. Kaplan and Melvin Roman, *The Organization and Delivery of Mental Health Services in the Ghetto: The Lincoln Hospital Experience* (New York: Praeger Special Studies, 1973).

47. Mullan, *White Coat* 139-141.

48. "Purposes of a Program in Community Pediatrics at Lincoln Hospital," September 11, 1969 (Mimeographed) 3; and Recruitment Brochure for Lincoln Hospital-Albert Einstein College of Medicine, House Officers Program, 1970-1971 and 1971-1972.

49. Mullan, *White Coat* 153.

50. The term was used by several interviewed and reflects the SDS influence.

51. Nick Egleson articulates this line of thought in "Letter to the Movement," *Liberation,* April 1970, 45-50. See Blum's account of the collective atmosphere in "New York: The Lincoln Collective"; and Mullan, *White Coat* chap. 8.

52. There is some discrepancy in numbers. Mullan says 29 housestaff; Health/PAC reports 32; and Blum says 30.

53. Blum, "New York: The Lincoln Collective."

54. For a detailed account, Health/PAC *Bulletin* 37; Mullan, *White Coat;* and Blum, "New York: The Lincoln Collective."

55. Mullan, *White Coat* 206. The Pediatric Department handbooks (1969-1975) describe the project over time, beginning with Dr. Einhorn's traditional format, the innovations of the Collective, and the assimilation of innovations within a more traditional framework.

56. Dr. Oliver Fein, Interview, July 25, 1978.

57. Mullan describes the situation in *White Coat* chap. 7. See also Health/PAC *Bulletin* 23.

58. Health/PAC *Bulletin* 23 gives a thorough description of this event.

59. Mullan, *White Coat* 147, describes this conference.

60. Health/PAC *Bulletin* 23:15, and Blum, "New York: The Lincoln Collective" 3.

61. Blum, "New York: The Lincoln Collective."

62. Mullan, *White Coat* 162-63.

63. Mullan, *White Coat* 63.

64. Mullan, *White Coat* 150; and Dr. Helen Rodriguez-Trias, Interview, July 19, 1978.

65. Mullan, *White Coat* 167; Dr. Helen Rodriguez-Trias.

66. See Mullan, *White Coat* chap. 10. Mullan says that as activists sensed the political revolt had failed, personal revolt against the system grew more appealing.

67. Mullan, *White Coat* 167.

68. Dr. Einhorn was dismissed, and Dr. Helen Rodriguez-Trias, a Puerto Rican physician, was appointed chief of service. The case made the front pages of New York City newspapers as an example of racially induced resignation. See Michael T. Kaufman, "Lincoln Hospital: A Case History of Dissent that has Split Staff," *New York Times*, December 21, 1970.

69. Mullan, *White Coat* 174.

70. Mullan, *White Coat* 143.

71. Mullan, *White Coat* 190.

72. HRUM statement quoted in Health/PAC *Bulletin* 37:16.

73. Mullan, *White Coat* 185-86, 193-95. "Third World" was the term used by the Lincoln Collective and activist groups to direct attention to internal

colonialism. For an account of HRUM, see Stephen Torgoff, "HRUM Sums Up Hospital Organizing," *Guardian,* December 27, 1972, 7; Cleo Silver, "Lincoln Hospital: Three Views," *Health Rights News,* January 1971; HRUM Statement, May 1971 (Mimeographed); and "Diagnosis Oppression: RX Revolution: Prognosis: Victory," *Liberated Guardian,* July 1972, New York.

74. Mullan, *White Coat* 193.

75. Health/PAC *Bulletin* 37:13.

76. Mullan, *White Coat* 195-96, taken from Minutes.

77. Dr. Oliver Fein described the Lincoln Collective in three phases: political confrontation, community outreach medicine, and in-patient medical reform, Interview, July 28, 1978. See also, Joan Salomon, "The Hospital," *The Sciences,* November 1972:21-27.

78. Mullan, *White Coat* 179.

79. Dr. Charlotte Fein, Interview, July 12, 1978.

80. Mullan, *White Coat* 200.

81. Dr. Helen Rodriguez-Trias.

82. Mullan, *White Coat* 195.

83. Mullan, *White Coat* 202. Also, interviews with Dr. Ken Rosenberg and Dr. Helen Rodriguez-Trias.

84. Mullan, *White Coat* 205.

85. Dr. Oliver Fein. See also the collective publication, *Temperature Rising,* Issues 1, 2, 3, 1974.

86. *Temperature Rising* 1:1 (April 1974).

87. *Temperature Rising:* 1:1 (April 1974).

88. David Bateman, "A New Member Speaks," *Temperature Rising* 1:1 (April 1974).

89. *Temperature Rising* 1:3, January 1975.

90. "Accreditation: What's Going On?" (Mimeograph). See also, Sandy Leff, "The Big White Wash," *Temperature Rising* 1:3, January 1975.

91. Dr. Oliver Fein argued that cuts in the public sector would not lead to community/worker support for these reasons.

92. Minutes of the Patient Care Committee, meetings and discussion; Patient Rights Booklet, August 27, 1973, first draft; and "A Proposal for a Patient Care Committee," October 12, 1973 (Mimeographed).

93. Jim O'Brien describes this period in "American Leninism in the 1970's" 27-30.

94. See Mullan's account of his work with Committee of Interns and Residents in *White Coat* 84-90; Peter Moyer, "Victory for Better Working Conditions," in *Temperature Rising* 1:1 (April 1974); Report on "On Call Room Struggle," February 11, 1974 (Mimeographed).

95. For the San Francisco General Hospital experience, see Tom Boden-heimer and Ken Barnes, April 1973, "Thursday Noon Committee—A First Attempt at Institutional Organizing, 1971-1972" (Mimeographed); Health/ PAC *Bulletin* 38 (February 1972).
For criticism of "critical mass," Minutes of a MCHR Regional Conference, New Haven, Conn., 1972, signed R. Kotelchuck, E. Messinger, A. Mazer, R. Leib, and M. Holliman; Letter from Tom Bodenheimer in response to Downington Conference, n.d.; and notes from the Downington Conference, held to discuss the merits of institutional health collectives.

96. Bodenheimer letter regarding the Downington Conference.

97. Dr. Peter Schnall, Interview, August 17, 1978.

98. For an overview, see Robert G. Harmon, M.D., "Intern and Resident Organizations in the United States, 1934-1977." April 1978 (Mimeographed) 7-10.

99. New York City's Committee of Interns and Residents struck first, followed by housestaff in Los Angeles and Chicago.

100. On the establishment of PNHA, see CIR *Bulletin* 1:1 (July-August 1972), and 1:2 (September-October 1972). On the decision to become a labor organization, see Tom Dorris, "PNHA Gets Teeth," *Hospital Physician* (November 1975):23, and "PNHA Forms a National Union," CIR *Bulletin* 4:10 (October 1975). Interview with Dr. Jay Dopkin, then president of PNHA and past president of CIR, July 31, 1978, Washington, D. C.

101. For example, Robert K. Match, Arnold H. Goldstein, and Harold L. Light, "Unionization, Strikes, Threatened Strikes and Hospitals: The View from Hospital Management," and Samuel Wolfe, "Worker Conflicts in the Health Field: An Overview," in *Organization of Health Workers and Labor Conflict*, ed. Samuel Wolfe (New York: Baywood Publishing Company, 1973).

102. For a review of the legal questions up to 1978, see Tom Dorris, "1978: The Year of the Housestaff Amendment?" *Hospital Physician* (March 1978):18.

103. *American Medical Association News* (March 6, 1981):1.

104. While most of these demands can also be viewed in terms of physician interests, my focus will be on the congruence of patient and physician interests.

105. Dr. Jay Dopkin, "History of CIR," CIR *Bulletin* 1 (1972).

106. Foreign medical graduates (FMGs) contributed to the increasingly political composition and outlook of housestaff. Encouraged by preferential immigration laws at a time of physician shortage, FMGs had become a secondary labor force by the early 1970s, comprising one-fifth of all practicing physicians and servicing the second-class institutions. With fiscal cuts and a shift of public concern from physician shortage to oversupply in the 1970s, their initially poor situation worsened. Between 1970 and 1975, a series of harsh professional and legislative policies were directed at them.

FMGs comprised between 40 to 70 percent of the staff at city hospitals and 45 percent of CIR membership. They needed due process and protection from racial discrimination. During the 1975 strike, the FMGs became a symbol and rallying cry. They also provided strong support for the strike. The hospitals, which went out with all housestaff, were predominately FMGs. Dr. Richard Knutson, Interview, November 20, 1975; and CIR *Bulletin* 3:8 (December 1974). On the general situation of FMGs, see Robert J. Weiss, et al., "Foreign Medical Graduates and the Medical Underground," and Robert J. Weiss, et al., "The Effect of Importing Physicians—Return to a Pre-Flexnerian Standard."

107. Mullan, *White Coat* 87.

108. This was certainly Health/PAC's view of CIR. While CIR was not abandoned, activists did not have great hopes for it and some, Mullan among them, shifted their focus to community/worker struggles such as the Lincoln Collective. Mullan, *White Coat* 86-90.

109. Mullan, *White Coat* 90.

110. CIR *Bulletin* 3:1 (1974), and Mullan, *White Coat* 84-90.

111. Dr. Richard Cooper, "Special Report on Hypertension," CIR *Bulletin* 2:5 (November-December 1973).

112. Editorial, "Who Ate the Job Lines," CIR *Bulletin* 3:2 (March-April 1974) and 3:6 (October 1974). On the impact on patient care see Richard Cooper, M.D., "Slave Labor Must End," CIR *Bulletin* 3:6 (October 1975).

113. Editorial, CIR *Bulletin* 3.6 (October 1974).

114. CIR *Bulletin* 4:8 (August 1975) and 4:11 (November 1975).

115. Interview with a striking housestaff member, March 18, 1975, New York. For a sense of how the leadership presented housestaff see "Presidential Message," Dr. Richard Knutson, CIR *Bulletin* 4:2 (February 1975); and Dr. Jay Dopkin, "Presidential Message," CIR *Bulletin* 6:3 (May 1977).

116. Dr. Richard Knutson, Interview, November 20, 1975.

117. CIR *Bulletins* 7:2 (April-June 1978) and 7:5 (November-December 1978).

118. For precedents there was President Kennedy's executive order regarding federal employees, and in New York State, the Wagner Act. Many states enacted labor legislation allowing for the unionization of hospital employees. Within the hospital, this was a period of unionization for nonprofessional workers as well as continued gains for nurses.

For housestaff, the key legislative act was the amendment of the Taft-Hartley Act in 1974, to cover employees of voluntary nonprofit hospitals. This was hailed as "dramatically expanding the rights of housestaff across the country to compel bargaining on wages, schedules, tenure, grievances, training and patient care." Murray Gordon, CIR *Bulletin* 3:5 (September 1974). Writing in the *New York Times* (November 16, 1975), A. H. Raskin said "collective bargaining would be for the seventies, what student activism was for the sixties."

119. The National Board of Medical Examiners issued a report which suggested that medical licensure be delayed until the completion of training. This would have cut off sources of independent income for housestaff and brought them under the control of the AAMC. The initially poor situation of FMGs worsened between 1970 and 1975, reflecting a series of harsh immigration policies and professional requirements. Finally, rising rates of malpractice insurance threatened housestaff along with other physicians.

120. Peter Kihss, "21 Hospitals here Hit by a Walkout of Housedoctors," *New York Times*, March 18, 1975.

121. The AMA issued a "surprise statement" calling the strike a "strike for better patient care" and stating that "overly long hours constitute a threat to the quality of care a patient is getting." This was an important policy statement because AMA endorsement represented a "clear reversal of position" and because "the strike represents a precedent-setting challenge to the traditional way in which specialists are trained." *New York Times*, March 19, 1975; and the *Times* editorial, " . . . AMA's militancy," *New York Times*, March 22, 1975.

122. Peter Kihss, "Pact Ends Doctor Strike, Staffs Return to Hospitals," *New York Times*, March 21, 1975.

123. CIR did not get specific limitations on shifts or a nondiscrimination clause.

124. Inspired by similar strikes on similar issues in San Francisco and Boston, CIR advocated more direct third-party benefits. During March 1981, CIR held an unsuccessful week-long strike at six city hospitals for better staffing and equipment levels in their contract.

125. The editorial in the *New York Post*, January 18, 1979, "The Wrong Weapon" condemns the one-day strike. See also *New York Times*, January 18, 1978.

126. Dr. Richard Knutson.

127. Dr. Knutson noted that during the 1975 strike the only hospitals with 100 percent support were heavily staffed by FMGs. Elite teaching institutions like NYU/Bellevue gave "terrible support." See also Lucinda Franks, "NYU Hospital Interns Bar Strike," *New York Times,* March 19, 1975.

128. David Fluhrer, "The Consequences of Bucking the System," *Hospital Physician* (November 1975).

129. See Dr. Jay Dopkin's editorial, "Invisible Ink," CIR *Bulletin* 4:8 (August 1975).

130. See CIR *Bulletin* 6:5 (May 1977); Tom Dorris, "The Consequence of Being Students," *Hospital Physician* (November 1976):40; Lawrence Boxt, "We've Come a Long Way," CIR *Bulletin* 6:7 (October-November 1977).

131. In January 1978, Dr. Martin Cherkasky, Mayor Koch's special advisor for medical affairs, proposed a plan to close one-half of New York City's municipal hospitals by 1982. *New York Times,* January 18, 1978.

132. Dr. Richard Cooper, Editorial, CIR *Bulletin* 4:9 (September 1975).

133. These strikes were illegal under New York State's Taylor Law which compels public employees to go to arbitration.

134. See Ronald Sullivan, "Doctors Offer Help in Suits Against City for Malpractice," *New York Times,* April 12, 1979.

135. "New York City Health Care Crisis," CIR *Bulletin* 4:5 (May 1975).

136. CIR *Bulletin* 8:1 (January 1979). The hospitals were able to gain the support of minority groups and leaders as part of an attack on the Koch administration in New York City.

137. CIR *Bulletin* 8:2 (February/March 1979). The coalition was called "The Coalition for a Rational Health Policy for New York City."

138. CIR *Bulletin* 8:2.

139. The CIR Political Action Committee recommended that CIR collect data on extra hospital beds to contradict official rationales for closures. CIR *Bulletin* 7:1 (January/March 1978).

140. See the Report of the CIR Political Action Committee, CIR *Bulletin* 7:1 (January/March 1978).

141. For an early history, see Peter Frishauf, "What's This Man Done For You," *Hospital Physician* (September 1975); Bottone, "Sorcerer's Apprentice" 28-29; and Harmon, "Intern and Resident Organizations" 9. See also *Hospital Physician* for May 1976, July 1976, April 1977, and August 1977.

142. Bruce Keppel, "LA Housestaff's Unique Patient Care Fund," *Hospital Physician* (September 1975):17; and *Hospital Physician,* November 1975.

143. *Hospital Physician* (July 1976):46-47 and (October 1976):54.

144. When CIR tried to make an issue of inadequate nursing staff, the issue was thrown out of collective bargaining on the grounds that nurses must make this demand themselves.

145. Keppel, "LA Housestaff's Unique Patient Care Fund" 17.

146. *Hospital Physician* (September 1977).

147. *Hospital Physician* (April 1977):45. Also, *Hospital Physician* (September 1977).

148. Although the housestaff successfully fought the medical school deans and the hospital administration to retain the fund, it was converted from salary to county budget and the county became partner to its management. Dr. Gregg Anderson, Los Angeles County Housestaff Association at the Patient Care Workshop, *Seventh National Assembly*, PNHA, May 5-8, Washington, D. C.

149. Dr. Dan Asimus, Chairman of the Joint Council of the Los Angeles Interns and Residents Association, quoted in *Hospital Physician* (November 1975):11-12.

150. Cook County Interns and Residents, Discussion of Patient Care, *Seventh Annual National Assembly*, PNHA.

151. Harold Levine, "Health Politics: Medicine at Another Level," *Hospital Tribune*, (February 8, 1971) 2.

152. Chicago was a center for SDS, the site of the 1968 Democratic National Convention and the SDS "Days of Wrath," as well as the national office. Chicago also had a history of medical activism on behalf of civil rights in the 1950s.

153. In the words of Dr. Terry Conway, president of the Cook County Housestaff Association during 1978, "We are the only public hospital and any cut to us is a cut to the medically indigent. We are the physicians for the South Side." *Seventh National Assembly*, PNHA, Panel on Public Hospitals.

154. The board had no union people and only one token community person. Dr. Nicholas Rango, Interview, May 29, 1979. Also, Levine, "Health Politics."

155. Roy Petty, "Behind the Cook County Strike," and Steve Diamond, "The Cook County Strike: A Diary," in *Hospital Physician* (November 1975):20, 47. Also, Dr. Nicholas Rango.

156. *Hospital Physican* (December 1975):32.

157. See Kindig and Lucas, Jr., "A New Alliance in Health Care," *Proceedings, First National House Staff Conference*, 1971, and David A. Kindig,

Letter to Edward D. Martin, President, in *Proceedings, First National Conference,* 1971 Appendix I.

158. For the AMA, housestaff represented a large untapped membership source. NARI was interested in selling insurance and services to housestaff.

159. See Harmon, "Intern and Resident Organizations" 13.

160. More controversial proposals to end excessive profitmaking in health care or to abolish the two-class health care system were rejected by the delegates.

161. See Peter Frishauf, "AMA Housestaff Unit Seized by PNHA Slate," *PNHA Newsletter* (February 1974); "Rango Condemns AMA Take-Over by PNHA Slate," *Hospital Physician* (February 1974):3; and Harmon, "Intern and Resident Organizations."

162. Dorris, "PNHA Gets Teeth," *Hospital Physician* (September 1975) and *Infusion for Housestaff* (February 1975).

163. In 1984, CIR spearheaded the revival of a national housestaff organization, The National Federation of Housestaff Organizations (NFHO), created along the lines of a federation model and composed of organizations which have collective bargaining agreements. CIR's position is that "the struggle for access to healthcare for all Americans is intricately linked to that of housestaff rights." David Marder, M.D., Editorial, NFHO *Newsletter* 4:1 (April 1987). Under CIR's leadership, NFHO has helped local organizations (Boston, Buffalo, New York, New Jersey, Chicago and California) build stronger ties with other health care unions both locally and nationally. CIR has a strong interest in affiliation with a national union for NFHO.

164. See CIR *Bulletins* 2:1 (1973); 2:5 (1973); 3:6 (1974); 4:4 (1975); and *Hospital Physician* (September 1975).

165. The movement of working-class populations out of urban areas and the entry of poverty groups also changed the constituency of particular hospitals and heightened the competition between surrounding public and private hospitals for reimbursable clients.

166. In 1957, interns in New York City earned $852 per year; residents, $1,260. By 1980, the starting range for salaries, now graded by years of experience, was from $16,505 to $20,705. In 1965, CIR negotiated a benefits fund for city paid housestaff that currently includes life insurance, disability coverage and dental, optical, psychiatric, and newborn care, in addition to basic hospitalization and major medical insurance.

167. This was true of Los Angeles housestaff who introduced the patient care fund and won adequate staffing and third-party rights. More recently, housestaff associations in San Francisco and Boston have gone on strike and won the inclusion of patient care items such as required levels of

staff and equipment in their contracts. In both cases, collective bargaining traditions have been weak, legislation has been less restrictive than in New York, and there was strong hospital, community, and trade union support.

168. "The NLRB Decision," *Hospital Physician*, May 1976, 50.

169. Dr. Jay Dopkin, then president of PNHA, interviewed in Washington, D. C., July 31, 1978; and Edward Gluckman, then executive director of CIR, interviewed in New York, April 26, 1978.

170. The AHA-AAMC brief was prepared by the "politically well-connected firm of former Watergate prosecutor, Leon Jaworski." *Hospital Physician* (May 1976).

171. Dr. Jay Dopkin, past president of PNHA, noted that PNHA did not really make use of the NLRB amendment legally; that it was only on the books for two years before being overturned; and that the five organizations that filed with the NLRB did so on their own. However, the NLRB decision had internal political consequences much like the impact of the ERA on the women's movement. It divided the movement, led to CIR's decision to leave PNHA, and PNHA's subsequent demise.

172. "The NLRB Decision," *Hospital Physician* (May 1976); Rex Greene, "Academia's Hidden Housestaff Agenda," *Hospital Physician* (July 1976); and Neil Shister, "The Move Against Housestaff Licensure," *Hospital Physician* (May 1977).

173. *Hospital Physician* (July 1976); also, the May 1976 and September 1975 issues.

174. Peter Frishauf, Editorial, "An Apple a Day," *Hospital Physician* (May 1976):5.

175. See, for example, "AMA Support for PNHA Bill in 1978," *Hospital Physician* (March 1978):20 and "AMA, AMSA, ANA," *Hospital Physician* (May 1977):46.

176. See Editorial by Dr. Richard Cooper, CIR *Bulletin* 4:9 (September 1975).

177. *Hospital Physician*, (December 1976):48. Also CIR *Bulletin* 4:4 (April 1975) for a discussion of PNHA's attack on the Health Manpower Bill.

178. Dr. Fitzhugh Mullan, *Seventh National Assembly*. PNHA, May 5, 1978, Washington, D. C.

179. Dr. Jay Dopkin, Interview, July 31, 1978.

180. Dr. Fitzhugh Mullan, *Seventh National Assembly*, PNHA.

Chapter 7

1. This is Lenin's vanguard. The question raised in *What is to be Done?* is how to generate political consciousness beyond economism.

2. Gorz makes this distinction in *A Strategy of Labor* 7-8. He emphasizes the importance of the analytic role—of examining reforms within their larger economic and political context so as to distinguish viable political alternatives.

3. UPA Minutes, January 7, 1975, Boston, Mass.

4. UPA Memo, "Structure in a Transitional Period."

5. The Housing and Community Research Groups, Urban Planning Aid, *Community Housing Development Corporations: The Empty Promise* 1, Cambridge, Mass. 1972. This pamphlet will be referred to as *The Empty Promise*.

6. Media was in-house work compared to the field orientation of the housing and prison projects.

7. In July 1976, one full-time and one part-time planner were the only professionals at UPA; in 1981, there were none.

8. Tom Gogan and Anne Meyerson's presentation of Homefront at the New York Area Network Conference, Columbia University, June 1976.

9. Discussion of the origins of the slide show project, Homefront Meeting, April 1976, New York.

10. Tony Schuman, Interview, May 12, 1976.

11. Homefront Agenda and Memo, "Consensus from an Evaluation of Homefront Practice," Homefront Meeting, May 1976, New York.

12. Homefront, "We Won't Move," a leaflet on the Morningside squatters, n.d. (Mimeographed).

13. The report went through three printings. Homefront also began work on an accompanying slide show that was not completed.

14. *Housing Abandonment in New York City* 126.

15. Homefront participated in a lively debate about building abandonment at the New York Area Network Conference, June 1976. See *Planners Network* #12:1 for the debate and the relation of activist intellectuals to self-help community efforts. See also #17:7 and #18:4. A similar discussion was held at the New York Area Network Conference, April 1977.

16. "Homefront—A Brief Description." March 1978 (Mimeographed).

17. On the In Rem Tenants Coalition and Union of City Tenants (UCT), interviews with Bill Borock, February 1981, and Tom Gogan, February 27, 1988.

18. See the *Planners Network* newsletter, particularly #1, August 4, 1975 and #3, November 6, 1975.

19. The mailing list had 300 names in 1977; 800 in 1979; and more than 900 in 1988.

20. David Gurin, *Planners Network* #1.

21. *Planners Network* #2:2.

22. *Planners Network* #1:3 and #2.

23. Renee Toback, *Planners Network* #2:3.

24. Alan Rabinowitz, *Planners Network* #2:3.

25. Compare Herbert Gans's preference to statements calling for an explicit radical identity. *Planners Network* #2:2.

26. Chester Hartman, *Planners Network* #1:2. For the following discussion see *Planners Network* #2:6, #2:7, #2:11.

27. Harvey, *Planners Network* #6:29. See also #2.

28. *Planners Network* #2:9.

29. More than one-half of those attending the first Boston and New York area meetings were unemployed or underemployed. Institutional affiliation was particularly important for unemployed professionals. Hartman commented: "Without an institutional identification, credentials of some kind may become of more importance to gain access to information." *Planners Network* #2:16.

30. Dave Ranney, *Planners Network* #1:5.

31. *Planners Network* #14:2.

32. See *Planners Network* #8 and #9.

33. Hartman suggested an organization similar to UPA in the Bay area. See *Planners Network* #2:18. On the importance of the International Hotel as a turf struggle, see *Planners Network* #10.

34. While UPA's struggle was a compelling local issue, it probably deterred advocacy.

35. See the letter by Michael Stone, reprinted in *Planners Network* #7.

36. See *Planners Network* #8:3, #9:2, and #10:2. A learning co-op, the Policy Training Center, was funded by NIMH in 1978.

37. The New York Area Network Conference, June 1976.

38. Tony Schuman, New York Area Network Conference, April 1977.

39. See the report from Bruce Dale, *Planners Network* #7:1; also #18:2 and #19:3.

40. *Planners Network* #14:1-2, 11-12.

41. *Planners Network* #19:1.

42. Chester Hartman, "Ten Years of Planners Network: Reflections and Ruminations," *Planners Network* #50:9. Subsequently, the Planners Network worked with a coalition to put together a conference (December 1986) in Washington entitled "Housing and Economic Development: State, Local and Grass Roots Initiatives." *Planners Network* #62:3.

43. One such example is Shelterforce, an organization defined by its issue focus (housing), not by profession.

44. In both New York and Boston, URPE was invited to early Network conferences to describe its own experience.

45. *Planners Network* #19:1.

46. Along these lines, the election of Network members and planning progressives to the board of the APA, the mainstream professional association, siphoned off some of the progressive energy.

47. Health/PAC subscription brochure, 1978.

48. Although Health/PAC's analysis did not remain static, Health/PAC is identified with the medical empires model.

49. Robb K. Burlage, *New York City's Municipal Hospitals: A Policy Review* (Washington, D. C.: Institute for Policy Studies, 1967).

50. 1971 marked the high point with a staff of 12 including three doctors.

51. See Health/PAC's *Annual Report, 1972,* for a description of the West Coast office under the direction of Dr. Tom Bodenheimer. Its publications include, Elinor Blake and Tom Bodenheimer, *Closing the Doors on the Poor: The Dismantling of California County Hospitals,* and *The Profit in Non-Profit Hospitals.* Health/PAC West also covered the development of doctor foundations and Kaiser-Permanente, the nation's model HMO.

52. The Health/PAC *Annual Report* for 1973 states: "This year we spoke to 62 groups and were asked to consult with 61 organizations. We developed materials for a lecture course on the politics of health care to present to activist groups at medical centers and hospitals, as well as teaching courses for workers on occupational health and safety. . . ."

53. Dr. Ken Rosenberg, Interview, May 23, 1978. Dr. Rosenberg was an SHO activist and, later, a Health/PAC staff member.

54. David Kotelchuck, Interview, March 22, 1978.

55. Ehrenreich and Ehrenreich, *The American Health Empire;* and David Kotelchuck, *Prognosis Negative: Crisis in the Health Care System* (New York: Vintage Books, 1976). As of 1986, *The American Health Empire* had sold 75,000 copies and *Prognosis Negative,* 30,000.

56. Health/PAC, *Annual Report,* 1976. See also Clark Proposal, 1976.

57. See, for example, the lead article "Profits in Medicine" *Bulletin* 72 (September/October 1976), written by Gelvin Stevenson, a member of URPE; Sander Kelman's critical book review of Robert Alford's *Health Care Politics* and of Health/PAC in *Bulletin* 70 (May/June 1976); and Meredeth Turshen on Occupational Health and Safety in Health/PAC *Bulletin* 71 (July/August 1976). These new voices reflected Health/PAC's participation in the URPE Conference on Health and in the ECHDG.

58. Health/PAC, *Annual Report,* 1973, 7.

59. David Kotelchuck, Interview, April 1978.

60. Health/PAC, *Bulletin* 1 (June 1968):1.

61. Health/PAC, *Bulletin* 1 (June 1968):2.

62. David Kotelchuck provided this overview, March 22, 1978.

63. Health/PAC promotional brochure 1971.

64. Health/PAC promotional brochure.

65. Health/PAC *Bulletin* 28 (February 1971). This and other guides were modeled after the North American Congress on Latin America (NACLA) research guide which had its roots in the critical sociology of C. Wright Mills.

66. Health/PAC *Bulletin* 28 (February 1971):1-2.

67. Dr. Desmond Callan was one of the directors of the NENA Health Center. Dr. Howard Levy spent several years at NENA. Drs. Oliver Fein and Ken Rosenberg were members of SHO and the Lincoln Collective.

68. On the Lower East Side, LENA was fighting for control of Gouverneur Hospital and NENA, for a health center. In Harlem, groups demanded control of Harlem City Hospital Center; in the South Bronx, for a community controlled mental health center against the Einstein-Montefiore Empire, and in Washington Heights, for a community controlled mental health center.

69. Health/PAC *Bulletin* 8 (April 1969).

70. Desmond Callan and Oliver Fein, "NENA: Community Control in a Bind," Health/PAC *Bulletin* 42 (June 1972):13. See also, *Bulletin* 37 and 42, and *The American Health Empire* chaps. 18-19.
For the impact of federal policy on community based activism see *Annual Report,* 1973, 6-8. It was important but not determinate.

71. Rhonda Kotelchuck, Interview, July 13, 1978.

72. Editorial, "Institutional Organizing," Health/PAC *Bulletin* 37 (January 1972):1.

73. Health/PAC *Bulletin* 3 (August 1968) raised the question, "New Breed of Doctors?" For CIR, see Health/PAC *Bulletin* 12 (September 1969) and for interns and residents at San Francisco General Hospital, Health/PAC *Bulletin* 22 (July/August 1970):17.

74. Health/PAC *Bulletin* 23 (September 1970). For a latter assessment of the Lincoln Collective see Susan Reverby and Marsha Handelman, "Emancipation of Lincoln," *Bulletin* 37 (January 1972).

75. Health/PAC *Bulletin* 23 (September 1970) and 29 (March 1971) on San Francisco General Hospital.

76. Health/PAC *Bulletin* 29 (March 1971) and 37 (January 1972).

77. On nursing, see Vicky Cooper, "The Lady's Not for Burning," Health/ PAC *Bulletin* 18 (March 1970):2, and Susan Reverby, "Health: Women's Work," Health/PAC *Bulletin* 40 (April 1972):15. For a general statement on the "unique" relation of women to the health system, see the Editorial, "Women and the Health System," Health/PAC *Bulletin* 40 (April 1972).

78. "What Course for Health Workers," Health/PAC *Bulletin* 22 (July/ August 1970):12.

79. David Gaynor,, et al., "RN's Strike," Health/PAC *Bulletin* 60 (September/October 1974):2, 14.

80. Rhonda Kotelchuck.

81. Health/PAC *Bulletin* 17 (February 1970).

82. Health/PAC *Bulletin* 19 (April 1970) drew on staff member Dr. Howard Levy's experience to discuss the army's use of medicine and medical personnel as a foreign policy tool in Vietnam. For drug addiction, see Health/PAC *Bulletin* 21 (June (1970), and for prison health care, Health/ PAC *Bulletins* 20 (May 1970), 21 (June 1970), and 53 (September 1973). A 1975 issue of the Health/PAC *Bulletin* 67 (November/December) devoted to the medical treatment of hyperactive children, went as far as Health/PAC was to go in a cultural Marxist direction. See the accompanying theoretical piece by Steven London, "Science as Ideology: Reflections on MBD" 10-11.

83. See Health/PAC *Bulletin* 40 (April 1972), "Women and the Health System."

84. See Health/PAC *Bulletin* 62 and 65 (1975) on sterilization. Health/PAC provided continuing coverage of abortion from 1969.

85. Compare Health/PAC *Bulletin* 33 (May 1971) with *Bulletin* 50 (March

1973) and 61 (November/December 1974). On the health labor force, compare *Bulletin* 22 (July/August 1970) with 40 (April 1972) and 46 (November 1972). Then compare these with the Braverman style analysis of hospital nursing in 66 (September/October) 1975.

86. Howard Levy and John Ehrenreich, "The Portal Vein Statement," New York, 1970 (Mimeographed).

87. For example, Sander Kelman's criticism in Health/PAC *Bulletin* 69 (March/April 1976).

88. Mike Clark, Interview, April 1978.

89. Rhonda Kotelchuck.

90. Health/PAC *Bulletin* 69 (March/April 1976).

91. David Kotelchuck, Interview, March 22, 1978.

92. Health/PAC *Bulletin* 69 (March/April 1976).

93. An example was the Clark Proposal, (March 1978) the first of two reports by the Preventive and Primary Care Project of Health/PAC.

94. Rhonda Kotelchuck speaking of 1976-1977.

95. This distinction is made by Levy and Ehrenreich in "The Portal Vein."

96. Levy and Ehrenreich, "The Portal Vein."

97. Levy and Ehrenreich, "The Portal Vein." Similar issues are raised in a 1975 critique of MCHR and of the Left in general. See Rhonda Kotelchuck and Howard Levy, "MCHR," Health/PAC *Bulletin* 63 (March/April 1975):27-29.

98. Dr. Howard Levy, Interview, July 25, 1978.

99. Dr. Oliver Fein, Interview, July 25, 1978.

100. Ehrenreich and Ehrenreich are examples with the publication of *The American Health Empire.*

101. Dr. Howard Levy.

102. Dr. Charlotte Fein, Interview, July 12, 1978.

103. Dr. Oliver Fein.

104. Dr. Howard Levy.

105. See for example, Health/PAC *Bulletin* 42 (June 1972) and 63 (March/April 1975).

106. This issue was raised back in 1970 by Levy and Ehrenreich in "The Portal Vein Statement."

107. David Kotelchuck, Interview, March 22, 1978.

108. See Rhonda Kotelchuck, "Government Cost Control Strategies," Health/PAC *Bulletin* 75 (March/April 1977).

109. "Report on the ECHDG," *HMO Packet* #1.

110. ECHDG cover letter (April 10, 1976) for *HMO Packet* #1. Except for the cover letter, these mimeographed packets are undated. They were produced by workgroups within the ECHDG and mailed to groups and individuals across the country on request. They will be referred to by number. Individual articles or contributions will be referred to by author and packet as the packets do not always have page numbers.

111. Joe Eyer, Interview, September 15, 1979.

112. Evan Stark "Introduction to the Special Issue on Health," entitled "The Political Economy of Health," *Review of Radical Political Economics* 9:1 (Spring 1977). Evan Stark was coordinator for the HMOs.

113. Evan Stark, cover letter dated January 1977, *HMO Packet* #2.

114. Among them, the role of the state, women and health, the health labor force, historical materialist epidemiology, ideology, corporate activity, and international health.

115. Several other packets were in process, on international health, the health labor force, and occupational health.

116. In making this and subsequent comparisons, I am using the health empires model as my baseline for Health/PAC. For a critique of the Health/PAC model by ECHDG members, see Evan Stark, "The State and Health," *HMO Packet* #1, and the book review by Sander Kelman, Health/PAC *Bulletin* 69 (March/April 1976).

117. See also, Stark, "The State and Health," and the bibliography, "Science is Social Relations," *HMO Packet* #4.

118. Hopper, "On HME: Notes from an East Coast Discussion Group Session."

119. David Gaynor and Joseph Eyer, "Materialist Epidemiology," *HMO Packet* #1.

120. David Gaynor and Joseph Eyer, "Materialist Epidemiology," *HMO Packet* #1.

121. See Peter Schnall, "An Analysis of Coronary Heart Disease Using Historical Materialist Epidemiology," in *HMO Packet* #2. Also, Howard Berliner, "Ideology in Medicine," *HMO Packet* #1.

122. Howard Berliner, "Notes on Historical Precursors of Materialist Epidemiology," *HMO Packet* #1.

123. Schnall, "An Analysis of Coronary Heart Disease."

124. Gayner and Eyer, "Materialist Epidemiology."

125. Howard Berliner and J. Warren Salmon, "Toward an Understanding of Holistic Medicine," *HMO Packet* #4.

126. *HMO Packet* #4. See also, Hopper and Guttmacher, "Suicide," for a discussion of HME as "social criticism."

127. Stark, "The Cutting Edge in Occupational Health."

128. Schnall, "An Analysis of Coronary Heart Disease," and Grace Ziem, "Toward a Historical Materialist Understanding of Rheumatoid Arthritis," *HMO Packet* #2. This critique occurred at a time of increasing public and professional discontent with the efficacy of traditional medical paradigms. Cancer was but one example.

129. Elizabeth Fee, presentation at a plenary on "Science," ECHDG meeting, September 16, 1979.

130. From the start, the ECHDG was divided between those who emphasized structural and those who emphasized cultural factors, and within the structural camp, between Old Left and New Left factions. Early on, this division was represented in alternating discussions of the state and HME, and in 1979, in the two workgroups, Health Services and Policy, and Sex, Culture and Everyday Life.

131. Kelman, "Definitions of Health."

132. Berliner, "Ideology in Medicine."

133. Berliner, "Ideology in Medicine."

134. J. Warren Salmon and Richard Garfield, "The Role of Ideology in Health Struggles in China," *HMO Packet* #4.

135. Sander Kelman, "Toward a Strategy of Health Protection," *HMO Packet* #3.

136. Demand for the HMOs was high, but there was no staff or budget to handle publication.

137. Many of the articles were printed in a final version in *International Journal of Health Services,* ed. Vincente Navarro, a founding member of ECHDG; also Health/PAC *Bulletin* and *The Review of Radical Economics.*

138. Stark, cover letter, *HMO Packet* #3.

139. Stark, cover letter, *HMO Packet* #3.

140. Stark, "The Cutting Edge in Occupational Health."

141. Berliner and Salmon, "Toward an Understanding of Holistic Medicine."

142. The September 1979 meeting was devoted to the question, "Where to?"

143. ECHDG meeting, October 4, 1978, New York.

144. ECHDG meeting, September 16, 1979, New York.

145. Elizabeth Fee, Presentation, ECHDG plenary "Science," September 16, 1979.

146. Dr. Vincente Navarro, Oral presentation, ECHDG plenary on "Science," September 16, 1979, New York.

147. ECHDG meetings, 1978-1979.

Chapter 8

1. Mancur Olson, Jr., *The Logic of Collective Action: Public Goods and the Theory of Groups* (Cambridge, Mass.: Harvard University Press, 1968) 14. Olson states that one must define the individual or collective nature of goods by reference to a given group.

2. NENA was an exception as were situations involving medical center expansion. In the case of NENA, community mobilization occurred because an asthmatic child almost died during a transportation strike. Cases involving medical center expansion were similar to urban renewal in that they posed threats to destroy surrounding homes and neighborhoods.

3. Olson, *The Logic of Collective Action*, 48.

4. Both Bell and Castells predicted a shift in the locus and nature of conflict from production and class to situs and distribution/consumption. Bell defines *situs* as the location of occupational activities within sectors—military, economic, or governmental, the university or the social complex. According to Bell, the emergence of a planned economy has brought formerly economic issues into the political realm. *The Post-Industrial Society* 37. Manuel Castells views governmental intervention as a form of legitimation necessitated by uneven development. He draws his examples from the service sectors: housing, transportation, and health. *The Urban Question: A Marxist Approach* (Cambridge, Mass.: MIT Press, 1977) Part V.

5. Castells, whose focus is primarily on urban political movements, makes this argument in *The Urban Question*.

6. Even activist doctors at Lincoln Hospital learned this lesson, for when housestaff suddenly resigned in protest of their political activities, the activists' victory turned into a defeat. See Chapter 6.

7. Ben-David, "Professionals and Unions in Israel."

8. "The Schools of the Minor Professions."

9. "Professions or Self-Perpetuating Systems?"

10. O'Connor, Habermas, and Castells use the term to refer to the contradictory functions of accumulation and legitimation for the expanding capitalist state. Castells specifically notes the impact of federal urban policy on minorities and the poor. In his scenario, uneven development led to a crisis of legitimacy and to urban conflict in the 1960s.

11. Robert R. Alford, *Health Care Politics: Ideological and Interest Group Barriers to Reform* (Chicago: University of Chicago Press, 1975) 14-17.

12. In the 1980s, a time of global economic restructuring, planning has become more central and contradictory for capitalism. See for example, Norman I. Fainstein, Susan S. Fainstein, and Alex Schwartz, "How New York Remained a Global City: 1940-1987," *Atop the Urban Hierarchy,* ed. Robert Beauregard (New York: Roman-Littlefield, 1989).

Chapter 9

1. Larson, *The Rise of Professionalism* Part I.

2. See Marie R. Haug and Marvin B. Sussman, "Professional Autonomy and the Revolt of the Client," *Social Problems* 17 (Fall 1964):153-61. While Haug and Sussman look cross-sectionally at client groups, they do not examine changing social composition. They also treat professional response summarily as cooptation.

3. A notable exception in the health movement was the community initiated health center, NENA, in New York City. See Chapter 5.

4. Well before the demand for Black Power became a general rallying cry, advocacy projects had generated their own community-advocate conflict.

5. See Rueschemeyer's criticism of Parsons for failing to examine the problem of value dissensus in the legal profession. "Doctors and Lawyers" 7-9. Along these lines, it is not so surprising to read, in 1989, that "some local health centers have become local power bases, at the expense of quality medical service." Lisa Glazer, "Community Health Centers Get a Check-up," *City Limits* (March 1989):13.

6. "The Professional Ideology of Social Pathologists," *AJS* 49:2 (September 1943).

7. Eliot Freidson, "Professionalization and the Organization of Middle-Class Labour in Postindustrial Society," *Sociological Review Monograph* 20 (1973):47-60.

8. Larson, *The Rise of Professionalism* 20.

9. Larson, *The Rise of Professionalism* 236-38.

10. Starr, *The Social Transformation of American Medicine,* Part II.

11. See Chapter 4.

12. Martin Rein, "Social Planning: The Search for Legitimacy."

13. "Professions or Self-Perpetuating Systems?"

14. Gorz, *A Strategy for Labor.* One example was the decision of a planning organization to pull back from its earlier involvement in community development housing and to organize tenants' unions. See Chapter 5.

15. Gouldner has noted that Marxism has many of the same defensive and offensive functions as traditional ideology. *Ideology and Technology, The Future of Intellectuals* and *The Rise of the New Class.*

16. Goode, "Theoretical Limits of Professionalization."

17. Johnson, *Professions and Power* and Larson, *The Rise of Professionalism.*

18. Wright, "Intellectuals and the Class Structure."

19. See Johnson, *Professions and Power* chap. 1.

20. Poulantzas, *Classes in Contemporary Capitalism* Part III, chap. 3 and Wright, "Intellectuals and the Class Structure."

Glossary of Acronyms

AAMC	American Association of Medical Colleges
AFSCME	American Federation of State, County, and Municipal Employees Union
AHA	American Hospital Association
AIP	American Institute of Planners
AMA	American Medical Association
ANA	American Nurses Association
APA	American Planning Association
APHA	American Public Health Association
ASPO	American Society of Planning Officials
BRA	Boston Redevelopment Authority
CAPE	Coalition of American Public Employees
CIR	Committee of Interns and Residents
ECHDG	East Coast Health Discussion Group
ERAP	Economic Research and Action Project
FMGs	foreign medical graduates
Health/PAC	Health Policy Advisory Center
HEW	Department of Health, Education and Welfare
HME	historical materialist epidemiology
HMO	Health Movement Organization
HRA	Health Revolutionary Alliance
HRUM	Health Revolutionary Unity Movement
JCAH	Joint Commission on the Accreditation of Hospitals
MCHR	Medical Committee for Human Rights
MDS	Movement for a Democratic Society
MLK	Dr. Martin Luther King, Jr. Health Center

NACLA	North American Congress on Latin America
NARI	National Association of Interns and Residents
NCUP	Newark Community Union Project
NENA	North East Neighborhood Association
NFHO	National Federation of Housestaff Organizations
NHCs	Neighborhood Health Centers
NIH	National Institute of Health
NIMH	National Institutes of Mental Health
NLRA	National Labor Relations Act
NLRB	National Labor Relations Board
NSF	National Science Foundation
NYC	Neighborhood Youth Corps
NYU	New York University
OEO	Office of Economic Opportunity
PEO	Planners for Equal Opportunity
PNHA	Physicians National Housestaff Association
PSRO	Professional Standards Review Organization
RMP	Regional Medical Program
SAMA	Student American Medical Association
SDS	Students for a Democratic Society
SHO	Student Health Organizations
SHPs	student health projects
SMC	Student Medical Conference
SNCC	Student Non-Violent Coordinating Committee
UTC	The Union of City Tenants
UFS	Urban Field Service
UPA	Urban Planning Aid
URPE	Union of Radical Political Economists
UU	Urban Underground
WHO	World Health Organization

Bibliography

Much of my source material consists of organizational records such as minutes, memos, letters, reports, leaflets, pamphlets, newsletters, and conference proceedings of health and planning organizations. This material was made available both by participants and organizations.

The following organizational publications have been cited throughout the text. Articles from these sources cited in the notes will not be listed separately in the bibliography:

AIMS *Interne*
Boston MCHR *Catalyst*
CIR *Bulletin* 1972-present
Civil Service Technical Guild, Local 375, AFL-CIO. *Building a City, Building a Union* 1987
HMO Packets #1-4
Health/PAC *Bulletin* 1968-present
Homefront *Housing Abandonment in New York City* 1977; pamphlets
Hospital Physician 1975-1977
Lincoln Collective *Temperature Rising*
MCHR *The Body Politic; Health Rights News* 1969-1971; newsletters and other publications
NCUP reports
PEO *Equalop* Bulletin 1965-1971
Planners Network Newsletter 1975-present
PNHA Proceedings of National House Staff Conferences 1971-1978
SDS Radical Education Project, *Selected Papers from Radicals in the Professions Conference,* 1967; *Liberation;* ERAP *Newsletter*
SHO *Bulletin* 1966-1969; *Encounter* 1966-1969; *Diffusion; Catalyst; Current;* Proceedings of National Assemblies
SHO Student Health Projects, Final Reports

UPA *Community Housing Development Corporations: The Empty Promise* 1973
UU pamphlets

The following abbreviations are used for commonly cited periodicals:
AJS   *American Journal of Sociology*
ASR   *American Sociological Review*
APSR   *American Political Science Review*
NEJM   *New England Journal of Medicine*
JAIP   *Journal of the American Institute of Planners*
IJHS   *International Journal of Health Services*

Ackerknecht, Erwin H. 1968. *A Short History of Medicine.* New York: Ronald
    Press.
Alford, Robert R. 1975. *Health Care Politics: Ideological and Interest Group Barriers
    to Reform.* Chicago: University of Chicago Press.
Alonso, William. 1963. "Cities and City Planners." Lynn 170-185.
Altschuler, Alan A. 1965. *The City Planning Process: A Political Analysis.* Ithaca,
    N.Y.: Cornell University Press.
American Medical Association. *AMA News* March 6, 1981.
Anderson, Martin. 1964. *The Federal Bulldozer.* Cambridge, Mass.: MIT Press.
Arnstein, Sherry. 1969. "A Ladder of Citizen Participation." *JAIP* 35:4. 216-24.
Aronowitz, Stanley. 1973. *False Promises: The Shaping of American Working Class
    Consciousness.* New York: McGraw-Hill.
Auerbach, Jerold S. 1976. *Unequal Justice: Lawyers and Social Change in Modern
    America.* New York: Oxford University Press.
Bach, Kurt W., et al. 1958. "Public Health as a Career in Medicine: Secondary
    Choice within a Profession." *ASR* 23 (October):533-41.
Banfield, Edward C., and James Q. Wilson. 1963. *City Politics.* Cambridge,
    Mass.: Harvard University Press.
Barber, Bernard. 1963. "Some Problems in the Sociology of the Professions."
    Daedalus 92 (Fall):669-88.
Barton, Basil E. 1954. "The Appreciation of Medical Politicians." *NEJM* 250:20
    (May 20):852-56.
Bazell, Robert J. 1971. "Health Radicals: Crusade to Shift Medical Power to
    the People." *Science* 173 (August 6):506-9.
Beard, Charles A. 1926. "Some Aspects of Regional Planning." *APSR* 22
    (May):276.
Beauregard, Robert. 1979. "Thinking about Practicing Planning." Cornell
    Conference "Planning Theory and Practice: Economic Context, Emerg-
    ing Coalitions, and Progressive Planning Roles." Ithaca, New York, April
    26-29.
Becker, Howard. 1962. "The Nature of a Profession." 27-46. *Education for the
    Professions.* Chicago: University of Chicago Press.
Bell, Daniel. 1976. *The Dialectic of Ideology and Technology.* New York: Seabury
    Press.
_____. 1973. *The Coming of Post-Industrial Society.* New York: Basic Books.
_____. 1960. *The End of Ideology.* Glencoe, Ill.: Free Press.

Bellush, Jewel, and Murray Hausknecht. 1966. "Entrepreneurs and Urban Renewal." *JAIP* 32:5. 289-97.

Ben-David, Joseph. 1965. "Professionals and Unions in Israel." *Industrial Relations* 5. 48-66.

Berliner, Howard. 1975. "A Larger Perspective on the Flexner Report." 5:4. 573-92.

Beyle, Thad L., and George T. Lathrop, eds. 1970. *Planning and Politics: Uneasy Partnership*. New York: Odyssey Press.

Bird, David. 1975. "The Sleepless-Nights Syndrome." *New York Times*. March 18.

Blake, Elinor, and Thomas Bodenheimer. 1975. *Closing the Doors on the Poor: The Dismantling of California County Hospitals, and the Profit in Non-Profit Hospitals*. Health/PAC Publication.

Blecher, Earl. 1971. *Advocacy Planning for Urban Development: With Analysis of Six Demonstration Programs*. New York: Praeger.

Block, Fred, et al. 1987. *The Mean Season: The Attack on the Welfare State*. New York: Pantheon Books.

Bloland, Sue and Harland Bloland. 1974. *American Learned Societies in Transition: The Impact of Dissent and Recession*. New York: McGraw-Hill.

Blum, Ron. 1970. "New York: The Lincoln Collective." *The New Physician* (October):829-31.

Bowles, Samuel, and Herbert Gintis. 1976. *Schooling in Capitalist America: Educational Reform and the Contradictions of Economic Life*. New York: Basic Books.

Braverman, Harry. 1974. *Labour and Monopoly Capital: The Degradation of Work in the Twentieth Century*. New York: Monthly Review Press.

Breines, Wini. 1982. *The Great Refusal: Community and Organization in the New Left: 1962-1968*. New York: Praeger.

Brown, E. Richard. 1979. *Rockefeller Medicine Men: Medicine and Capitalism in America*. Berkeley: University of California Press.

Bruce-Briggs, B. ed. 1979. *The New Class?* New Brunswick, N. J.: Transaction Books.

Bucher, Rue, and Anselm L. Strauss. 1961. "Professions in Process." *AJS* 66:4 (January):325-34.

Burlage, Robb K. 1967. *New York City's Municipal Hospitals: A Policy Review*. Washington, D. C.: Institute for Policy Studies.

Burnham, James. 1941. *The Managerial Revolution*. New York: Penguin Books.

Burrow, James G. 1977. *Organized Medicine in the Progressive Era: The Move Toward Monopoly*. Baltimore, Md.: Johns Hopkins University Press.

Caplow, Theodore. 1964. *The Sociology of Work*. New York: McGraw-Hill.

Carlson, Rick J. 1975. *The End of Medicine*. New York: Wiley-Interscience.

Carr-Saunders, A. M., and P. A. Wilson. 1933. *The Professions*. London: Oxford University Press.

Castells, Manuel. 1977. *The Urban Question: A Marxist Approach*. Cambridge, Mass.: MIT Press.

Clark, Colin. 1940. *The Conditions of Economic Progress*. London: Macmillan.

Clark, Michael. 1977. "The Impact of the Fiscal Crisis on Publicly Supported

Primary and Preventive Health Care Services in New York City: A Proposal." New York: Health/PAC (Mimeographed.)

Cloward, Richard A., and Frances Fox Piven. 1975. *The Politics of Turmoil.* New York: Vintage Books.

_____. 1971. *Regulating the Poor: The Functions of Public Welfare.* New York: Vintage Books.

Cogan, Morris L. 1953. "Toward a Definition of Profession." *Harvard Educational Review* 23 (Winter):33-50.

Cohen, Henry. 1970. "The Changing Role of the Planner in the Decision-Making Process." Erber. 174.

Cunningham, M., H. Sanders, and P. Weatherly. 1967. "We Went to Mississippi." *American Journal of Nursing* 67. 801.

Davidoff, Paul. 1975. "Working Toward Redistributive Justice." *JAIP* 41:5. 305-18.

_____. 1965. "Advocacy and Pluralism in Planning." *JAIP* 31:4. 334.

Davidoff, Paul, and Linda Davidoff. 1977. "Advocacy and Urban Planning." Paper submitted to symposium on "Advocacy and the Disciplines." Society for Applied Anthropology. June 6. (Mimeographed.)

_____. 1970. "Advocacy Planning Polarizes the Issues." Forum "Whom Does the Advocate Planner Serve?" *Social Policy* 1:2 (July/August):34-5.

Davidoff, Paul, Linda Davidoff, and Neil Newton Gold. 1970. "Suburban Action: Advocacy Planning for an Open Society." *JAIP* 36:1. 12-21.

Davidoff, Paul, and Thomas Reiner. 1965. "A Choice Theory of Planners." *JAIP* 31:4 331-38.

Davis, Karen, and Cathy Schoen. 1978. "A New Approach to Health Care Delivery." *Health and the War on Poverty.* Washington, D. C.: The Brookings Institution. 161-202.

Derber, C., ed. 1982. *Professionals as Workers: Mental Labor in Advanced Capitalism.* Boston: G. K. Hall.

_____. 1982. "The Proletarianization of the Professional: A Review Essay." Derber. 13-33.

Downey, Gregg W. 1971. "Medical Rights Committee Plans Crusade for Medical Justice." *Modern Hospital* (June).

Dugan, Timothy F. 1977. "Consumer Control: Real or Imagined?" Paper presented to Residency in Social Medicine. Montefiore Hospital. August 26. (Mimeographed.)

Durkheim, Emile. 1957. *Professional Ethics and Civil Morals.* London: Routledge and Kegan Paul.

_____. 1949. *The Division of Labor in Society.* New York: Free Press.

Dyckman, John W. 1961. "What Makes Planners Plan." *JAIP* 27:2.

Edelman, Murray. 1964. *The Symbolic Uses of Politics.* Urbana: University of Illinois Press.

Efthim, Alex. 1970. "Report on Study of the Social Service Work in the NENA Health Center." June 15. Detroit, Mich. (Mimeographed.)

Egleson, Nick. 1970. "Letter to the Movement." *Liberation* (April):45-50.

Ehrenreich, Barbara. 1987. "The New Right Attack on Social Welfare." Block, et al. 161-95.

Ehrenreich, Barbara, and John Ehrenreich. 1979. "The Professional-Managerial Class." *Between Labor and Capital.* ed. Pat Walker. Boston: South End Press. 5-45.

———. 1970. *The American Health Empire: Power, Profits and Politics.* New York: Vintage Books.

Ehrenreich, Barbara, and Deidre English. 1973. *Witches, Midwives and Nurses: A History of Women Healers.* Old Westbury, N. Y.: Feminist Press.

Erber, Ernest, ed. 1970. *Urban Planning in Transition.* New York: Grossman Press.

Etzioni, Amitai, ed. 1969. *The Semi-Professions and Their Organization.* New York: Free Press.

Fainstein, Norman I., and Susan S. Fainstein. 1974. *Urban Political Movements: The Search for Power by Minority Groups in American Cities.* Englewood Cliffs, N. J.: Prentice-Hall.

Fainstein, Norman I., Susan S. Fainstein, and Alex Schwartz. "How New York Remained a Global City: 1940-1987." *Atop the Urban Hierarchy.* ed. Robert Beauregard. New York: Roman-Littlefield, 1989.

Faludi, Andreas. 1973. "Expansion of Planning as a Bureaucratic Function of Urban Government." *A Reader in Planning Theory.* ed. Andreas Faludi. Oxford: Pergamon Press. 232.

Fellman, Gordon, and Barbara Brandt. 1973. *The Deceived Majority: Politics and Protest in Middle America.* New Brunswick, N. J.: Transaction Books.

Flexner, Abraham. 1910. *Medical Education in the United States and Canada.* Bulletin 4. New York: Carnegie Foundation for the Advancement of Teaching.

Franks, Lucinda. 1975. "NYU Hospital Internes Bar Strike." *New York Times* March 19.

Freidson, Eliot. 1986. *Professional Powers: A Study of the Institutionalization of Formal Knowledge.* Chicago: University of Chicago Press.

———. 1985. "The Reorganization of the Medical Profession." *Medical Care Review* 42:1 (Spring):11-35.

———. 1973. "Professionalization and the Organization of Middle-Class Labour in Postindustrial Society." *Sociological Review Monograph* 20:47-60.

———. 1970. *Profession of Medicine: A Study of the Sociology of Applied Knowledge.* New York: Harper and Row.

———. 1970. *Professional Dominance: The Social Structure of Medical Care.* New York: Atherton Press.

———. 1961. *Patients' View of Medical Practice: A Study of Subscribers to a Prepaid Medical Plan in the Bronx.* New York: Russell Sage.

Frieden, Bernard J. 1967. "The Changing Prospects for Social Planning." *JAIP* 33:5. 311-23.

Fuchs, Victor. 1968. *The Service Economy.* New York: Columbia University Press.

Galbraith, John Kenneth. 1967. *The New Industrial State.* New York: Houghton Mifflin.

Galper, Jeffrey H. 1975. *The Politics of Social Services.* Englewood Cliffs, N. J.: Prentice-Hall.

Gans, Herbert J. 1975. "Planning for Declining and Poor Cities." *JAIP* 41:5. 305-7.

_____. 1968. *People and Plans: Essays on Urban Problems and Solutions.* New York: Basic Books.

_____. 1962. *The Urban Villagers: Group and Class in the Life of Italian-Americans.* New York: Free Press.

_____. 1959. "The Human Implications of Current Redevelopment and Relocation Planning." *JAIP* 25:1. 15-25.

Geiger, H. Jack. 1971. "Hidden Professional Roles: The Physician as Reactionary, Reformer, Revolutionary." *Social Policy* (March/April): 24-33.

Gelfand, Mark I. 1975. *A Nation of Cities: The Federal Government and Urban America, 1933-1965.* New York: Oxford University Press.

Gilb, Corinne Lathrop. 1966. *Hidden Hierarchies: The Professions and the Government.* New York: Harper and Row.

Ginzberg, Eli. 1977. *The Limits of Health Reform.* New York: Basic Books.

Ginzberg, Eli, and Alice M. Yohalem, eds. 1974. *The University Medical Center and the Metropolis.* New York: Macy.

Glaser, Barney G., and Anselm L. Strauss. 1967. *The Discovery of Grounded Theory: Strategies for Qualitative Research.* New York: Aldine.

Glasscote, Raymond M., et al. 1975. "The Beginnings." *The Alternate Services.* Washington, D. C.: American Psychiatric Association. 7-12.

Glazer, Nathan. 1974. "The Schools of the Minor Professions." *Minerva* 12:3 (July):346-63.

_____. 1959. "The School as an Instrument in Planning." *JAIP* 25:4. 191-96.

Godschalk, David, ed. 1974. *Learning from Turbulance.* Washington, D. C.: American Institute of Planners.

Goode, William J. 1969. "The Theoretical Limits of Professionalization." Etzioni.

_____. 1961. "The Librarian: From Occupation to Profession?" *The Library Quarterly* 31 (October):306-20.

_____. 1960. "Encroachment, Charlatanism and the Emerging Profession: Psychology, Sociology and Medicine." *ASR* 25 (December):902-14.

_____. 1957. "Community Within a Community: The Professions." *ASR* 22 (April):194-200.

Goodman, Robert. 1971. *After the Planners.* New York: Simon and Schuster.

Gorz, André. 1976. "Technology, Technicians and Class Struggle." *The Division of Labour.* ed. André Gorz. Sussex: Harvester Press.

_____. 1967. *A Strategy for Labor.* Boston: Beacon Press.

Gouldner, Alvin W. 1979. *The Future of Intellectuals and the Rise of the New Class.* New York: Seabury Press.

_____. 1976. *The Dialectic of Ideology and Technology.* New York: Seabury Press.

Gramsci, Antonio. 1971. *Selections from the Prison Notebooks.* New York: International Publishers.

Greenwood, Ernest. 1957. "Attributes of a Profession." *Social Work* 2 (July): 44-55.

Grupenhoff, John T., and Stephen P. Strickland, eds. 1972. *Federal Laws: Health*

Environment, Manpower. Washington: Science and Health Communications Group.

Habermas, Jürgen. 1975. *Legitimation Crisis.* Trans. Thomas McCarthy. Boston: Beacon Press.

————. 1970. *Toward a Rational Society.* Trans. Jeremy J. Shapiro. Boston: Beacon Press.

Hall, Richard H. 1968. "Professionalization and Bureaucratization." *ASR* 33 (February):93-104.

Hancock, John L. 1967. "Planners in the Changing City: 1900-1940." *JAIP* 33:5. 290-304.

Harmon, Robert G., M.D. 1978. "Intern and Resident Organizations in the United States, 1934-1977." (April):7-10. (Mimeographed.)

Harrington, Michael. 1976. *The Twilight of Capitalism.* New York: Simon and Schuster.

Harris, Richard. 1969. *A Sacred Trust.* Baltimore, Md.: Penguin Books.

Hartman, Chester W. 1975. "The Advocate Planner: From 'Hired Gun' to Political Partisan." Forum "Whom Does the Advocate Planner Serve?" *Social Policy* 1:2 (July/August):37-9.

————. 1971. "The Harvard Urban Field Service: A Retrospective View." *11 Views: Collaborative Design in Community Development.* ed. D. Batchelor. Durham: North Carolina State University School of Design. 119-30.

————. 1971. "The Urban Field Service." *The Architectural Forum* 135:2 (September):50-53.

Harvey, David. 1976. "Planning the Ideology of Planning." Paper presented at conference "Planning: Challenge and Response." Center for Urban Policy Research. Rutgers University. New Brunswick, N. J. (Mimeographed.)

Haugh, Marie R. 1977. "Computer Technology and the Obsolescence of the Concept of Profession." *Work and Technology.* eds. M. R. Haugh and J. Dofny. Beverly Hills, Calif.: Sage Publications. 215-28.

————. 1975. "The Deprofessionalization of Everyone?" *Sociological Focus* 3:197-213.

————. 1973. "Deprofessionalization: An Alternative Hypothesis for the Future." *Sociological Review Monograph* 20:195-211.

Haugh, Marie R., and Marvin B. Sussman. 1964. "Professional Autonomy and the Revolt of the Client." *Social Problems* 17 (Fall):153-61.

"The Health Needs of the Nation." Editorial. *NEJM* 248:2 (1953):77-78.

Hershey, Cary. 1973. *Protest in the Public Sector.* Lexington, Mass.: D. C. Heath.

Heydebrand, Wolf V., and James J. Noell. 1973. "Task Structure and Innovation in Organizations." *Comparative Organizations: The Results of Empirical Research.* ed. Wolf V. Heydebrand. Englewood Cliffs, N. J.: Prentice-Hall. 294-322.

House, Jonathan. 1979. "Periled City Hospitals." *New York Times* January 17.

Hughes, Everett C. 1958. *Men and Their Work.* Glencoe, Ill.: Free Press.

Jacobs, Jane. 1961. *The Death and Life of Great American Cities.* New York: Random House.

Jacoby, Russell. 1975. *Social Amnesia.* Boston: Beacon Press.

Jamous, H., and B. Peloille. 1970. "Professions of Self-Perpetuating Systems: Changes in the French University Hospital System." *Professions and Professionalization.* ed. J. A. Jackson. Cambridge: Cambridge University Press. 111-52.

Johnson, Terence J. 1977. "The Professions in the Class Structure." *Industrial Society: Class, Cleavage and Control.* ed. Richard Scase. New York: St. Martin's Press. 93-110.

———. 1972. *Professions and Power.* London: Macmillan

Jordan, Edwin P. 1954. "Group Practice." *NEJM* 250:13 (April 1):558-61.

Kaplan, Seymour R., and Melvin Roman. 1973. *The Organization and Delivery of Mental Health Services in the Ghetto: The Lincoln Hospital Experience.* New York: Praeger.

Kasparson, Roger E., and Myrna Breitbart. 1974. "Participation, Decentralization, and Advocacy Planning." Resource paper no. 25. Washington, D.C.: Association of American Geographers.

Katznelson, Ira, and Mark Kesselman. 1975. *The Politics of Power: A Critical Introduction to American Government.* New York: Harcourt Brace Jovanovich.

Kaufman, Jerome L. 1974. "Contemporary Planning Practice: State of the Art." Godschalk. 111-37.

Kaufman, Michael T. 1970. "Lincoln Hospital: A Case History of Dissent that has Split Staff." *New York Times* December 21.

Kelman, Sander. 1971. "Toward the Political Economy of Medical Care." *Inquiry* 8 (September):30-37.

Kett, Joseph. 1968. *The Formation of the American Medical Profession: The Role of Institutions, 1780-1860.* New Haven, Conn.: Yale University Press.

Kihss, Peter. 1975. "Pact Ends Doctor Strike, Staff Returns to Hospitals." *New York Times* March 21.

———. 1975. "New Offer Made in Doctor Strike." *New York Times* March 19.

———. 1975. "21 Hospitals Here Hit by a Walkout of Housedoctors." *New York Times* March 18.

King, Lambert. 1969. "SHO Business: A New Role?" *Medical World News* (May 9):23.

Knowles, John H. 1977. *Doing Better and Feeling Worse: Health in the United States.* New York: W. W. Norton.

Kotelchuck, David. 1976. *Prognosis Negative: Crisis in the Health Care System.* New York: Vintage Books.

Koziol, Ronald. 1969. "Radicals Get One Million from HEW." *Chicago Tribune,* December 7.

Krause, Elliott A. 1977. *Power and Illness: The Political Sociology of Health and Medical Care.* New York: Elsevier.

Krumholz, Norman, Janice Cogger, and John Linner. 1975. "The Cleveland Policy Planning Report." *JAIP* 41:5 (September): 298-304.

Kumar, Krishan. 1978. *Prophecy and Progress: The Sociology of Industrial and Post-Industrial Society.* London: Penguin Books.

Lane, Robert E. 1966. "The Decline of Politics and Ideology in a Knowledgeable Society." *ASR* 31:5 (October): 649-662.

Langer, Elinor. 1966. "Medicine for the Poor: A New Deal in Denver." *Science* 153 (July 29):511-12.

Larson, Magali Sarfatti. 1980. "Proletarianization and Educated Labor." *Theory and Society* 9 (January):131-75.

———. 1977. *The Rise of Professionalism: A Sociological Analysis.* Berkeley: University of California Press.

Lefcourt, Robert, ed. 1971. *Law Against the People.* New York: Vintage Books.

Lenin, V. I. 1969. *What Is to Be Done? Burning Questions of Our Movement.* New York: International Publishers.

Levine, Harold. 1971. "Health Politics: Medicine at Another Level." *Hospital Tribune* (February 8):2.

Levy, Howard. 1971. "Counter Geiger." *Social Policy* (May/June):50-57.

Long, Norton. 1959. "Planning and Politics in Urban Development." *JAIP* 25:4. 167-9.

Long, Priscilla, ed. 1969. *The New Left.* New York: F. Porter Sargent.

Lowinger, Paul. 1968. "The Doctor as a Political Activist? Progress Report." *American Journal of Psychotherapy* 22:4 (October):616-25.

Lubove, Roy. 1967. *The Urban Community: Housing and Planning in the Progressive Era.* Englewood Cliffs, N. J.: Prentice-Hall.

Lynd, Staughton. 1965. "The New Radicals and 'Participatory Democracy.'" *Dissent* 12:3. 324-33.

Lynn, Kenneth S., ed. 1963. *The Professions in America.* Boston: Beacon Press.

MacIver, Robert M. 1922. "The Social Significance of Professional Ethics." *Annals of the American Academy of Political and Social Science* (May):101. 5-11.

Mallet, Serge. 1975. *Essays on the New Working Class.* ed. and trans. Dick Howard and Dean Savage. St. Louis: Telos Press.

Marcuse, Peter. 1974. "The Ethics of the Planning Profession." Working Paper DP 43. Los Angeles: University of California, School of Architecture and Urban Planning.

Marris, Peter. 1963. "A Report on Urban Renewal in the United States." *The Urban Condition.* ed. Leonard J. Duhl. New York: Basic Books. 113-34.

———. 1962. "The Social Implications of Urban Redevelopment." *JAIP* 28:3. 180-6.

Match, Robert K., et al. 1973. "Unionization, Strikes, Threatened Strikes and Hospitals: The View from Hospital Management." Wolfe.

McGarvey, Michael R., Fitzhugh Mullan, and Steven S. Sharfstein. 1968. "A Study in Medical Action: The Student Health Organization." *NEJM* 279:2 (July 11):74-80.

McKinley, J. B., "Toward the Proletarianization of Physicans." Derber. 37-62.

Merton, Robert K. 1957. "Some Preliminaries to a Sociology of Medical Education." *The Student Physician: Introductory Studies in the Sociology of Medical Education.* ed. Robert K. Merton, et al. Cambridge, Mass.: The Commonwealth Fund. 3-79.

Metzger, Walter P. 1975. "What is a Profession?" *Seminar Reports.* Program of

General and Continuing Education in the Humanities, Columbia University. September 18.

Meyerson, Martin. 1956. "Building the Middle-Range Bridge for Comprehensive Planning." *JAIP* 22:2. 58-64.

Miliband, Ralph. 1969. *The State in Capitalist Society.* New York: Basic Books.

Mills, C. Wright. 1969. *The Power Elite.* New York: Oxford University Press.

––––––. 1956. *White Collar: The American Middle Classes.* New York: Oxford University Press.

––––––. 1943. "The Professional Ideology of Social Pathologists." *AJS* 49:2 (September):165-80.

Mollenkopf, John. 1975. "The Post-War Politics of Urban Development." *Politics and Society* 5:3. 247-95.

––––––. 1975. "Theories of the State and Power Structure Research." *The Insurgent Sociologist* 5:3 (Spring):245-64.

Moore, Barrington, Jr. 1972. *Reflections on the Causes of Human Misery and upon Certain Proposals to Eliminate Them.* Boston: Beacon Press.

Moore, Wilbert E. 1970. *The Professions: Roles and Rules.* New York: Russell Sage.

Moynihan, Daniel P. 1969. *Maximum Feasible Misunderstanding: Community Action in the War on Poverty.* New York: Free Press.

Mullan, Fitzhugh. 1976. *White Coat, Clenched Fist.* New York: Macmillan.

––––––. 1968. "A New Mood in Medical Students." *Medical Opinion and Review* 4:3 (March):18-25.

Murray, Charles. 1984. *Losing Ground: American Social Policy, 1950-1980.* New York: Basic Books.

Needleman, Martin L., and Carolyn Emerson Needleman. 1974. *Guerrillas in the Bureaucracy.* New York: John Wiley and Sons.

NEJM. 1953. "The Health Needs of a Nation." 248:2. 77-78.

Nocks, Barry C. 1974. "Case Studies: A Decade of Planning Education." Godschalk. 206-29.

O'Brien, Jim. 1978. "American Leninism in the 1970s." *Radical America* (November 1977/February 1978):27-62.

O'Connor, James. 1973. *The Fiscal Crisis of the State.* New York: St. Martin's Press.

Offe, Claus. 1972. "Advanced Capitalism and the Welfare State." *Politics and Society* 2:4 (Summer):479-88.

Olson, Mancur, Jr. 1968. *The Logic of Collective Action: Public Goods and the Theory of Groups.* Cambridge, Mass.: Harvard University Press.

Oppenheimer, Martin. 1973. "The Proletarianization of the Professional." *Sociological Review Monograph* 20 (December):213-28.

Parsons, Talcott. 1968. "Professions." *International Encyclopedia of the Social Sciences.* ed. David L. Sills. New York: Free Press. 12:536-47.

––––––. 1954. "The Professions and Social Structure." *Essays in Sociological Theory.* 2nd ed. Ed. Talcott Parsons. New York: Free Press. 34-49.

––––––. 1951. "Illness and the Role of the Physician: A Sociological Perspective." *American Journal of Orthopsychiatry* 21 (July):452-60.

Peattie, Lisa. 1968. "Advocacy Planning in the United States." (Mimeographed.)
Perloff, Harvey. 1956. "Education of City Planners: Past, Present and Future." *JAIP* 22:4.
Perloff, Harvey, and Frank Klett. 1974. "The Evolution of Planning Education." Godschalk. 161-80.
Piven, Frances Fox. 1975. "Planning and Class Interests." *JAIP* 41:5. 308-10.
———. 1966. "Professionalism as a Political Skill." *Personnel in Anti-Poverty Programs: Implications for Social Work Education.* New York: Council on Social Work Education.
Poulantzas, Nicos. 1975. *Classes in Contemporary Capitalism.* London: New Left Books.
Progressive Architecture. 1968. "Advocacy Planning: What it is, How it Works." (September):102-15.
———. 1968. "ARCH: Black Advocates." (September):107-111.
Pynoos, Jan. 1969. "Urban Field Service." *Planning Comment* 5:2. 56-62.
Quigg, Newton. 1957. "Planning Comes of Age." *JAIP* 23. 185-91.
Rabinowitz, Francine. 1969. *City Politics and Planning.* New York: Atherton Press.
Rayack, Elton. 1967. *Professional Power and American Medicine: The Economics of the American Medical Association.* Cleveland, Ohio: World Publishing.
Rein, Martin. 1970. *Social Policy.* New York: Random House.
———. 1969. "Social Planning: The Search for Legitimacy." *JAIP* 35:5. 233-45.
Rosen, George. 1974. "The First Neighborhood Health Center Movement: Its Rise and Fall." *From Medical Police to Social Medicine: Essays on the History of Health Care.* ed. G. Rosen. New York: Science History Publications. 304-27.
———. 1974. "What is Social Medicine? A Genetic Analysis of the Concept." *From Medical Police to Social Medicine: Essays on the History of Health Care.* ed. G. Rosen. New York: Science History Publications. 60-119.
———. 1963. "The Evolution of Social Medicine." *Handbook of Medical Sociology.* eds. Howard E. Freeman, et al. Englewood Cliffs, N. J.: Prentice-Hall. 23-50.
———. 1963. "The Hospital: Historical Sociology of a Community Institution." *The Hospital in Modern Society.* ed. Eliot Freidson. New York: Free Press. 1-36.
———. 1958. *A History of Public Health.* New York: M. D. Publications.
Rosenkrantz, Barbara G. 1972. *Public Health and the State: Changing Views in Massachusetts, 1842-1936.* Cambridge, Mass.: Harvard University Press.
Rothman, R. A. 1984. "Deprofessionalization: The Case of Law in America." *Work and Occupations* 11 (May):183-206.
Rothstein, Peter. 1966. "The Community Health Center." Institute for Policy Studies. Washington, D. C. (Mimeographed.)
Rothstein, Richard. 1969. "Evolution of the ERAP Organizers. Priscilla Long. 272-88.
Rothstein, William G. 1972. *American Physicians in the Nineteenth Century: From Sects to Science.* Baltimore, Md.: Johns Hopkins University Press.

Rueschemeyer, Dietrich. 1964. "Doctors and Lawyers: A Comment on the Theory of the Professions." *The Canadian Review of Sociology and Anthropology* (February):17-30.

Ruzek, Sheryl Burt. 1978. *The Women's Health Movement: Feminist Alternatives to Medical Control.* New York: Praeger.

Sale, Kirkpatrick. 1974. *SDS.* New York: Vintage Books, 1974.

Salomon, Joan. 1972. "The Hospital." *The Sciences* (November):21-27.

Schumpeter, Joseph A. 1942. *Capitalism, Socialism and Democracy.* New York: Harper and Row.

Schwartz, Harry. 1983. "A Medicare Standoff with Doctors Looms." *Wall Street Journal* November 3.

Scott, Mel. 1971. *American City Planning.* Berkeley: University of California Press.

Seeley, John. 1959. "The Slum: Its Nature, Use, and Users." *JAIP* 25:1 7-14.

Shyrock, Richard H. 1967. *Medical Licensing in America, 1650-1965.* Baltimore, Md.: Johns Hopkins University Press.

_____. 1966. *Medicine in America: Historical Essays.* Baltimore, Md.: Johns Hopkins University Press.

Sibley, John. 1972. "Interns and Residents Plan National Organization." *New York Times* March 6.

Simmons, Leo and Harold G. Wolff. 1954. *Social Science in Medicine.* New York: Russell Sage.

Somers, Anne R., and Herman M. Somers. 1967. *Medicare and the Hospitals: Issues and Prospects.* Washington, D. C.: The Brookings Institution.

Spencer, James A. 1979. *Credentials for Professional Planners: A Study of Certification and Its Implications.* Washington, D. C.: American Institute of Certified Planners.

Stark, Evan. 1977. "Introduction to the Special Issue on the Political Economy of Health." *Review of Radical Economics* 9:1 (Spring).

Starr, Paul. 1982. *The Social Transformation of American Medicine.* New York: Basic Books.

_____. 1978. "Medicine and the Waning of Professional Sovereignty." *Daedalus* 107:1 (Winter):175-93.

Stevens, Robert, and Rosemary Stevens. 1974. *Welfare Medicine in America: A Case Study of Medicaid.* New York: Free Press.

Stevens, Rosemary. 1971. *American Medicine and the Public Interest.* New Haven, Conn.: Yale University Press.

Stinchcombe, Arthur L. 1978. *Theoretical Methods in Social History.* New York: Academic Press.

Strickland, Stephen P. 1972. *Politics, Science and Dread Disease: A Short History of United States Medical Research Policy.* Cambridge, Mass.: Harvard University Press.

Sullivan, Ronald. 1983. "Priorities Revised in City's Hospitals." *New York Times* August 20.

_____. 1979. "Doctors Offer Help in Suits Against City for Malpractice." *New York Times* April 12.

Susskind, Lawrence E. 1976. "Citizen Involvement in the Local Planning Process." Prepared for the Citizen Involvement Network. Washington, D.C.

———. 1974. "The Future of the Planning Professions." Godschalk. 138-59.

Susskind, Lawrence, and Anne Aylward. 1976. "Comprehensive Planning: A State-of-the-Art Review of Concepts, Methods, and the Problems of Building Local Capacity." Prepared for the Advisory Commission on Housing and Urban Growth. American Bar Association. January 29. (Mimeographed.)

Thabit, Walter. 1960. "Renewal—A Planning Challenge." *JAIP* 26:2. 84-88.

Tichy, Noel M. 1977. *Organization Design for Primary Health Care: The Case of the Dr. Martin Luther King, Jr. Health Center.* New York: Praeger.

Time. 1975. "The Doctors Union." (October 27): 81.

Toren, Nina. 1975. "Deprofessionalization and Its Sources." *Sociology of Work and Occupations* 2 (November):323-37.

Torgoff, Stephen. 1972. "HRUM Sums Up Hospital Organizing." *Guardian* (December 27):7.

Touraine, Alain. 1971. *The Post-Industrial Society.* New York: Random House.

Urban Planning Aid, Inc., Housing and Community Research Groups. 1973. *Community Housing Development Corporations: The Empty Promise.* Cambridge, Mass.

Vollmer, Howard M., and Donald L. Mills. eds. 1966. *Professionalization.* Englewood Cliffs, N. J.: Prentice-Hall.

Waitzkin, Howard. 1978. "A Marxist View of Medical Care." *Annals of Internal Medicine* 89:264-78.

———. 1970. "Expansion of Medical Institutions into Urban Residential Areas." *NEJM* 282:18 (April):1003-7.

Weaver, Robert C. 1965. "Social Issues: The Disadvantaged and the Amenity Seekers." in *The Metropolitan Future: California and the Challenge of Growth.* Berkeley: University of California Press, 1965.

Webber, Melvin M. 1963. "Comprehensive Planning and Social Responsibility: Toward an AIP Consensus on the Profession's Roles and Purposes." *JAIP* 29:4.

Weiss, Robert J., et al. 1974. "The Effect of Importing Physicians: Return to a Pre-Flexnerian Standard." *NEJM* 290:26 (June 27):1453-58.

———. 1974. "Foreign Medical Graduates and the Medical Underground." *NEJM* 290:25 (June 20):1408-13.

Wiebe, Robert H. 1967. *The Search for Order, 1877-1920.* New York: Hill and Wang.

Wilensky, Harold L. 1964. "The Professionalization of Everyone?" *AJS* 70 (September):137-58.

Wilensky, Harold L., and Charles N. Lebeaux. 1958. *Industrial Society and Social Welfare.* New York: Free Press.

Williams, Roger M. 1977. "The New Urban Pioneers." *Saturday Review* (July 23):8-14.

Wilson, James Q. 1966. *Urban Renewal: The Record and the Controversy.* Cambridge, Mass.: MIT Press.

Wolfe, Samuel, ed. 1973. *Organization of Health Workers and Labor Conflict.* New York: Baywood Publishing.

———. 1973. "Worker Conflicts in the Health Field: An Overview." Wolfe.

Wolfe, Samuel, and Hila Richardson Sherer. 1977. *Public General Hospitals in Crisis.* Washington, D. C.: Coalition of American Public Employees.

Wood, Edward W., Jr., Sidney N. Brower, and Margaret W. Latimer. 1966. "Planner's People." *JAIP* 32:4. 228-34.

Wright, Erik Olin. 1979. "Intellectuals and the Class Structure of Capitalist Society." *Between Labor and Capital.* ed. Pat Walker. Boston: South End Press. 191-211.

———. 1979. *Class Structure and Income Determination.* New York: Academic Press.

———. 1976. "Class Boundaries in Advanced Capitalist Societies." *New Left Review* 98 (July/August):1-41.

Wright, P. and A. Treacher, eds. 1982. *The Problem of Medical Knowledge.* Edinburgh: Edinburgh University Press.

"The Wrong Weapon." 1979. Editorial. *New York Post* January 18.

Yarmolinsky, Adam. 1978. "What Future for the Professional in American Society." *Daedalus* 107 (Winter):159-74.

Index

Los Angeles County Interns
and Residents; Physicians
National Housestaff
Association (PNHA)
Housing Abandonment in New York City,
152
Housing Act (1949), 33
Housing and Urban Development,
Department of (HUD), 34
Housing developments, 149-50
See also Communities, low-
income and minority; Urban
renewal
Human Sciences Press, 161

Ideological autonomy, 202, 203
Ideology 175
of social transformation, 199-200
Information gathering by SHO, 92
Innovations, control functions of,
117
In Rem Tenants Coalition, 153
Institutionalization
of community fieldwork, 54
of planning, 11
of scientific model of medicine, 14
Institutional organizing, 115-18
Institutional strength, 183-84
Institution building, 201
Institutions, defined, 109
Insurance, hospital, 38
Interns, 40
Interviews, 27-29

Jacobs, Jane, 36
Jamous, H., 185, 200
Job centers, health care facilities as,
99, 182
Joint Housestaff/Attendings
Standards and Grievance
Committees, 134
*Journal of the American Institute of
Planners (JAIP)*, 36, 37

Kasperson, R.E., 117
Kelman, Sander, 175
King, Lambert, 92
Knowledge, 183-84, 191-204
autonomy issue and, 202-4
as central attribute, 3
change and, 19
critical vs. traditional views of,
6-7
demystification of, 108, 109
dysfunctional role of narrowly
defined, 185
expertise as, 6
of medicine, 17-18
models, 12, 14-15
new clients' challenge to, 191-94
of planners, 12, 17-18
politicization and nature of, 185
radical critique of, 194-204
deprofessionalized strategies
and, 196-98
political implications of,
200-201
reprofessionalization and,
198-200
scientific, 14
self-control and, 208n4
stability of, 6, 194
Kotelchuck, Rhonda, 147

Landlord abandonment, 152
Larson, M.S., 194
Lathrop, G.T., 34
League of Voluntary Hospitals, 134
Leavitt, Jacqueline, 55-56
Legitimacy
for change, bases of, 198-200
conferred by clients, 197-98
crisis of, for medicine and
planning, 186-87
"Letter to the Movement" (Egleson),
75
Lincoln Collective, 22, 118-31
budget cut threats and, 125, 127,
128

2018